D1203509

TALKING OF MUSIC

Neville Cardus

TALKING
OF
MUSIC

COLLINS
ST JAMES'S PLACE, LONDON

FIRST IMPRESSION   NOVEMBER, 1957
SECOND IMPRESSION   FEBRUARY, 1959

The essays in this book are based
on material originally published in
the *Manchester Guardian*.

PRINTED IN GREAT BRITAIN
COLLINS CLEAR-TYPE PRESS: LONDON AND GLASGOW

TO

SIR THOMAS BEECHAM
with thanks for much instruction
and wit

CONTENTS

PART ONE

CONDUCTORS AND CONDUCTING

Arturo Toscanini	*page* 13
Sir Thomas Beecham at Seventy-five	18
Sir Malcolm	24
Furtwängler	29
The Hallé Orchestra	34
The Orchestral Conductor	39
More About the Conductor	44

PART TWO

COMPOSERS

Approaching Mahler	51
Mahler's Ninth Symphony	55
Igor Stravinsky	59
Sibelius at Ninety	64
Mozart the Unparalleled	69
Schönberg and Berg	74
Anton Bruckner	78

7

CONTENTS

Ralph Vaughan Williams   *page* 83

Of Richard Strauss

    1. A FEW LAST WORDS   88

    2. " CAPRICCIO AND DANAE "   93

    3. RICHTER AND STRAUSS   98

    4. STRAUSSIANA   103

A Note on Berlioz   108

A Connoisseur Symphony   113

The Genius of Liszt   118

Chopin and Pianists   122

Brahms and the Piano   128

The Songs of Hugo Wolf   133

PART THREE

ABOUT OPERA

The Tragic Sense in *Carmen*   139

Verdi's Masterpiece   144

Return to Vienna   149

Words and Music in Opera   168

Of British Opera   172

Let's Make an Opera   181

CONTENTS

PART FOUR

TRADITION AND EXPERIMENT

" Contemporary " Music   *page* 187
Revolt and Tradition   192
The Pioneer's Dusty Way   196
Relative Values   201
Music and Literature   207
Music and " Meaning "   212
Music and Nature   217
What is a Banal Tune?   222
Composer and Public   227
Content and Technique   231
Fabricated Music   236

PART FIVE

ENGLISH MUSIC

What do the English People really Sing
    To-day?   243
Period Music   248
The English and Music   253
Contemporary English   259
Words and Music   263

9

CONTENTS

PART SIX

CRITICISING THE CRITICS

Criticism with Humour   *page* 269

The Objective Ear   274

Criticising the Critics   278

Shaw as a Music Critic   283

The Critic and Beethoven   289

Arthur Johnstone   294

Erich Hartleibig   299

TAILPIECE

A Rare Memory of Gigli (1935)   309

Index   313

PART ONE

CONDUCTORS AND
CONDUCTING

Arturo Toscanini

ARTURO TOSCANINI achieved a renown and authority never shared by any musician not a composer and definitely creative. Yet it is more than likely that if he had died in 1918 he would to-day be mainly remembered as a great conductor of opera. Few musicians outside Italy and America—and America at this time was not supposed to have come to musical enlightenment—associated Toscanini with the symphonic masterpieces. Beethoven and Brahms were at this time the perquisites of German, Austrian or Central European interpreters. The war of 1914–18 brought to an end the Teuton and Central European way of subjective or romantic expression. The " new age " saw the dwindling of emotion and armament in all the arts: the fashion was now for the angular if not the flat, for severe lines and—to use the cant current term—for objectivity. The hour was ripe for the mature Maestro, who in La Scala had come to lay first importance on strictness of tempo and restraint of tone and scrupulous observance of the written note, not as a result of æsthetic philosophising on his part but because of his need to tame vocalists and quell them into some respect for musical values. During this same period of reaction against romantic indulgence of expression, America was bringing orchestral technique to an accuracy and polish not dreamed of in

Europe, let alone attempted. It was when Toscanini found the almost flawless instrument in New York that his fame widened the world over and he became the final authority in the growing school of interpretation which sought first and last " to see the object as in itself it really is "; in other words, to play the music as written down in the score.

He has frankly been the victim of the lavish praises reserved in other years for the prima donna. The irony is that Toscanini himself seldom could be content or happy with his own interpretations. He was one night visiting a friend and he entered the room while a gramophone record was playing a Beethoven symphony. Toscanini listened a while, then smote the furniture. " It does not go! No legato. Basta! " With some natural trepidation his host told him the record was one of Toscanini's making. " I don't care! " snapped Toscanini. " It is still no good all the same! " He represented the non-romantic view of musical interpretation, which is another piece of irony; for unmistakably he was Italian to the bone, and he emerged from La Scala. He has been acclaimed as the one and only conductor who could hear a score " objectively " and sought relentlessly to reproduce the music as written down in the composer's lifetime. Nobody who is not prepared to look metaphysics brazenly in the eye and then pass by will, without a pause praise Toscanini, or anybody else, on the strength of his power to penetrate the heart of the " object as in itself it really is."

Toscanini, no more than any other great artist, could or would, an' he could, deny a personal urge or conception; he had a wider range than all his contemporaries simply because of his greater age and experience. His fanatical insistence on clearness throughout a performance, and on tempi as logical as a mathematical proposition, did not suit every composer. I have heard *Tristan* under Toscanini sound as much lacking in nervous tension and tragic shadow as I have heard *Meistersinger* under Furtwängler lacking in steadiness of pulse and geniality of diction. Toscanini usually presented a composer above life-size; as he grew older he could not relax the wheel of his rhythm—more than once it seemed to go round like the wheel of Ixion bearing the bound orchestra. His presentation of Mozart wanted a certain elegance and disarming courtesy. His Beethoven was incomparably majestic; his encompassing of *The Ring* of Wagner was large, magnanimous, and epic; the vast shapes merged into a single mighty range. He was unexcelled for grasping a gigantic structure as though seeing from the first beat the end in the beginning. But when all is said it was in Verdi's music that he was incomparable. Sometimes it was as though he were putting the music under an X-ray; notes and figures seldom if ever heard in average performances could now be identified as individual groups. Occasionally the question came to mind: " Did the composer intend us to hear these subsidiary figures as consciously as all this? " He was always the serious expositor, never using music for purposes of self-exhibition or even of a justifiable self-catharsis. Beecham conducts like the connoisseur serving a wine for our and his own delight. Toscanini was the vintner.

He was his severest critic; he never rested on any oar of self-satisfaction. His assets are seldom found assembled together in one conductor: immense knowledge and experience, a natural way of absorbing tone, a keen ear, a prodigious memory, great force of personal will and conviction, and—greatest of all—a simple honesty equal to

Verdi's. His interpretations were direct and unambiguous; he was incapable of that subtlety which depends on the oblique approach. The score for him was holy writ; it was as though he were telling us that by his taking heed of the letter the spirit would take care of itself. " Who am I to interpret Beethoven? "

Most of us, even though possibly touched with more than talent, fall by the way at the moment when the strain is at its most challenging. Says the Lord to Mephistopheles in the " Prologue in Heaven " in Goethe's *Faust*, " Man's efforts sink below his proper level, and as he seeks for ease too soon, I send him a dæmon for companion to spur him on." Idealism for most of us is not enough; artistic integrity and zeal for discovery are not enough. The ego must take part, ambition if you like. Toscanini certainly housed a dæmon. Some years ago he revisited Milan. He has told the story—in his own way: " I go to La Scala to hear the *Trittico* of Puccini. But Puccini and I—we have long not spoken. A silly quarrel. So I go to La Scala incognito, in the gallery, alone. *Suor Angelica*—no good! *Il tabarro* also no good. But *Gianni Schicchi* . . ." he waved a kiss with his hand—" a little masterpiece. Lofely! So I think now I go round to artists' room and embrace the Maestro and kees him and forget all these silly quarrel. And I go down the stairs queek and round the theatre to the stage door. . . ." He stopped and scowled at himself. " But no! "—and he struck himself a terrific blow over the heart—" No! This Toscanini "—and another blow over the heart—" this Toscanini "—he spat at himself and delivered another blow—" he says no! So I go away, back to my hotel, and next morning I fly to New York, and a few months after-wards Puccini die and I never see him again. Ach! This

16

Toscanini "—another blow—" this devil Toscanini ! "—
and another blow and more spit. He was a conductor in
thrall: that is why for a lifetime he could not stop, cease,
or find satisfaction.

So it happened that the dreaded Maestro, before whom
the most high-handed virtuosi would tremble and the most
hardened of streamlined orchestras would obey with fear
and respect—this Toscanini was the most humble conductor
of them all in the presence of the immortals; he was there
to do their will. That is why nobody of intelligence ever
spoke of Toscanini's " Ninth " Symphony, or of Toscanini's
Brahms. As far as it is possible for human beings to achieve
abnegation and at the same time retain the style that is the
man himself, Toscanini succeeded in subduing his hand to
what it worked in. He was not infallible; and only the
least understanding of his followers ever wished him to be.

Sir Thomas Beecham at
Seventy Five

ON 29TH APRIL, 1954, Sir Thomas celebrated his seventy-fifth birthday, and most of the rest of us celebrated it with him. Panting time and the first violins toil after him in vain. He may nowadays walk to the conductor's desk less jauntily than of yore; he may carry more of mortal flesh. He has actually taken to using musical scores in public, and no doubt he is finding them engrossing, holding his attention from first page to last. In such unimportant ways he renders unto time some of its dues; but the wit and the mind and the spirit and the informing imp of the man are fresh as ever. He renews himself morning after morning, better still, he enjoys himself. His brown eyes seem never tired; there is speculation in them always; they quiz and question and open wide, and some look of pain enters them at expressions of foolishness. Then, suddenly, they will withdraw and become veiled; you will understand now why Beecham, artist in panache, can get to the heart of Delius.

Doctor Johnson wrote that if anybody had met Burke taking cover from rain only for a moment in a shed he would have said, " There is a remarkable man." The same compliment could fairly be spoken of Sir Thomas, whether or not he were inexplicably to be found one day sheltering in a shed. What indeed would Doctor Johnson have to say could he but see Sir Thomas at work with the baton, coaxing the fiddlers, smoothing the lines of melody into a sort of orchestral permanent wave, urging the brass to higher peaks and clouds of resonance. " Why, sir," we can perhaps hear him saying, " a giant might lift heavy weights and drop them on his feet, or a man might blow himself out prodigiously and burst from more ambition than is in nature; but this conductor of Musick is bound by a Constitution; the players, sir, have they not their notes in front of them? " It is historical fact that Sir Thomas was born in St. Helens. At the first sight or sound of him the truth of this might not be suspected, for he is urbane and of the world of civilised men and women, conscious of poise and his own irony, more Oxford in accent than Wadham. Yet he cannot altogether put us off the scent. The humour and pertinacity of his native county creep in, so that we can realise with content that in spite of all temptations to belong to an exclusive stratum of society he remains a Lancashire man. It is significant that for all his affectation of disdain and his magisterial way of administering correction to bourgeoisie and *hoi-polloi* alike, he is known among orchestral players as " Tommy." They admire him, they find him occasionally trying, capricious, earnest, conscientious and evasive, in swift sequence. They always find him amusing and, when all is said and done, kind. I have known him for a quarter of a century, and not once have I heard him speak unkindly or meanly of anybody. He has scarified ignorance and incompetence, yes, using names of the culprits more or less in the manner that we refer to abstract personages of a morality play.

19

I have known him perform acts of graciousness and courtesy almost obsolete at the present time.

Sometimes his tongue is cruel simply because he cannot resist the crack or snap of his own wit. At a certain concert, a pianist played abominably, with Sir Thomas conducting. At the end of the performance the piano men came to the platform to move the instrument away. " I don't think," said Sir Thomas to them, " I don't think you need waste your energies on this occasion. Just leave the instrument alone a few minutes longer and I fancy it will slink off on its own accord."

He has lived to know his legend, which of course tells only the half-truth:—our most brilliant conductor and wit, a character and a personality from the beginning, now one of the nation's gallery of persistent and necessary Grand Old Men. He once said to me: " I am generally admired and rendered notorious for all sorts of doubtful qualities and doings, but I never receive recognition of the one gift which I command beyond any other—my gift for industry, patient industry." I have met him in most circumstances, in trains, ships, hotels, concert-halls, in his bedroom, in his bed, morning and night, but never have I found him idle. His talk is part of his activity; it is never " small," never about things, never what Kant would have called " descriptive." He is constantly relating idea to idea, mood to style. He will range rapidly from Mozart to wine, from cricket and Cliquot to Montaigne, from George Robey to the Elizabethan and Restoration playwrights, from pinpush to poetry. For all his supposed irreverence and his delight in shocking the complacent and the conventionally traditional, he is, like every man of comedy, serious at bottom. If he loves a composer, a book, a picture, a play, he loves wholeheartedly. He is in the truest sense of an abused word, the perfect amateur. I am fond of making contrast between Toscanini and Beecham by saying that Toscanini is the experienced and wise vintner, but Beecham personally flavours the wine, like the connoisseur of cellarage.

No other conductor shares Beecham's delight in his own work; no other conductor takes his gay view of music. He does not worry about inner meanings, philosophy, and the rest of it. " Music," he argues, " must sound well, brilliant, or beautiful. It must sing." He once asked for a dance orchestra to be stopped in the Mirabell Gardens at Salzburg, so that he might demonstrate, with his own vocal examples, and at supper, too, with champagne, the beauty of the opening horn melody of the C major symphony of Schubert. Sufficient for Sir Thomas are the curvings of melody, the mingling of instrumental colours, the dancing of symmetrical patterns round a point of rest. He gets his effects mainly by trusting to his natural instincts, to his exquisitely sensitive ear. Sometimes his enthusiasm carries him away in a quick movement; enthusiasm of itself is usually dangerous in the arts. But he is never mediocre; if he fails, he fails grandly. He is not naturally given to music excessively contrapuntal. He prefers Handel to Bach, and will not be thought the worse of on that account hereafter. He abhors the portentousness which comes from too much stress and gravity in the handling of rhythm. He apparently believes that if a conductor applies himself to the freeing of the main melodies, to a clear and winging flight, with the basic rhythms also unburdened, then the details of texture may confidently be left to fall into place. His performances usually have a spontaneous sound; if he here and there lightens a harmonic mass or even appears to fillet certain German compositions—" take them off the hone sir," as the waiters say—he goes in front of all other conductors in his power to express the felicity and ease which are the certain signs of greatness and mastery in music. His range, from Sibelius to Delius, from Mozart to the Strauss of *Elektra*, from Rossini to the Beethoven of the *Eroica*, is unequalled. For years he held English opera aloft on his own shoulders. And never in this country has a sustained opera season surpassed in variety and fineness of style the Beecham opera of his heyday.

The public forgets. Many of us to-day are still in debt to Sir Thomas; he led us out of the Teutonic captivity. He showed us other and more sensitive worlds. He introduced us to Russian ballet and opera and to the more stylish of the French masters of lyric opera. He boxed the compass on voyages of gorgeous discovery: *Louise*, *Tiefland*, *A Village Romeo and Juliet*, the best of Mozart and Strauss: opera from every land: *Naïl*, *Pearl Fishers*, Stanford's *The Critic*, the first English performances which were at all like the original of *The Tales of Hoffmann*. At Covent Garden he conducted *The Ring* with less than the Wagnerian forging energy, but I shall never forget his treatment of *Siegfried*. Instead of a great musical bas-relief, he gave us a succession of beautifully-painted, not to say tinted canvases, all set before us in a row, a Wagner of taste and poise! It is an irony which he, no doubt, is the first to appreciate that for years Covent Garden Opera, once on a time his oyster, is closed to him. None the less he has prevailed. Age cannot wither him; it is his privilege to do the withering. And his bark is worse than his bite. He has worked without surcease or stint for music everywhere. And if anybody should ask, in the manner of the stuffy individual in Arnold Bennett's *The Card*, " With what great cause has he been identified? " the answer in Sir Thomas's behalf is the same: " Why, with the great cause of cheering us all up."

The universal congratulations that reach him every birthday will mingle affection and admiration. It was on his seventieth birthday that Sir Thomas was entertained to lunch by a host of music-lovers; and telegrams came in shoals from distinguished folk unable to be present. The chairman read them one by one, to tumultuous applause. " Felicitations," " To a Maestro," from every famous name . . . Schönberg, Strauss . . . then, finally, from Sibelius. Vast cheering, at the end of which Beecham looked up to the chairman from his place at the table, and, with a slightly pained expression, asked " Nothing from Mozart? " What a man. Long may he be preserved.

23

Sir Malcolm

Time does not even pant after Sir Malcolm Sargent in vain; it has apparently given up the chase. We might as well add up the birthdays of springtime or the quavers and semiquavers in Mozart. If he changes at all it is only to remain the same—at any rate, to look at; slim, stiff, and angular yet elegant, the freshest carnation can hardly live up to him. The black polished hair, the dark twisted handsome ugliness of his visage (it is not merely a face), the swiftness of his glances, the simple splendour of his clothes, which fit him so perfectly that they seem physically as well as psychologically part of him and we cannot imagine him naked. No wonder that at a Promenade Concert the young boys and girls lean over the bar in the area and gaze at him: well they might.

His vitality is iridescent. Sir Thomas Beecham, not as unkindly as custom has made the remark appear, once called him " Flash." He is affectionately known by orchestral players by this vivid term. Recently he conducted in Tokio with his usual effect of spectacular ignition; and Sir Thomas, on hearing of this latest of Sir Malcolm's triumphs, could not resist the comment: " Flash in Japan, I suppose."

But Beecham years ago knew the worth of Sir Malcolm when he appointed him conductor in reserve of the London

Philharmonic Orchestra, which Beecham created in the 1930s. Of all our native conductors, Sir Malcolm is probably the finest musician; he is a pianist of skill and character, and once on a time he was actually an organist. He reads a score at sight and knows the grammar and syntax which constitute a composer's style. Orchestral players admire what they call his " stick " technique. No conductor surpasses him in the handling of a large choir. To see and hear him rehearsing a large choir is to understand why and how he can put them all, especially the sopranos and contraltos, under a spell. At a dubious moment he will interrupt, break the course of the music and say, fingering his tie, " But really, really, my dears—we can't sing out of tune, now, can we, really, not really, can we? Let's try again—te-de, te-do, te-he." In 1931 he conducted the first of all performances at the Leeds Festival of Walton's *Belshazzar's Feast*. Seldom has a conductor, in one comprehensive stroke and flash of musical-dramatic vision, more powerfully put a new work " across "—I can use no phrase more expressive than this of what I am trying to say. It was an act of spontaneous creation and spontaneous combustion achieved at one and the same time. In 1939 Sir Malcolm conducted a performance of *The Dream of Gerontius* in the Royal Albert Hall. I have not heard an interpretation since which so eloquently and poignantly took the measure of Elgar's masterpiece; and I had not heard one as good before. Toscanini was in the audience and after the performance he ran round to the artists' room and embraced Sir Malcolm, who we may be sure accepted the compliment and the way it was tendered, with the right modest concealment of embarrassment. It is in a reminiscence of this superb performance that Sir

Malcolm will sometimes tell of a tenor who was rehearsing with him the part of Gerontius. Sir Malcolm found it was necessary to give this tenor a certain interpretative clue. "You see, my dear fellow, Gerontius in Part Two is dead and he is about to go into the presence of an angel. On earth he of course believed as a good Catholic in angels, but now he is actually in the presence of an angel. So, my dear fellow, you must find a different, a more awed tone. . . ." And the tenor said, "Ah, I understand, Sir Malcolm—thanks very much," and he took out his pencil and wrote on his vocal score, at the appropriate bar: "Meet angel."

When Sir Malcolm was a young man he was with the British National Opera Company, and one of his first appearances in Manchester was as conductor of Vaughan Williams's *Hugh the Drover*. He was described by Langford in the *Manchester Guardian* as more than promising. In the decades since then he has had little experience at all in the opera house yet only the other year he was called on to conduct the first performance of William Walton's *Troilus*, and again he was not found wanting. Such is Sir Malcolm's and the Englishman's gift for rapid adaptability and improvisation in the arts.

He has gone beyond the scope of music in the expression and fulfilment of his personality; he has taken his place in the portrait gallery of the nation's imagination and notion of *flair* in the best places. He has helped, as no other musician except Sir Henry Wood, to remove native distrust of music known as "classical." Once on a time, the general public in these isles were not willingly drawn to Bach, Beethoven, and the rest; some of them unwittingly echoed Zuleika Dobson whenever they confessed that they knew nothing about music but knew what they liked. Sir Malcolm dispels austerity and aloofness. He introduces the various composers to us as so much excellent company; sometimes he might seem even to transform the function of conducting into a sort of musical salesmanship " Brahms on the second floor, Mod'm. Beethoven on the seventh." The flair and confident gesture are deceptive; they entirely mislead the superior people who love to think they can dismiss a thing with the term " little bourgeoisie." Sir Malcolm has a critical sense, scholarship, and wit which would put nearly all of his detractors to flight. Let us hope that one day we shall see and hear him actually routing them—on television. He refuses to take a dreary view of life or the arts to suit or conform to the contemporary æsthetic, which still persists in believing that a long face denotes a profound and up-to-date view of life. Sir Malcolm has passed through bitter enough experiences, has suffered bruises to body and heart. It seems only yesterday that we had given him up for dead in some sanatorium at Davos. Deep personal loss did not cause his spirit to droop depressingly; out of it he composed his orchestral version of the *Four Serious Songs* of Brahms, one of the most apt of all orchestral transcriptions.

Versatility and enthusiasm in themselves can often do harm in the arts; they need the disciplined rein of self-criticism and technique. Greatness itself—a vague term to use in a description of an interpretative artist, and maybe vague in any context—insists on much solitude, on indifference to the large public's applause and to the conventionally polite way of doing things. Sir Malcolm doesn't take a dæmonic view of music or of any art. He seems to regard them all and love them all with ethical, patriotic, and social connotations. Well, ethics, patriotism, and good breeding and manners in the drawing-room of civilised men and women are necessary and valuable adornments to existence. But I must bring my tribute to an end, or I shall be dragging into it Sir Willoughby Patterne himself!

Furtwängler

THE OBITUARY notices of Furtwängler were grudging of praise in this country, and when Strauss died he too had a poor press here; but recently English criticism has sentimentally made amends, praising the later Strauss rather beyond his deserts. On the whole the contemporary critical attitude everywhere is allergic to German music, and to musicians deriving from nineteenth-century romanticism, or the German way of subjective and personal expression. The fashion now is for the " pattern," for " objectivity," to use a term which no metaphysician would lightly employ as a convenient label. Furtwängler was almost certain to get on the wrong side of a school of thought that regarded a musical score as a fixed and final statement. " A conductor," he argued in his *Gespräche*, " can only prepare ' finish,' and estimate details (at rehearsal); a whole work on the other hand, complete in itself, always retains something imponderable. Anyone who believes this imponderable element to be essential and of ultimate significance will never overestimate the importance of rehearsals." In a recently published biography (" *Wilhelm Furtwängler*," by Curt Riess), the author quotes Weber, who lamented that it was difficult to interpret music in the spirit in which it had been conceived by the composer—" For these problems there are no words to express what we mean. The meaning can be found only in an understanding human heart, and if this feeling is lacking, a metronome cannot really help us. And the score is no help either."

Furtwängler could probably have answered the critics who complained against the liberties he apparently took with tempi and dynamic indications, but he despised critics. Being a thorough German, he certainly could have produced arguments, metaphysically well-grounded to demonstrate how hard it is to discover the " objective truth " of a musical score, or of anything else, save by some assistance from the subjective self. His pianissimi were frequently challenged by London critics; he might—given a sense of humour, but he hadn't much—have retorted: " Are you sure your ears are objectively in order to-night? " " Is your position in the hall the throne and seat of objective truth? "

We need only consider the notebooks of Beethoven to realise how little he trusted to written crotchets, quavers and the rest, to serve as final statements. Furtwängler believed in a necessary act of improvisation at the creative point, the point where the interpreter finds the wave-length to the composer's " station " so to say. " The essentials of a performance cannot be determined in advance," writes Mr. Riess, paraphrasing Furtwängler. " For Furtwängler the actual performance was decisive. He learned to assume responsibility afresh at every concert; he conducted every work as though he had never conducted it before." On the only occasion I met and spoke to Furtwängler he complained of English critics, who attacked him because year after year he included in his programmes the same Beethoven symphonies. " But they are never the same to me," he replied. " Each time, I live through them I seem to get closer to the music—but it is still far distant! "

He was at Toscanini's extreme and a poet highly strung. Toscanini was the great architect or builder, working from the blueprint. In music Furtwängler sought a solution for all his problems of spirit; he even believed that by the power of music he could defend Germany against the Nazi ideology. " I did not directly oppose the party," he said to Mr. Riess, " because I told myself this was not my job. I should have benefited no one by active resistance. But I never concealed my opinions. As an artist, I was determined that my music, at least, should remain untouched. Had I taken an active part in politics, I could not have remained in Germany. I knew that a single performance of a great German masterpiece was a stronger and more vital negation of the spirit of Buchenwald or Auschwitz than words. Please understand me correctly; an artist cannot be entirely unpolitical. He must have some political convictions, because after all, he too is a human being." (The naïveté here is quite touching!) " As a citizen it is an artist's duty to express these convictions. But as a musician I am more than a citizen. I am a German in that eternal sense to which the genius of great music testifies."

It is not generally known that Furtwängler's heart's desire was to compose. Middle-class pride prevented him from taking a risk with his livelihood and the family esteem; then rapid advance as a conductor stemmed a talent which was as reproductive as creative. His second symphony in E minor, is eloquent of a resigned loneliness. He always seemed " lost " or alone. When he came on to the platform and bowed, just once or twice at the audience, in polite acknowledgment of applause, he seemed a man apart. His unfulfilled wish to compose was no doubt the cause of his extremely personal treatment of a well-worn masterpiece. He was trying to share the processes of creation. Never did he conduct in a routine way. None but a superficial view of Furtwängler has ever attributed his occasional excesses of tempi and shading to rhetorical or applause-catching display. Furtwängler conducted as though no audience were present behind his back. A player in the Berlin Philharmonic Orchestra told me that Furtwängler conducted like a sort of musical vampire. " He draws the blood and life out of you, so that we can't make music for ourselves—after a concert with Furtwängler I can't even take part in a chamber quartet for days and days."

It is a limiting view of a composition which argues that there is only one way of interpreting it. I should say myself that only good second-rate composers, Saint-Saëns or Rimsky-Korsakov, can be performed and their music realised to the full by a strict literal observance of the score and its directions. Certainly a symphony of Beethoven is not exhausted spiritually or musically by one superbly comprehensive inventory taken by Toscanini. No dramatic critic insists that all contemporary interpretations of Hamlet should begin and end with Sir John Gielgud's. " I had to discover the true interpretation of masterpieces," said Furtwängler, referring to his early experimental years: " I had to study the entire world repertory. I repudiated every schematic pattern of interpretation, every so-called tradition, which to-day enables many conductors to evade personal interpretation." The frustrated composer in him would not sit back and allow the interpreter in him the detachment of the " score as objective truth " school. " I cannot," he confessed, " adjust and transform myself as easily as a man can who is only a conductor." It was as absurdly narrow to think of Furtwängler mainly as a conductor as it was to think mainly of Schnabel as a pianist. He was an artist for whom music was the chief mode of consciousness, a necessary way of life. Like any other artist, he enjoyed the public's admiration and support, but he did not set himself to serve them or any critic or fashion. As a conductor and artist who seemed to go into the creative forge, he must be counted the greatest since Mahler and Nikisch. There is only Klemperer left to us from this Faustian tradition. It is a school with limitations, maybe —but, as the greatest of Faustians has told us, it is within limitations that the master finds himself.

The Hallé Orchestra

THE HALLE ORCHESTRA is forging full steam and healthfully towards its hundredth birthday. When I first heard a Hallé concert Richter conducted, and the year was 1907. So I have known the orchestra for nearly half of its lifetime. The inevitable question arises: how would Richter's Hallé Orchestra sound to-day compared with Barbirolli's?

The style under Richter was, of course, different and mainly German. From the view of technical performance, it is pretty certain that the Hallé of 1957 would surpass Richter's combination even at its best, simply because all orchestras of the present are able to rehearse oftener together than was possible in Richter's, or even in Harty's period. I can never cease to feel amazement when I remember that under Harty most Hallé concerts enjoyed only one rehearsal weekly—on Thursday mornings a few hours before the beginning of the concert itself. Yet in Harty's day we heard first performances in Manchester of nearly all the Sibelius symphonies, the fourth and ninth symphonies of Mahler, as well as *Das Lied von der Erde*. Round about the late 1920s Stravinsky conducted the Hallé Orchestra in a programme of some of his own compositions; and he was delighted and astounded at the ease and facility with which the Hallé players read the notes at sight, and changed them into music. It is because the Hallé orchestra

34

has grown up " the hard way " that it is representative of Manchester and Lancashire life and character. It is not the product of a luxurious " culture "; it is not like an orchestra in, say, Philadelphia, streamlined and expensive, so much so that a cloth is thrown over it at the end of a concert on cold nights to protect the engine.

The Hallé Orchestra belongs to a definite soil and air, and has a masculinity handed down from a long distant past in which the country's common sense made a good working-alliance with German thoroughness. The Hallé Orchestra (we called it a " band " when I was a boy running wild in Oxford Street and All Saints) is not a thing apart from Manchester's general and institutional consciousness; indeed it *is* an institution in and of Manchester, part and parcel of the physical and spiritual environment, co-existent with the Rylands Library, the *Guardian*, the Ship Canal and the " United," not to mention (in these days) the " City."

I have known a time in Manchester and Lancashire when a man turned or " took to " a fiddle or a trombone as another man to pigeons and whippets. A Hallé player's pride—and he has a right to it—doesn't mean that he considers himself the superior of any other Manchester or Lancashire man or character—say an outside-right or a wicket-keeper at Old Trafford. He is satisfied to contribute his share to the day's work and recreation, to the job of cheering us all up. That is why the Hallé Orchestra is never dull or anonymous of voice or accent; it does not depend, to make its presence felt, on its superb technique alone. Whether playing at top form or a little below top form, it always means something in terms of county character and tradition.

Under different conductors, naturally, any orchestra cultivates different traits of style. Under Sir John Barbirolli I think the Hallé players have acquired an almost Latin clearness and brightness; Sir John, in a way, has " Mediterraneanised " Manchester's music—to use the expressive language of Nietzsche. He has, for our epoch and for the present generation, made the Hallé Orchestra his own—as much his own as it was ever Richter's. I wish gramophone recording had been generally in use in Richter's day, so that we could now compare Richter and his Hallé with Barbirolli's. Can a boy's memory be trusted? The impressions made on a youthful mind and sensibility have a power to last long after middle-age has forgotten yesterday's happenings. But may we trust the memory of a boy in a period of very poor orchestral playing, taking this country by and large? I was little more than a boy when I first heard the Hallé Orchestra under Richter, and I had until then heard hardly any music at all, unless performed by the " Besses o' th' Barn Band," which, of course, taught me to tolerate none but the finest brass in the world.

It was the glorious brass of the Hallé under Richter that thrilled me and struck awe into my innocent heart and ears when I heard the orchestra in the overture to *Die Meistersinger*, and in the Prelude of Act III of the same opera. Majestic yet heartening, genial in the overture, and broad as the sea in full foam at sunrise; sad and solemn yet benign in the wise, slow-moving Prelude of Act III; I can't believe this *Meistersinger* music has ever since been heard in this country as nobly and beautifully intoned as by the Hallé of my boyhood.

During the war of 1914–18, Sir Thomas Beecham, like Sir John Barbirolli during the Second War, came to the rescue of the Hallé in a crisis threatening disintegration; but Manchester must never forget the power behind the throne then, the name of Behrens, just as it must never forget the name of Godlee. Sir Thomas *cosmopolitanised* the Hallé, if I may use a word of my own in this particular context. Under Richter, the Hallé seldom played Mozart really well; Richter heard all music through ears tuned to the stature of tone of Beethoven and Bayreuth. Beecham brought poise and style to Mozart in the Free Trade Hall; also he brought out of the players gorgeous colour—much as a warm fire renders invisible ink visible.

I remember a certain " popular " Saturday-night Hallé Concert; towards the end of the programme the Barcarolle from *The Tales of Hoffmann* was due for performance. I, after the manner of a born music-critic, planned to get out of the hall before this hackneyed piece began. At the pinch, my retreat was cut off and I was obliged to stay and listen near one of the exits. I was enchanted; the Barcarolle, conducted by Beecham and played by the Hallé, was re-created, made new and magical, alluring, haunting. It was at this same concert, if I am not mistaken, that Beecham caught sight of me as I stood at the exit-door when he was in the crescendo of the " William Tell " Overture, the final piece of the evening. And as he saw me, and as he increased an already terrifically quick tempo, he gave me a delicious and naughty wink.

The wit and civilisation of Beecham, assimilated into the heart and bone's marrow of the Hallé, were more than ready to respond to Harty's sensibility. He was one of the most poetic conductors ever nurtured in these islands. He widened the expressive range of the orchestra, so that it could play Berlioz and Brahms, Strauss and Sibelius, second to none. Harty should never be forgotten for a moment when we are admiring the Hallé Orchestra and contemplating its rich heritage of tradition and culture from the years of the founder, Charles Hallé to the present day's consummation achieved by Sir John Barbirolli. What's bred in the bone comes out in the performance of the shortest—even the latest composition.

The Orchestral Conductor

THE ORCHESTRAL conductor has to-day usurped the position on the concert platform once occupied by the prima donna; in fact, he might truly be described as the masculine gender of the same collective noun. He is nearly as expensive too, if not as spacious, though not as expensive as the spectacular Italian soprano who came to see Colonel Higgins, then director of Covent Garden. She asked for a colossal nightly fee, and Colonel Higgins said: " But, my dear, I only want you to sing."

The fashionable conductors of the present time, like the surviving members of the school of the prima donna, attend to their personal appearance in the mirror of public adulation. A decade or two ago all conductors were fat and philosophical; they are now elegant and obviously eligible. So with women singers. In other years, nature has exacted a severe price from women for the gift of a good larynx; what was given by the one hand was taken away by the other. The golden tone was encased in much solid flesh. Nowadays our finest women singers are not only beautiful to hear but beautiful to look at. Even Wagnerian singers need not be hidden in the twilight of the gods. When the Vienna Opera visited London the other autumn, the loveliness of Lisa della Casa, Seefried and Jurinac more than matched their singing. Indeed, I found myself obliged to go to the same opera twice; once to look at these wonderful creatures, then to listen to them. At the first sight of each of them beauty wooed all sentience and sensation to one channel of visual perception. It was impossible to see and hear them simultaneously.

Not even the most beauteous prima donna can now vie with the orchestral conductor in point of box-office appeal, or in any sort of appeal that counts for much from the box-office point of view. In the vast streamlined emporium which is the contemporary musical scene he is the immaculately dressed shopwalker saying: " Brahms on the second floor, sir. Mozart on the sixth. Vaughan Williams in the hardware department, mod'm, very durable." The new public which has filled concert-halls in the television epoch wishes to use eyes as well as ears. The orchestral conductor is the focal centre. He has conquered the crowd and has his fans; he is also apparently taking possession of the great composers. " But have you heard MY ninth symphony? "—meaning Beethoven's. Years ago Toscanini took exception to a certain conductor in America and would not consent to appear in any opera scheme with him. Months later Toscanini was invited to a private dinner, and when he arrived his host was entertaining the other guests on the gramophone. Toscanini listened carefully, then said: " Very good, who is it that conducts? " The host was embarrassed, for the conductor was none other than the one Toscanini had dismissed with contempt. But the truth had to be told. " What? " expostulated Toscanini, " that mountebank? Ach, it is as I always say, anybody can conduct! "

The rise of the orchestral conductor as a spectacle of the concert-hall is due to the relation of function to structure, if we may deal biologically with a subject so delicate and decorative. During the last quarter of a century the orchestra has developed enormously in numbers, scope and technique. The public has become orchestra-conscious as never before. To take charge of the magnificent instrumental machine some virtuoso control was necessary, if only for the needs of salesmanship. When I was a youth, a whole column of music-criticism might appear any Friday morning in the *Manchester Guardian* signed " S. L.," ending with the sentence " Dr. Richter conducted." Simply that and nothing more; no other mention of the most renowned conductor of his period. A conductor of the present would feel like calling the law of libel to his aid if he were not regarded by the critic as the pivot and pilot of the programme. To say the truth, the orchestral conductor as we know him now is the sign of an improved musical taste at large—in spite of his many vanities and hints of charlatanism. He is at least a more musically civilised tyrant than the old-time prima donna was, with her dreadful and limited vocal repertory. The conductor to-day cannot drop lower than, say, Tchaikovski in his quest for easy " acclaim "; but the prima donna of yesterday was expected to sing Tosti, or even " Home, Sweet Home." I retain a recollection of once seeing Clara Butt advance massively down the centre of the platform, to the uttermost edge of it, there to bow and condescend to the audience, before singing " Dear Little Jammy Face."

There is no doubt, too, that orchestral playing has improved everywhere in quality of blended tone and assembled skill. The wonder is not that orchestras in the past frequently sounded thin and out of tune but that they sounded many times as though they really were good orchestras.

(I am referring, by the way, to English orchestras.) Rehearsals were often meagre and casual. Sir Hamilton Harty was obliged to content himself usually with one rehearsal for each Hallé concert; possibly an " extra " would be put at his disposal for the first performance in Manchester of the ninth symphony of Mahler. Such were Harty's gifts that he maintained a very high standard of execution with the Hallé Orchestra, and at the same time made his audience acquainted with all the Sibelius symphonies, all Berlioz, while it is to be doubted if Manchester has ever heard Brahms played with more warmth and more range of expression than by the Hallé under Harty.

Harty was an extraordinary musician and man; other conductors not his equal were unable to cope with our empirical orchestras of those years. Much as many of us admired Landon Ronald's sensitive ear, we cannot believe that he would survive comparison with standards of conducting developed since his death. Yet he was regarded as an outstanding interpreter of Elgar. Certainly he rose head and shoulders above one or two of his predecessors and contemporaries. Who would credit the fact, if there were not historical evidence in support of it, that once on a time the lists of prominent British conductors included Sullivan, Cowan, Manns, and . . . ? One night a trombonist came home more than usually exhausted after a concert, and his wife asked him what was his opinion of the new conductor. " Tell you the truth, my dear, I didn't have time to notice him." The orchestral conductor is now expected to give us more than a performance that makes an inventory, so to say, of the notes as written down on paper; it is assumed that he will interpret a work with relevance to style. He must understand that no metronome

42

can indicate the difference between an adagio movement by Mahler and one by Brahms.

Sometimes, naturally enough, conductors take themselves too seriously. One of them addressed the New York Philharmonic Orchestra on the evening before a performance of the ninth symphony of Mahler. " Gentlemens," he said, " to-morrow when we play, in the owdience will be Alma Mahler, who was the Geist, ze inspiration, of thees immortal Meisterwerk. Now gentlemens, I want der performance to be more as a performance; I want it to be a Konzeption, so that Mahler's vife, his guter Geist, will feel that in the hall is the Geist of Mahler *selbst*—'imself. So I leave no stones unturned to make thees performance komplet, immaculat'. From my own expense I give yet anozer rehearsal if necessary. So I ask you, gentlemens, to give me now any advise, any leetle advise, about bowing or phrasings. I am modest man. I listen."

He bent his head and waited. Not a sound. So he spoke again. " Komm', don't be shy. I am humble man. Any leetle advise from you; you are all very great musicians. Speak, I leave no stones unturned . . ." There was more silence, then from the trombones came a voice. " Why, Doc.—send for Bruno Walter! "

More about the Conductor

WE CANNOT very well leave our discussion of the conductor as prima donna without raising the old question, " Should he have the score in his head or his head in the score? " In other words is it an advantage to conduct from memory? Most of the virtuosi conductors dispense with score, at any rate while at work in public, where they can be seen and generally admired. Some of them, Toscanini and Mitropoulos for example, are equal to the achievement of a detailed rehearsal, all from memory. Only one English conductor so far has consistently dispensed with the score; and even he, our greatest, has recently taken the precaution of using the score at concerts, where he may be seen turning over the pages most diligently.

One of our newest and most promising aspirants to orchestral conductorship, Thomas Matthews, sometimes dispenses not only with score but with baton. The Russian Safonov was perhaps the first conductor without baton. Hans Richter, most conservative of conductors, invariably laid the baton down on his desk during the five-four movement of the " Pathétique " Symphony of Tchaikovski, probably because in his period five-four was a tempo likely to be considered eccentric on the whole. There are in fact, no hard and fast rules governing the use of the score or baton. Much depends on the size of the orchestra, and also much depends on the character of the music. If a work is in the chamber category, the use of a score by the conductor evokes a sense of modest impersonal music-making necessary to the style. In a Brandenburg concerto of Bach, say, a conductor by using a score relates performance to an unselfconscious absorption in the notes and patterns for their own sake as music which is content with beauty not obviously " expressive." Only in music calling for dramatic or pictorial or histrionic presentation may a conductor not use a score tastefully and justifiably. Obviously he discards the score so that he might the more freely bring into play his gestures and other aids to personal expression and interpretation. In strictly classical music, in Bach especially, any personal nuance is hurtful to style; " expression " imposed egoistically from the outside is distracting in Bach, if it is not positively misleading. The conductor as a deliberately personal interpreter was born, or was the consequence of, the Romantic movement of the nineteenth century. Clearly, then, the style of most classical or classically derived music is bound to seem post-dated by conducting which even obliquely hints of a virtuoso technique or of a personal view of its emotional content. A conductor should suggest to us that he is part of the musical ensemble in all works which are related to the concerto style. It is a rather vulgar sight to see a conductor directing orchestra and pianist through a concerto, and not admitting his place in the scheme, one among many, by " following " or seeming to " follow," the printed notes. Whether the pianist should play from memory in a concerto is another matter; but it is not necessarily a sign of indifferent musicianship or artistry in a pianist if he or she likes to have a score within sight. Dame Myra Hess is not above this act of conscience.

For the purposes of an orchestral work of unmistakably dramatic intent, or a work at all histrionic in its emotional appeal, the conductor who is in any degree a personal genius at interpretation will find a score in front of him a hindrance and source of frustration. He is now in the position of and performing the function of an actor. Whenever I see English conductors referring to the score while they are supposedly in charge of Strauss's "Don Juan" or the "Pathétique" Symphony of Tchaikovski, I feel that both himself and myself are somehow being kept outside the inner dramatic world of the music; there is a wall or veil of academic concern in the way of full imaginative realisation. With a Furtwängler, a Bruno Walter, a Klemperer, the gestures and every physical movement of a conductor are as the gestures and every physical movement of a Gielgud; they are essential accessories to an interpretation which is almost as much histrionic as it is musical. Music goes through these conductors stimulating dramatic or pictorial conceptions, even as words and poetry pass through the mind of a great actor, to take the shape of the varieties of tone and the tempo of his speech and movements, all making for personal interpretation.

I have never understood why many music critics protest whenever a conductor in the romantic or non-objective tradition comes to us with an interpretation of a symphony by Beethoven or Brahms which departs from general usage of the score at points, introducing here an uncommon emphasis, there an unfamiliar delay or indulgence. We don't expect every Hamlet to toe a rigid line of observance to the letter. So long as the style of a work is respected, there are as many occasions and opportunities for "personal" interpretation in Beethoven as there are in Shakespeare.

The greater the work, the more it will accommodate or stimulate different " meanings " or different " imputations," to use Professor Samuel Alexander's term. Whether the conductor buries his head in the score, or carries it about with him in his head, he should not regard it too literally. Not all the music is in the notes; in fact, all the music is in the style. Certainly there is no finality to be got from the metronomic court of appeal. Consider merely the matter of tempo indications. Adagio in Mozart must sound or seem to move on lighter feet than in Brahms. A middle-aged, middle-class, and rather corpulent man walking alongside a young aristocrat of no superfluous flesh is obviously going at a more burdensome pace; even if he is not lagging behind his companion he is apparently not accustomed to a tempo of pedestrianism which his companion would scarcely call adagio at all! The question of weight of harmony must enter the conductor's mind and imagination as he decides points of tempo. The score is sometimes addressed as much to the imagination as to the strict musical eye. In all music demanding for its performance a large orchestra dating its period of origin Romantic or post-Romantic, the conductor will the more comprehensively get to the heart of the matter if he does not bury his head in the score; all the more so if he is so hypnotic that he can momentarily make us feel that the printed notes are not in existence at all, anywhere. To perform as remarkable an act of suggestion as this, he will most emphatically need to have the score in his head.

47

PART TWO

COMPOSERS

Approaching Mahler

MAHLER IS still not really liked or understood in this country at large. There is a big and growing appreciation of him in America; for the conductors there are mainly of Continental origin and training, consequently they learned to approach Mahler very early in life. Few English conductors seem to have the faintest clue to Mahler. Neglect of Mahler here is most time excused by reference to the expense involved by the large orchestra he needs, and to the number of rehearsals required, and so on. Mahler certainly does, in nearly all his works, call for lavish instrumental forces; also he expects as much imagination and passion as technique. But Henry Wood conducted the first symphony of Mahler at a Promenade Concert in 1903, and the First and Seventh in 1905 and 1913 respectively. Hamilton Harty gave performances of the fourth and ninth symphonies, and *Das Lied* at Hallé concerts some twenty years ago, with one or two rehearsals for each at the most. No; we needn't carry our investigation too far as we seek the cause of the average English conductor's shyness in the presence of Mahler.

The bulk of the writing about Mahler in English reveals much the same innocence or ignorance. Some of it strikes me as having been written about another composer altogether. Mahler is sometimes described in English as though in a Teutonic tradition (" long-winded and meta-physical "). A composer less Teutonic than Mahler, in mental tissue or orchestral method, has never lived. He is supposed to have written perpetual " swans-songs " of nineteenth-century Viennese and Central European culture; yet he opened up " new paths," and you will hear his influence at work, assimilated by nothing less than genius, in, for instance, the orchestral preludes of *Peter Grimes*. He is persistently linked to Bruckner, even as Bruckner is linked by the half-educated to Wagner. Mahler and Bruckner are both marked off from Wagner by the basic fact, that neither is erotic in the least. And Mahler is marked off from Bruckner by Bruckner's absolutely sure faith and patience. Bruckner is integrated—by God, as he himself would surely say. Mahler, in spite of his colossal Catholic *mise-en-scène* and " properties," dis-played on the canvas of the eighth symphony, subsided into the autumnal pessimism of *Das Lied* and the slow movements of the Ninth and Tenth symphonies. More than any other composer, not excepting Wolf, he lived on his nerves; his music is, so to say, very frequently so many exposed nerves. Even in the Adagio of the ninth sym-phony, where at last Mahler achieves a full, broad simple contained close harmony, he is soon impelled into the familiar tense reachings upward in the strings: a sort of ache of aspiration, then a quiver of an appoggiatura. Through music, Mahler tried to find himself and integrate his mixed elements. Thirty-three years ago, the first of discerning English writers on Mahler nearly touched the spot: " To be naïve and to be direct are not quite the same thing, though Mahler did all that was possible to make them so, and a writer may be both and yet come short of the sincerity of emotion without which nothing is true or enduring in the arts. There are some grounds for suspicion of Mahler's emotional sincerity in his art, in spite of his naïvety and ruthless directness of style. He is a Jew and a Catholic, and while there is every reason why a Jew should show some sympathy with Christianity from its origin and make it prominent in his art, the Jewish-Catholic standpoint is complex to the normal sensibilities." Thus Samuel Langford in 1920; nobody since has got closer than " S. L." to the core of the matter in Mahler.

I don't agree, none the less, that Mahler was ever insincere. Only in the eighth symphony are we likely to be worried about the Catholic-Jew complex. His trouble was not insincerity but a frustration which receives so powerful an expression, in the finale of the first symphony for example, or the " Stürmisch bewegt " movement of the Fifth, that we may even think of this frustration as a source of inspired greatness. The fury is terrific, and takes the shape of bare, steely harmony. " Pitched battles against the world and the demons of life," wrote Langford of these movements; and who that has written on music since has written half as well? Inspiration seldom fell on Mahler by grace; he had to " hammer it out." But the ring on the anvil, though many times jarring and discordant, is desperately honest. Sometimes the true and right idea eluded him, so he resorted to gestures. He was by nature unable to wait patiently during a dry creative period, wait like Bruckner, strong in the faith that, as Goethe told Eckermann, ideas come when they will, and you'll find them one morning sitting on your shoulder like children from God, saying: " Here we are."

But I am making the common mistake of talking of

Mahler as though he were mainly a pathological case, and not a composer of immense range, worth endless study as musician and music-maker. There is in him occasionally an invention so sharp that it almost stings, and a reckless profusion of energy properly to be called dæmonic. The Rondo-Finale of the fifth symphony, with its triple fugue, is an example of the Dionysiac (but I had better say " Walpurgisnacht ") aspect of Mahler. The Rondo Burleske of the Ninth is as though all that we associate with the style of the grotesque scherzo had been let loose in a gigantic scornful flagellation of notes. Mahler was imprisoned in the shackled rhythmical periods of his times; he tries hard to break the bars. As early as in his second symphony, he changes his time-signature twenty-three times in thirty-six rehearsal " measures " in the fourth movement. Flexibility of rhythm is not one of Mahler's strongest points; he was temperamentally taut. And nothing appears in Mahler's music that is not true to the man himself. His influence on orchestral technique has been greater already than that of any other composer since Berlioz. In another piece, I shall hope to go thoroughly into Mahler as a composer who wrote music not for the enlightenment of other composers as different one from the other as Shostakovich, Britten and Aaron Copland, but for all of us who are willing to lend ears to a very human artist, whose world was the symphonies made out of his sweat and blood and essence.

Mahler's Ninth Symphony

THIS COPIOUS work has not often been presented to London
audiences, but one or two critics have dealt with it severely,
dismissing the music as tasteless and extravagant. Taste-
lessness is very much a matter of taste, so for want of room
we must pass this objection by. Extravagance, a risky word
to use in any context nowadays, refers no doubt to Mahler's
fulsomeness of expression, to his uninhibitedly romantic
attitude to his art, and to the eighty-or-so minutes' traffic of
the four movements of the ninth symphony. One of the
metropolitan bloodhounds sniffed out the resemblance of
the theme of the adagio to *Abide with me*. The sternest
self-denial is needed to resist pointing out the resemblance.
Many have noted it; but many more have kept the discovery
to themselves. It is as common nowadays to chastise
Mahler for vulgarity as once on a time Charles Dickens
was taken to task for the same reason. Not that there is
any other thing that Mahler shares with Dickens, except
genius. (If an approach to Mahler could be helpful by way
of a novelist, Dostoevsky might be suggested.)

There are, of course, reasons for complaints against
Mahler on grounds of familiar cadences and inflections,
banal refrains and rhythms. His view of music was not
strictly that of the artist; he did not detach himself from his
art and the material of it and contemplate from an æsthetic

distance the touch and proportions of his handiwork. He would have been mystified at the contemporary æsthetic of music as a matter of abstract patterns, music *qua* music. Mahler lived in and on music; so soaked was he in its substance, as his school and period knew and felt it, that all its elements, every tone, harmony, and instrumental timbre, had its association-values, its " meaning," its power to be identified with his own psychosis, his emotional modes of existence, his fantasies. Music was in fact sacramental for Mahler, and he no more looked consciously at the quality or pedigree of any of his own themes and symphonic material than the priest inquires whether the bread has been freshly baked, or whether the wine is a 1941 Châteauneuf du Pape. A curious and significant point in Mahler's creative processes is that often he begins from a melody or figure which is definitely and disturbingly familiar; then the artist in him gets to work in a series of transformations, each reaching to a finer imaginative and musical ether. It is as though the ancient beads having been devoutly counted, the egoism of the artist could now be given licence. But first of all is the ninth symphony a confessional, with no reservations. The paradox is that Mahler, who made capital out of his sense of loneliness in the world, was essentially a histrionic composer whose music is always making gestures. The sincerity of these gestures is beyond question, and they have become so habitual as to suggest unself-consciousness. Throughout the considerable output of Mahler we find the same clues to what he is saying; he is constantly aiming at a personal communication. The rising figure of the Adagietto of the fifth symphony is Mahler's main spiritual and psychological leitmotiv. We hear it completely realised in Mahler's most beautiful song " Ich bin der Welt abhanden gekommen," where once and for all he expresses his uncharted drifting state. No composer has associated as unambiguously as Mahler certain conditions of mind and feeling—known as " ideas " in music—with a more easily recognised set of tone symbols. Mahler called on words and the human voice in five of his large-scale works, and he was frequently using cuckoo calls, fanfares for trumpets, bringing back echoes of military music from the barracks heard in his boyhood. But it is an error to count him among writers of programme music; even the finale of the second symphony, with its " Resurrection " clamour and bell-ringing, is no more imitative of external phenomena than the finale of Beethoven's Ninth; it is a musical, or at any rate an instrumental, apotheosis.

He not only wore his heart on his sleeve; he exposed lungs and liver. His crescendi are as so many nervous reactions. No music in existence is as un-English as Mahler's, so ungentlemanly in its want of reserve. He strips himself naked. In his efforts to harmonise his mind and nature, to mingle the sharpness of his Jewish intellect and his general nervous reflexes, his love and his hatred of life, he wrestles with music with a tormented ecstasy that is unparalleled in symphonic composition. At the height of the argument of the first movement of the ninth symphony a trumpet sounds an obvious " fate " theme; the tumult of the orchestra is strenuous; swirling figuration threatens the tonal centre. The drum cracks: gunshot and despair and ghostly muted brass. It is passages in Mahler such as this that cause judicious and formal musicians to grieve; they maintain that Mahler's counterpoints are of the kind which " fit in " if they happen to " stick."

But it is not with Mahler, as it is with Tchaikovski (who purely as a musical artist was Mahler's peer), a case of physical frenzy. Mahler's ecstasy and anguish alike are of the spirit and sensibility. Another paradox about Mahler is his reputation in certain places for melodic banality— dripping with portamento—and the solemn truth that his approach to music was really austere, religious, unerotic. When he does smile it is with a twist and a grimace. He was antipodal to Strauss, who probably enjoyed the act of composition and creation more than any other musician; Strauss was perfectly and comfortably integrated as man of the world. The intense soaring strings of Mahler, aching their way upward, the last squeezing out of an appoggiatura—in all parts of the orchestra—hint less of rest at last than of resignation and exhaustion. I find the ninth symphony deeply moving as expression, and fastinating as art; for Mahler's movements around the tonal centre, especially in the Adagio, are preparing the way for later experiments. He glances back as man and poet in the Ninth; as musician he looks prophetically forward. And as Dr. Mosco Carner has pointed out, Mahler had foreboding of the twilight about to fall on Austria and on many a favourite god. Whether a man " likes " Mahler or not is one question, and a personal matter. It is nonsense to question his sincerity; and it is pure ignorance to suggest that as a craftsman of the orchestra he had anything to learn from anybody. Maybe he knew too much.

Igor Stravinsky

It was in a very remote past that the present writer, with countless other young intellectuals, found in Stravinsky's music a rallying-point for all our libertarian enthusiasms. Stravinsky was for us the avatar of our æsthetic adolescence. Compared with him, Strauss was already old-fashioned and bourgeois. Stravinsky was like astringent air coming through a heavily-furnitured and Teutonic music-room; he put the orchestra to austere physical drill, reduced its weight and removed fleshiness by means of drastic and brutal rhythmical emphasis. He led for us an after-war exacerbationary nervous reaction.

Yet it was this same Stravinsky who, while we were even younger—by a few years—had ravished us with the orchestral iridescence, the flashing sensuous appeal of *L'Oiseau de Feu*. In our ecstasy, as Karsavina danced in this ballet, we could not stay to bear in mind that it was, after all, resplendently fresh from the Rimsky-Korsakov workshop of many colours. *Petroushka* completed the spell; we all became balletomanes now, finding in it something of the salt of humanity coming out of the pathos and tears of the puppet. We could not guess or dream then that the day would dawn on which our magician would renounce or deny his own witchery, and, stripping his art naked of all allurements to eye and sense, give us the

Symphonies pour Instruments à Vent, and generally assume a more and more objective, not to say hieratic, point of view. Sufficient for the day the orgy of *Le Sacre du Printemps*, which lifted from us a burden of rhythmical inhibitions inherited from slow-breathing Germans. The *Great Sacred Dance* was an escape for countless sedentary adolescents who for long had yearned to live dangerously (if, all the same, respectably). The ironical fact is that Stravinsky provides much the same rallying-point for the young avant-garde of 1957. He has shed many skins of style; he has seemed to encompass all musical worlds, seeking a fresh mask, now back to the classics, now some dalliance with Glinka, now a reaction to Lully, to Pergolesi and, as though in despair, a return to himself. " Il est permis de violer à condition de faire un enfant," he has himself argued; rape is justified by the creation of a child. But the more he has changed school and technical procedure, the more he has remained the same Stravinsky. The rake has, on the face of it, made little progress.

It is easy to fall into banality while discussing Stravinsky this way. A composer is free to compose in any form or idiom at hand, though the greatest have usually made forms of their own, or given new twists or direction to them, as Stravinsky himself has done in his master-works *Petroushka* and *The Rite*. He is a genius, we all know; and at bottom he is a Russian uprooted and rendered by circumstance the cosmopolitan prophet of the latest metamorphosis of what is known as the " contemporary scene," which also remains the same the more it seems to change. A composer is related to and under the influence of his social and economic environment. Different conditions produce or encourage the production of a Haydn and a Bruckner. The more closely he is connected with his public the more obliged a composer is to address himself to his listeners in a language he knows they will understand. The musical scene or habitat has disintegrated in recent years; there is no main contemporary musical language, familiar at once to a public at large.

Stravinsky has, at any rate, avoided extremes of tonal unfamiliarity; he has written with increasing solicitude for shapes and patterns tolerably traditional. The question is whether neo-classicism, no matter how broadly viewed, will accommodate itself to the Stravinsky conception of rhythm and instrumentation. Only by some arbitrary act of theoretical or æsthetic purpose could a modulation be made to neo-classicism from the stupendous orchestral dynamics and percussion of *Le Sacre*. Where is the nexus, the bridge-passage from that work of supreme genius to the *Apollon Musagète*, the third symphony, and *The Rake's Progress*?

A new conception of any musical element or material, whether of rhythm, melody, or harmony, calls for a new mould or some instinctive transformation of an old form. Theory or *a priori* thinking is of little use here. The power and plasticity of Stravinsky's rhythm and orchestration in *Petroushka* and *Le Sacre* knock us over; argument about it is overwhelmed. But it is a kind of rhythm which, by explosion, tends soon to exhaust itself. It scarcely waits on the more or less orderly key-transitions that go hand in hand with melody, or the thematic sequences of the kinds of music classically derived. The probability is that the right approach to Stravinsky has been hindered by the excessive claims on his behalf by uncritical followers. In Stravinsky's audiences to-day some of the Elders among

61

those present can look on at the applauding " young bloods " and relive old egoisms of exclusive adoration and comprehension. The greatest geniuses turn upon themselves as they grow old, wisdom enters, and even the platitudinous is risked. I know of no music by Stravinsky which causes me to think of ripeness and of simple, unself-conscious fulfilment. But maybe we do him wrong to apply to him a test of musical greatness relevant enough in past years. He is the complete contemporary composer, plus genius; he is as contemporary in the nineteen-fifties as he was more than forty years ago, when *Le Sacre du Printemps* first set the cat amongst the pigeons.

When Sir Arthur Bliss presented the gold medal of the Royal Philharmonic Society to Stravinsky he said that future musical generations " would have to reckon with the disturbance of his personality," which was very finely said. The programme on this occasion, brilliantly played by the Royal Philharmonic Orchestra conducted by Stravinsky himself, consisted entirely of ballet music, as though the composer were attempting to anticipate posterity's valuation of his genius. The latest music given, the *Orpheus* of 1947, opens no fresh creative vein, but now and again solemnity touches some depth of emotion, and the composer conducted with an eloquence of gesture which openly contradicted his own theory of objective, non-emotional interpretation. The evening began with the charming *Divertimento* arranged from the ballet *The Fairy's Kiss*, and two of my colleagues listened to the music, which is based on pretty tunes selected from Tchaikovski, with their eyes glued to the printed score. It is certain, surely, that Stravinsky has more wit and sense of humour than has been given by nature to his average admirer or disciple. *Petroushka* brought a distinguished concert to a brilliant end, and once again the feeling came over me that I was reliving olden times, revisiting distant scenes and glimpses of the moon— the same dazzling orchestral choreography and mimicry of forty years ago, the same cascades of arpeggi, the same fanfares, the same incisive, liberated, yet iron-gripped rhythms and accents, the same Stravinsky and—the same audience.

The occasion rendered due honour to the greatest composer of ballet; whatever the future may decide about his musical limitations, the first to relate ballet to a serious world of imagination and satire, the boldest and most entertaining of innovators, fascinating even while he is clinical, and so Protean or versatile that the Stravinsky enigma still waits the solution; behind all the masks, which is the face, lined with the soul and experience?

Sibelius at Ninety

SIBELIUS AT the age of ninety has produced no music of importance for a quarter of a century, and so has lived long enough to enjoy a larger portion of his own posterity than any other composer, with the exception of Charpentier, who (as far as my knowledge goes) is still alive, though born in 1860* and musically silent or extinct these forty-odd years. Sibelius, once famous by the seductions of the *Valse Triste*, is regarded in this country and America as one of the great symphonists, classic in æsthetic and mental fibre if not in his treatment of forms and formulæ. But he has not yet conquered in all the civilised places; in fact, a few years ago a celebrated conductor described Sibelius to me in these terms: " The ideal composer for countries not truly musical." His disregard of alluring cantabile long-phrased melody keeps the Italians at a distance; his lack of charm and cosmopolitanism makes the French uncomfortable; the Austrians and Germans expect from music either the poise of a Mozart, the geniality and warmheartedness of a Schubert, the wordly sensuousness of a Strauss, the heroic gesture of a Beethoven, or the piety of a Bruckner.

Sibelius deals in none of these familiar characteristics and material. He once expressed his point of view as

*Charpentier died in 1956.

64

follows: "It strikes me more particularly that musicians are still writing in the post-Wagner style, with the same laughable pose and the still more laughable would-be profundity." His fourth symphony, which is positively antithetical to the romantic or picturesque symphonic style, is more than forty years old. The reaction against the subjectively emotional and the didactic kind of symphony cleared the air, so that in certain latitudes could be seen the rugged summits of the Sibelius masterpieces, "bald as the mountain tops are bald," bald almost as the man Sibelius himself. He seems in his mature works to compose from the rawest material of music, out of simple scale-passages, fragments of themes, insistent rhythms, thrummings in the violins, cluckings and whirlings in the wood-wind, brass suddenly played crescendo, horn cadences. The usual symphonic procedure, statement-development-and-recapitulation, is either telescoped or treated elliptically; the short themes fall naturally into germ-cells, then the whole tissue of the music expands, with little waste matter. Out of a mist of string tone and wood-wind croaking like frogs in a winter marsh, brass will emerge as a sun of copper, if not of gold. Then abruptly, with a few imperious chords rudely off the beat, Sibelius will bring the symphony to an end, dismissing us with a peremptory: "Take it or leave it."

A man might as well hang himself as look for a conventionally extended line or sequence in a Sibelius symphony (excepting in the first two of his seven), even as, according to Dr. Johnson, a man might as well hang himself as look for a story in a novel by Samuel Richardson. Yet the music of Sibelius is thoroughly consecutive; in fact it is tight in its relevance and interdependence, bar by bar. Every note falls into pertinent position. The seventh symphony consists of only one movement played, of course, without a break. It lasts not much more than twenty minutes. None the less it creates the effect of an unfolding musical and orchestral grandeur, with unity in variety and contrast and development, the end foreseen and sown in the beginning. Usually a ground bass or encompassing fundamental tone binds the texture or acts as the germinating source of the whole content of the great Sibelius. His personal ways of using the materials of music, the thought-processes weaving mosaic into mountain, have nothing to do with what is known as "modern" music. Beethoven would have understood the vocabulary, the diction, and the logic of Sibelius, who has not listened uncreatively to the last quartets of Beethoven. The short cuts taken by Sibelius in his way of symphonic thinking do observe, if we look closely into it, that logic of musical argument which seems part of our habit of musical cerebration; but he gives to all his sequences such a continuity and concentrated order that the different paragraphs are concealed. It is rather like great prose written in short paragraphs, with no full stops and only semicolons, until the clinching decisive full stop at the end. Rhythm and orchestral dynamics are his hammer and anvil; they happen to be just those qualities in music to-day, from the lowest kinds to the highest, which are intelligible at once to a public that is not always sure to respond to the subtlest melodic or harmonic changes.

This original musical faculty of Sibelius, and the highly personal art and technique which have served it, has produced the impression of nature music, brooding and omnipresent; not nature expressed by "picturesque" associations and tone-equivalents or images, but by absorption of Sibelius's mind and imagination into the atmosphere and setting of his physical habitat and home. It is, in a great and poetic sense, national, even regional, music. There are no men and women in the world in Sibelius; no earthly or temporal passions spin the plot. If I may quote from myself (for I cannot put the idea into other words):

" It is the music of animism. In Sibelius the forces of nature seem to live more and have being of their own as they are changed into orchestral sounds. It is as if the sights and sounds of his country, the air and the light and darkness, the legends and the history, had by some inner transforming force become audible in terms of rustling violins, horn-calls out of a void, brass that swells in short gusts, beginning and ending almost as soon as heard; oboes and flutes that emit the clucking of weird fowl; bassoons from the darkness of swamps." One of the earliest works of Sibelius is called *En Saga*. The same title could be applied to each of his masterpieces. His mind and vision have followed a single track, and as the fashions change some of his music may take a place in a less than universally arresting company of masterpieces.

There is a natural tendency, whenever we are trying to make an estimate of a great artist, to dwell on his greater and more portentous aspects to the neglect of less imposing but not less human characteristics. Sibelius is a full man who has lived an experienced life. He can unbend; he has humour, if we can get through the clefts in the rock. The Intermezzo movement of the fifth symphony is an exquisite miniature, delicate in touch, and bred in the fancy. There are long-breathed and striding tunes in the first and second symphonies; even at the noble ending of the seventh symphony a splash of colour reminds us that once on a time

67

Sibelius wrote a *Valse Triste*. In the incidental music to *The Tempest*, Sibelius shows his hand at characterisation of the grotesque and the engagingly femine—Caliban and Miranda. In a little song, *Tennis at Trianon*, he is swift in his vocal and piano etching of cut and thrust and service and volley in the sunshine. A setting of " Come Away Death " by Sibelius is one of the very greatest Shakespeare songs extant. We must try to see Sibelius in the round, his bulk and large assemblance.

The influence of his methods, his technique, individual attitude, and use of the stuff of music, have already changed the course of the symphony, in shape and plasticity. At the age of ninety, Sibelius can take satisfaction in the knowledge that in places he is revered as a classic, and in others as a contemporary and productive force.

Mozart the Unparalleled

OVER TWO HUNDRED years ago Mozart was born at Salzburg on 27th January. His star was temporarily obscured by the post-Beethoven Wagnerian æsthetic, dramatical-symphonical, quasi-symphonical, heroical-ethical and pastoral, the æsthetic of the fertilisation of music by drama. But to-day it shines more luminously, certainly more constantly than any other in the sky. Hans Richter was once asked to name the composer who, in his opinion was the greatest of them all. Without hesitation he said, " Beethoven, undoubtedly." The questioner expressed surprise at a reply so positive. " Undoubtedly, Herr Doktor? But I thought you might have considered Mozart." " Oh," replied Richter, " I didn't understand that you were bringing Mozart into the argument; I thought you were referring to the rest."

Less than half a century ago, in fact in the lifetime of many of us not yet tottering, Mozart's position in musical history had once and for all been established by the authorities as " classical "; he was almost docketed a " period " composer, plus genius, a genius no doubt having gifts towards drama as well as for the strictly musical forms, but born as an opera composer perhaps too soon; for not yet had the expressive and plastic technique of music-drama been brought under control. Mozart was obliged to compose operas in forms derived very much from instrumental music. " Mozart's most dramatic finales and concerted numbers," wrote Bernard Shaw, " are more or less in sonata-form, like symphonic movements . . . and sonata-form dictates repetitions and recapitulations from which the perfectly unconventional form adopted by Wagner is free." Shaw admits, with an insight uncanny half a century ago, that Mozart was a dramatist comparable to Molière. I shall try to show presently that as a dramatist he, in his own art, went beyond Molière.

The great miracle of his achievements, most of them a separate miracle, is that though bound to his period's " absolute " patterns of music, undramatically shaped, he composed opera which in 1957 we can see, now that the Wagnerian mists are clearing and we can dwell on other peaks in the range, as unparalleled for breadth of character-isation in all phases of human activity, from the ridiculous to the sublime, from Papageno to Sarastro, from the comedic to the pathetic, from Figaro to the Countess, from the rogue-picaresque to the traditional romantic seducer, from Lepor-ello to Don Giovanni. He can embody in a melody which an infant can sing the vivacity of a Zerlina, or the awakening ardours of the boy Cherubino. By a few chords in the trombones Mozart can evoke the shape and presence of the majestically spectral; in simple notes for a bass singer, almost displaying the lowest spectacularly, he wrote for Sarastro the only music which, as Shaw said, we might decently conceive coming out of the mouth of God. The " Non mi dir " air in *Don Giovanni* is none the less expressive and in character even if it does end in virtuoso vocal embellishments. Mozart had no need to invent leading-motives to identify his characters; all the music each of them sings is nearly always in character. I cannot explain—and nobody has enlightened me on this point—why " Lá ci darem " comes naturally from the mouth of Don Giovanni though really it is the most childlike of tunes, ideal for performances on the chimes which on sunny afternoons at Salzburg have delighted the ear as we have sat outside the Glockenspiel café. The strains of the March of the Priests in *Zauberflöte* evoke feelings of awe and majesty, of solemn temples and the insubstantial pageant; yet they are strains of a harmony scarcely going beyond the stage of study reached by the first-year pupil coping with elementary inversions. Other composers, Bach and Gluck for example, had composed dramatic music before Mozart came to the scene, using forms not fashioned or evolved from a dramatic intent or impulse. But they had been obliged by the limitations of the dominant musical patterns to confine themselves to a general and not particular dramatic suggestiveness. Mozart, with much the same material and moulds, created a whole " Comédie Humaine." This was the wonder, the miracle, of him. His instrumental works, his " absolute " compositions, are for all their perfection of style and diversity to be explained in terms of a flowering to genius of an eighteenth-century musical culture. By means of forms and tones not yet associated with precise expression, not yet rendered dramatically significant and plastic, he breathed life into figures which in their different libretti are more or less the lay stock puppets of the hack theatre scribbler.

He was the least consciously expressive as he was the most comprehensively ranged composer. He contributed to every kind and shape of music, secular and sacred, opera and symphony, all manner of chamber combinations, all manner of concerted pieces, all manner of " occasional " pieces, including a composition for a musical clock. He seldom went to work directed by an æsthetic theory. No sweat of notebooks for him. " I made it a little long on purpose," he writes to his father of an aria he had written for Raaff the singer, " for it is always easy to cut down, but not easy to lengthen." If the tenor engaged to sing in *Don Giovanni* is unequal to " Il mio tesoro," well then let him try " Dalla sua pace." If Elvira wants another " number " perhaps she will be placated by " Mi tradi." And if " Mi tradi " does not quite seem to fit into the context, heard only with the ear of logic and dramatic sequence, the Mozartian style will in time reconcile the irreconcilable. All is changed in the twinkling of an eye from earth to heaven. Shaw, as we have seen, compared Mozart as a dramatist to Molière, and he was right to think of him as a being essentially informed by the Comic Spirit. Whether the characters in Mozart's operas are living vitally in laughter, or suddenly softened by pathos, or possessed by the dæmonic, or harried, like Elvira, by jealously outraged pride and contumely which are ironically a proof of the love that is a constant wound to the self, no matter how often these people may strike home to our ordinary hearts, yet we can never come truly to know them, any more than we can come to know Mozart. They are aloof, masked like their creator, who surveys his work as though " sub specie æternitatis." Mozart transcended the comedy of Molière; and he brought to it a Platonic ideality and finality.

He would be moved to astonishment and perplexity if he could revisit us and learn that he is safe with the greatest of those who have illumined and transfigured existence here below. His attitude to his art was almost professional; he composed much as craftsmen making Chippendale. He described himself as " soaked " in music; he composed habitually. In the last year of his life he composed *La Clemenza di Tito* and *Zauberflöte*, the *Requiem*, the E flat Quintet, an adagio for harmonica, a work (K.617) for harmonica, flute, oboe, viola and 'cello, three pieces for a mechanical organ, his last piano concerto, the clarinet concerto, the beatific " Ave verum corpus." In six weeks he composed the E flat, G minor and C major symphonies.

> I gave to-day to the mail coach the symphony which I composed in Linz for Old Count Thun, and also four concertos, I am not particular about the symphony, but I ask you to have the four concertos copied at home, for the Salzburg copyists are as little to be trusted as the Viennese. . . .

This is another passage in a letter to his father; and the symphony he thought of little value, tossed off for the " Old Count," is as near to perfection as human genius can reasonably hope to approach. Sometimes Mozart's inexhaustible gift to compose had inevitably to nourish itself on notes and ingenuity. The flawless execution happened as instinctively as the weaving of a bird's nest, which of course is one of the wonders of creation. He remains the most enigmatic and inexplicable of composers; we shall not know his like again. That a Mozart was born once, and once and for all, is a happening and consummation which beggars understanding and all known science, all psychology, biology, physics and metaphysics, and all cosmogony whatsoever.

73

Schönberg and Berg

THE TALKS in the Third Programme on Arnold Schönberg and his music may have helped listeners to prepare themselves for the first stage performance in England of Alban Berg's opera *Wozzeck*. Berg was a student of Schönberg and was proud to say the he could hide a twelve-note series in a composition and defy detection.

The difficulty facing an attempt at verbal exposition of the twelve-note technique—conveniently, if wrongly called atonalism—is that, like relativity, it can be discussed only in terms of its own formula, terms comprehensible to none except those who know all about it already. It is a theory calculated to the end of freeing music of the limitations of the major and minor system; twelve-note technique is egalitarian, each note as " dominant " as any other, with no common rabble of subdominants, mediants, and all the servile rest. But exactly as relativity has not so far palpably affected our everyday conduct and thinking processes, so atonalism has not yet changed the general procedure among musicians who are not working in a provincially doctrinaire circle.

Much too much is made of the twelve-note technique in considering the music of Schönberg that matters. It became an " *idée fixe* " with him only after he had exhausted himself creatively. He was the last great romantic. Ernest

Newman has finely described *Das Lied von der Erde* as the "swan song" of romanticism in music. And *Pierrot Lunaire* of Schönberg is the "Danse macabre." From *Verklärte Nacht* onward to the change of artist to theorist, Schönberg was musically akin to Mahler. It is superficial to say that in *Verklärte Nacht* he received any really seminal urge from Wagner: the melodic line in *Verklärte Nacht*, the cantilena of the "Woman's" music, has an elastic tense sensitiveness not known in Wagner, whose lyricism usually has a good middle-aged "spread" over its nerves.

The curious fact about Schönberg and Berg is that underneath all the "progressivist" technique of composition, the atonalism and so forth, the imaginative material of both often reminds us of the old-fashioned melodrama with—as it was called in my young days—"slow music." Hidden nocturnal horrors, dank pools, women in white searching for lost lovers in woods at midnight, green sickness on faces not necessarily at the window; guilt and insanity, the bizarre and the sadistic—all the romantic stock-in-trade now in a condition of decadence, all rather uncivilised, lacking style or poise, or the restraint of health and breeding. Schönberg, in his works that have meaning for us as music and art, tried desperately and courageously to make a synthesis of romanticism and the pathological sophistication of Vienna during the years of incipient disintegration. Then the genius, the virtue and the evil, went out of him. And when the devil is ill the devil a monk would be. Schönberg found refuge and a new life in science. In the monastic confines of atonalism he told over and over again his twelve-note rosary: "Grundgestalt: Cancrizans: one in twelve and twelve in one." Schönberg, the born melodist and humane musician, who as late in his development as

75

the F Sharp minor Quartet, op. 10, could warm us with the beauty of the vocal movement " Ich fühle Luft von anderen Planeten," settled down to a pedantry fearful to contemplate. In his prime he became cut off from the world; his genius was rendered doctrinaire, arbitrary, not intuitive.

Nobody has more concisely, ruthlessly, and wittily put the case against atonalism as a fruitful source of music than Constant Lambert. It is an inspiration to quote him in this context.

> There is one objection to atonalism so simple and childish that no one seems to have had the courage to make it. Although atonalism has produced complications and objective fugal structures that can with justice be compared with the " Art of Fugue " of Bach; subjective and neurasthenic operas that can be compared with *Tristan and Isolde* and *Parsifal*, it has produced nothing that we can set beside Chabrier or Offenbach, let alone the comic operas of Mozart. An atonal comic opera is a chimerical thought, and though it is unlikely that either Schönberg or Berg would in any case wish to attempt such a genre, the mere fact that the task would be impossible is a proof of the narrow emotional range offered by their idiom.

> No atonal music has so far been written to express pride or joy in life or wit or charm or any of the exchanges of mind and sensitiveness which bring civilised men and women together. When atonal music has not been associated with an obviously melodramatic or lurid stage action or lurid literary text, and has needed to survive as music standing on its own feet, it has failed to hold the attention of any large number of listeners anywhere, though it has

76

been before the public, with much propaganda on its behalf, for thirty years at least. We are, of course, assured by the advocates that atonalism is the music of the future, that the twelve-note technique is in advance of its time. But who can say what sort of music the future will wish to hear? And is it any more likely that posterity will welcome a system of music from which key distinctions have been eliminated, and in which every note is of equal importance, than posterity will welcome a social system in which there are no class distinctions and everybody's somebody? The fact needs to be kept in mind, too, that while a new language is being put together, experimented with and made intelligible, the chance that a masterpiece will emerge from it at the same time is extremely remote.

Berg escaped the hieratic specialism of Schönberg's later periods. His atonalism in *Wozzeck* is frequently not more than skin deep. The score is a skilful summing-up of orchestral and operatic formulæ from many sources, from *Tristan* to *Pierrot Lunaire*, plus, of course, Berg's own genius in full flower. When he is moved by his theme to forget all theory Berg composes in a stark, unambiguous, gripping way. Nobody else has got into music Berg's atmosphere of pathological swamps corrupting to body and soul while the moon glows red as blood. But it is lucky for Berg that atonalism was at hand while he was working on *Wozzeck*. If the ordinary tonal methods had been risked wholesale, cheerfulness might have crept in—and that would never have done.

Anton Bruckner

As WE have here recently been discussing Mahler, we might profitably go on to a consideration of Bruckner, if only to try once again to correct the notion, still generally held in this country, that these composers shared anything in common, except that they both lived in Vienna. Mahler was thirty-six when Bruckner died at the age of seventy-two in 1896. Mahler was in every way at Bruckner's extreme; he was uncharted in the world, restless, living on his nerves, idealist and pessimist, and not integrated psychologically—which is not to say that he was disintegrated as a maker of music, as one of our brisker young critics seemed, the other week, to think I was saying. Mahler belonged in his maturity to the sophisticated and cosmopolitan world, in spite of all the recurrent " Wunderhorn " echoes in his music. His mind had so fine a subtlety that, compared with a development section in a Mahler symphony, a development section in a symphony of Brahms is straightforward and strophic. Bruckner was described by Mahler himself as " half simpleton, half God," an exaggeration in both directions of the metaphor. The naïveté of Bruckner has been overdone; Mahler himself (of all men!) once used to be called naïve by English musicians brought up on the undoubted intellectual complexities of, say, Sir Hubert Parry. Bruckner was no inspired country schoolmaster. Though he remained to the end of his life untroubled of mind and heart about the meaning of the world, for he was " God-intoxicated " and humble but reliant of faith, his ways of thinking in music, his symphonic syntax and logical procedure, his use of a three-theme group in a first movement, were far from simple. The apparent sameness of tone in his symphonies, of technical procedure—pedal-points, bustling string tremolandos, surging scale unison passages broad and confident, brass chordings which only superficial ears will relate to Wagner, suddenly detached wood-wind, repeated phrases and sequences, finale climaxes built on fanfares, and more and more string figurations racing along to a decisive clean-cut tonic—these traits of style, so direct and reliant at one moment, so withdrawn to the solitude of the organ-loft the next, are the marks of a genius not moving along a single track of the imagination. If he was not a full man, he was broad of vision enough to praise his God and his country in symphonies of vast tonal canvas and multitude.

We must bear in mind that Bruckner was not of the German but Austrian habit of symphonic composition, not at all kindred to the " thoroughly composed " or *durchkomponiert* method. He has the length, heavenly or other, of Schubert, with deep religious inwardness, and an equally religious enjoyment of the landscape of his " Heimat," his countryside, not perceived or felt as scenery or atmosphere, though there is plenty of both in a Bruckner scherzo, but as a way of worshipping God in nature: God, in fact, as peasant. Moreover, he has nothing to do with the heroic-ethical " humanity " or " brotherhood " (" Menschlichkeit ") symphony which the Ninth of Beethoven threatened for a while to perpetuate. In Bruckner there is no struggle against fate or doubt; man is safe with God in Bruckner. But though the sound of the Bruckner orchestra, with its rich string melodies, deep-toned brass, and the organ registrations of wood-wind, tell of a man sure of soul and faith, there is no smugness, nothing suggestive of a comfortable bourgeois pew. It is risky even to call Bruckner a romantic; his symphonies stem from the nature romance of Schubert, but he is never the full-throated lyrist, never consciously in search of sensuous beauty. His diction is rather that of musical prose than of musical poetry. It is, of course, stupid to link him to Wagner, merely on the strength of his use of the tuba. Almighty God Himself could not create two minds, two natures, as opposed as those of Bruckner and Wagner—Bruckner who never wore a mask, never the Tarnhelm, but was always himself.

The duration of a Bruckner symphony is not for clocks to measure. Bruckner in his music dwells on big and not small matters: and the shaping of his structures was controlled in the main by his conception. Like any other composer, excepting Beethoven, he is sometimes put into chains by obligations to form as a thing in itself; but on the whole he fills his capacious surfaces pertinently enough. His redundancies, his sudden full-stops, his fallings back on the familiar devices, inversions and imitations, are part of his make-up as a man and artist. I know no other composer in whose style it is as difficult as in Bruckner to suggest how the " faults " might have been remedied without concealing the Bruckner some of us have come to love. I have no time for any kind of musical analysis, or any way of writing about music, that does not get through the technical apparatus to the spirit and the substance which make all the difference between one kind of skill and another. In the best, indeed the only, essay in English that understands Bruckner, Mr. Richard Capell truly and eloquently writes:

> His uniqueness is this: that in the century par excellence of individualism he achieved a major work—major and original by the century's own standards—by applying himself, with no deliberate aim at originality, no conscious exploiting of his personality, to a job of work, the writing of symphonies to the glory of God in the frame of mind of any honest craftsman.

But we should not emphasise Bruckner's austerity. He can sing a broad-chested song; the length and extent of his adagio movements are a consequence of the span of his melody. His scoring for strings is frequently rich and ornamental. (Why, by the way, are conductors nowadays ruining the ineffable second melodic subject of the adagio of the seventh symphony by taking it too quickly, without leisure for cadences and the lovely wood-wind echoes?) His scherzi are vigorous and genial. No composer has written music of happier heart than Bruckner's, or music more lovable. He is not witty, clever, or agile; he cannot run faster than Wagner, which is the only characteristic the two composers share; and on a first hearing there is a certain sameness about all his symphonies. He was not Protean. But use him well and he can be vastly satisfying.

Composers in different periods feel or react to the material of music in different ways. Bruckner was concerned mainly with tone, blending orchestral and organ textures; for he was a master of both instruments. Rhythm in Bruckner is secondary to song and to contrasts of sound

values. Tone, rather than rhythm, is the musical symbol
for the Brucknerian moods of meditation and of thanks-
giving. He made the adagio the crisis or centre of interest
of a symphony. That is why more than once a Bruckner
finale comes to us as an anti-climax. Only the adagio of
the Ninth Symphony of Beethoven will survive comparison
with a Bruckner adagio for sustained raptness of song;
but Bruckner was denied Beethoven's genius for transition.
He is constantly coming to a full stop, then beginning again.
A man at his devotion, communing and praying and contemplating, is not particular about logic, the clause of the
excluded middle, and what not. The impression sometimes got from Bruckner's music is an unawareness on the
composer's part of the fact that anybody is listening.
Bruckner is aloof from the little battles of the hour; he
stood apart from the romantic wallowings and the nineteenth-century crowings of the Uebermensch or his
prophets. He was a great composer, none the less great
for being a good man; which at the present time seems
a curious saying.

Ralph Vaughan Williams

An orchestral piece by Ralph Vaughan Williams, O.M., was performed at Bournemouth half a century ago, and there is no reason why he shouldn't run on the heels of Saint-Saëns, Strauss, and Verdi over the distance of more than fifty years of sustained creative work. He has left Sibelius well behind. He is certainly the only composer who has written an "a cappella" Mass and also a Romance for the harmonica of Larry Adler. He has gone his own absorbed ways for so long and the fame and honours showered on him in the course of time may easily have embarrassed if not bewildered him. Nothing of an obviously popular order has come from his pen, no tune for average vulgar ears, no oratorio wearing the right and proper crêpe on its sleeve and the recognisable white choker, no patriotic stuff. A ballet or " masque" on the theme of Job might sound less than alluring to the crowd. His best-known song, *Linden Lea*, has been mistaken for the chastest folk-song. If *The Lark Ascending* is becoming nearly as well known as *The First Cuckoo in Spring*, the reason most likely is the brilliant playing by Paul Beard or Thomas Matthews or Laurance Turner of the solo part. Elgar has been called a " one tune " composer, and with equal point Vaughan Williams can be called a one-theme composer—as related to Tallis. But the Elgarian is able

to find individuality in a family likeness; so it is with those
who really know Vaughan Williams. To the townsman all
sheep in a flock look the same; the shepherd knows each
at sight. The range of Vaughan Williams is wide, even if
he doesn't at once woo the impressionable senses. There
are no sensual men and women in his music, none, that is,
smacking of the contemporary world. The *Five Tudor
Portraits* in themselves tell of an abounding nature and
bloodstream. But even here the common touch is not to
be felt as strongly as the integrity of the art by which the
portraits are presented. Integrity in fact is the word that
springs to mind as soon as the music of Vaughan Williams
is discussed. He is as English as Thomas Hardy. I can't
imagine Italians or Spaniards or Frenchmen revelling in
Vaughan Williams. He is none the less worth our while
on that account. The stuff of his work is national in the
truest way, and not as a by-product of the study of folk-
song. The Englishry of this music is of the man himself,
as unselfconsciously put on as his clothes—which is to say
much.

Reflection is not readily separable from feeling in Vaughan
Williams; there are no personal approaches, no egoisms.
Each of his works seems more and more to open out the
scene of English field and dale and sky and village and
town and lawn; and the emotion and passion which give
identity and life to the atmosphere are traditional and part
of our history. It is, generally speaking, timeless music,
never going into the air or drawing-room of socially civilised
men and women. It inspires affection; it strengthens but
does not nervously excite. It can achieve nobility and
sound the note of power. Yet we are never addressed
rhetorically; in fact, something of humbleness is there,

making for greatness. The eruption of the fourth symphony came as a shock. We had not been warned. The third symphony of Vaughan Williams, the *Pastoral*, was described by Samuel Langford as a work of " general slowness, lacking arresting features. One might as well look for an instantaneous change of the weather as for an arresting contrast in this music." It was possibly the *Pastoral* Symphony that encouraged a witty critic to say of Vaughan Williams's music that it put him in mind of a cow looking over a fence. The remark need not necessarily be taken as of unkind intent.

After the *Pastoral* came the explosive, harsh, protesting discords of the fourth symphony, bitter, ironical, brutal, definitely ungentlemanly. We couldn't get it into the canon. But the dæmon was soon exorcised; the fifth symphony reposed and reposes in the bosom of John Bunyan. Not long ago, the story goes, Vaughan Williams was conducting his rude imperious and acrid fourth symphony at a rehearsal. When the final chords had been savaged out he put down his baton and, as he walked from the platform, turned to the orchestra saying: " Well, gentlemen, if that's modern music, you can have it."

In all things he goes about his work like a big man. During his formative years music was steeped in many strange dyes. The bedazzlements of Strauss and Rimsky-Korsakov, the pervasive odours of Scriabine—many were lured to destruction. Vaughan Williams remained outside the circle, though in no backwater. The force of his own genius and its plasticity are apparent in every score from him that followed the *Sea* Symphony. There are many transformations of psychology, many sheddings of skins. Genius, and nothing else, is the common denominator of works as different one from the others in vision, thought processes, and musical construction, as the *London* Symphony and *Riders to the Sea*, the fourth and fifth symphonies, the Mass in G and *Job*, the *Serenade to Music*, and the *Five Tudor Portraits*.

A surface monotony, a natural consequence of the use of modal harmony, with its associations of austerity and remoteness, must not deceive us. Vaughan Williams is not all high-noon serenity and spaciousness of tempo; there is rough weather enough in his music, moments when the amenities are ignored and mischief enters. Even in the fifth symphony, " the symphony of the Delectable City," the cloven hoof shows itself in the middle of the Scherzo; Pan thrusts his head through the horse-collar at the height of bucolic revels. During the course of the opera *Hugh the Drover*, delightful, amiable, and picturesque, something of the grimness of the old English ballad tinctures the flavours of open air. The fifth symphony, with its echoes of Alleluia, seemed to bring Vaughan Williams full circle in his seventieth year; the onward flowing music surely contained his testament. It sounded ripe as fulfilment. But the sixth symphony, produced in 1948, landed us at the end in dark metaphysical limbo. The Epilogue, to use the composer's own language, " drifts about contrapuntally." The tone is as though disembodied; the colour is dark and enigmatical. Two chords, E flat major and E minor, move like shadows of each other, and die into a void. Vaughan Williams defies augury. In his eighty-first year, when his seventh symphony was produced, he still had us on tiptoe.

More than any other English composer he has liberated music from forms and procedure grown arbitrary. Binary

86

contrast and fission, this theme and that theme in opposition or conjunction, do not suit a propulsive polyphony or development in lines. At its best, the music of Vaughan Williams is woven rather than moulded. It unfolds as though from an inner coil. The polyphony has a choral richness of expression, as in the Finale of the fifth symphony. Melody in Vaughan Williams becomes ornamented within the range of restricted intervals, and there is usually a hint of a fundamental " earth " tone. Art and nature go hand in hand; fine art and simplicity, strength and not infrequently clumsiness. The portraits of Vaughan Williams the man reveal the style itself. He has in a way transcended music and gone into the nation's consciousness and fibre, kindred with Wordsworth, Hardy and Edward Thomas.

Of Richard Strauss—I

A FEW LAST WORDS

IT HAS long since been a sentimental conceit among writers
about music that the last works of certain composers contain
premonitions of the end and are touched with shadows.
Mozart did indeed suffer such a premonition, as we may
guess from a letter written by him in 1791; but the fact
that he was round about this time working on the *Requiem*
has nothing to do with the case. An artist scarcely needs
prompting from the grave to get into a *Requiem* mood if he
has already undertaken to deliver a *Requiem* to order on set
terms. Mozart actually interrupted the composition of
the *Requiem* to write an opera for the Coronation of Leopold
II, at Prague. Verdi's last music was of a religious cast,
but all his life, as a composer, he had been in the midst of
death, drastic and sudden, in Italian opera. The dark and
backward abyss into which we are taken during the scherzo
of the C major Quintet of Schubert is inexplicable and
bodeful; but after all " Tod " is one of the first words
babbled by any German or Austrian baby in his cradle,
alternating with " Schicksal," " Schlaf," and " Mädchen."
A few weeks before his death, Schubert was thinking of
taking lessons in counterpoint.

If Bruckner was inspired to his ninth symphony by

thoughts of the mortality of all flesh, he must also have believed that he would take an unconscionable time dying; and if Mahler was really taking a farewell from the world in the " Lied von der Erde " and his ninth symphony, we must suppose that he prepared himself well in advance very much after the manner of Captain Hook in *Peter Pan*, who seizes the opportunity of some leisure moments in the busy traffic of a Pirate King to deliver his dying speech lest, when dying, he " should have no time to make it." *Parsifal* is not so much the work of a genius conscious that he is about to experience physical dissolution as one by a man of deep-troubled experience, and by an artist revelling in the rich dyes his hand is still working in. Wagner was contemplating an attempt at a new form of symphony towards his end. The shades certainly fall on the four last songs of Brahms; but even these, grave and beautifully resigned though they are, can as music be linked in style and significance to the Brahms of the *Requiem*, composed in the prime of his life.

The perfect " last works " left to us by a composer are, of all men's, Strauss's four last songs, each written after his eighty-third year, and three of them almost within his closing year, in 1949; *Im Abendrot* was finished In May 1948, *Frühling*, June 1948, *Beim Schlafengehen* in August 1948, and *September* in September 1948, The words of these songs, deliberately chosen for treatment by a ripe master never given to indulgence in unnecessary unworldliness, all tell of fulfilment and readiness to depart; even the *Spring* setting glances back on rapture not to be recaptured. In *Im Abendrot*, deep in the glow of the setting sun, the voice sings of tired wandering; and on a poignant darkened rising interval asks, " Is this perhaps death? "—

"ist dies etwa der Tod ?" Then, in the orchestra, the horn quotes from *Death and Transfiguration* and two larks sing as the music goes into silence. In *Beim Schlafengehen* the words tell of the day that " has made me tired," the hand is ready to cease from labour, the brain from all thinking, all the senses willing to sleep. And in the last of all Strauss compositions, *September*, the farewell is a twilight piece in the autumn garden. Here, in these four last songs, is the most consciously and most beautifully delivered " Abschied " in all music.

Here, also, is the essence of Strauss. The old familiar artistry is here, too, even more consummate than before, because now it is refined with an economy and poetic sensibility not always characteristic of Strauss. The soprano solos are exquisitely melismatic, with a lovely floating *bel canto* purity, yet thoroughly Straussian in flavour. *Frühling* is rather cruelly high in tessitura, but on the whole the vocal writing is inseparable from the orchestration, which is perfectly blended in its intimate sonorities and traceries. The familiar Straussian tone remains—the familiar devices of divided strings and horn cadences, the familiar rise and fall to a flattened note, the familiar sudden changes from and back to a diatonic harmony. The instrumental prelude to *Im Abendrot* emulates *Danae*, which was the opera Strauss loved perhaps the best amongst his later stage productions. But everything has been changed in the four last songs to mellowness; it is as the colours and patterns and the sap of late autumn to the colours and patterns and the sap of spring. The leaves are brown as they fall. Strauss has put off his armour. The man of the world reveals his heart to us; and we can hear the beat and feel the warmth. I know of no old man's music as lovable as this. He does not call on the consolations of religion, or dwell on hopes of a blessed resurrection. In *Beim Schlafengehen* the soul goes winging in the magic circle of the night. The songs are dedicated to the beauty of the world and nothing less. I find difficulty in suggesting by words the raptness of the soprano's exalted melody, as she sings " Und die Seele unbewacht, will in freien Flügen schweben, um im Zauber-kreis der Nacht, tief und tausend-fach zu leben "; the curve of the voice and the tone of mingling instruments suggest the night's endless purpled dome.

There is not a note too many in the four songs. The patterns are cunning; long experience has taught Strauss to use instinctively his store of technique, and to select from it exactly what he needs to answer the promptings of his imagination. We do not usually associate Strauss with the wisdom that comes of a spiritual intensity and absorp-tion. But in these songs the long familiar vocal and instru-mental style and the musical material of it are spiritualised, yet with no weakening of Strauss's own ardour, impulse, and appeal to heart and senses, *Beim Schlafengehen* is, for me, one of the most magically beautiful songs I know, To hear it sung by Lisa Della Casa, and to hear it played by the Vienna Philharmonic Orchestra, is to come upon, at the crest of a lifetime of music, something much to be grateful for, a song to be blessed, and one which changes years of admiration of Strauss to affection. I am not sure that I would not give the whole of *Elektra* for these four last songs. They have been recorded by Decca, with Della Casa and the Vienna Philharmonic, the flawless artists. *Beim Schlafengehen*, in its general manner and arrangements, recalls *Morgen*. There is to begin with a likeness in a vocal

91

recitative which exquisitely hovers between song-speech and song. Then a solo violin of " echt " Straussian tone and feeling prepares for the entry of the voice, which carries on the violin's opening phrase at the words " Und die Seele."

The instrumental score for these songs contains two flutes, two piccolos, two oboes, celesta, English horn and tuba. *September* has a coda in which the horn, always essential to a Strauss apotheosis, is now used with a tenderness that causes the term " apotheosis " in this connection to seem a very hard one. Here is " transfiguration " indeed; here is the benedictory dying-fall, and the readiness. To think of the young eagles of Strauss, the flight to the sun in *Don Juan*, then to know the calm fulfilled peace, beauty and plenty of these songs! He made a good end, after all.

Of Richard Strauss—II

"CAPRICCIO AND DANAE"

A RECENT Strauss season at Covent Garden has apparently left unsatisfied that increasing body of critics which regards opera or any other form of art as an object in time and space, unrelated to the mysterious vagaries of genius, and to be contrasted one with another, like the latest Citroën and Renault car. *Arabella* is belittled because it doesn't come up to expectations based on long acquaintance with *Rosenkavalier*; *Die Liebe der Danae* is dismissed impatiently because parts of it weary the listener who is not interested in the machine or mill of Strauss's technique, whether there is corn in it to grind or not. The evolution of a great artist's mind is more and more fascinating to study the older he grows and, it may seem paradoxical to say, the fascination becomes stronger if, with the accumulation of years and experience, our genius is unable to find any new seam to open in his creative mine.

Strauss, unlike Verdi, discovered in himself no new soil or territory, could not shed the old skin; he continued to the end to play with, and arrange, the old material, the old stuffs so deeply and richly dyed, with his hand entirely subdued to a lifetime's working in it. He subtilised his touch; in *Capriccio* he puts familiar material through a

93

connoisseur sieve and achieves a fastidiousness we scarcely
expect from any German and Bavarian. Strauss in his last
years was once chided for his habit of persistent composition, week in and week out, even though he had no new
things to say. He defended himself with a charming amia-
bility. " Well," he said, " a man can't play Skat all day,
can he?" In *Die Liebe der Danae* he is to be discovered
going to the extreme of his ingenuity to substitute contriv-
ance for invention, and by a virtuoso pride, ease, and recklessness of taste in his orchestration to conceal his boredom
with a libretto not tangibly human enough for his essential
worldliness. Years ago Strauss wrote to Hugo von
Hofmannsthal, saying he was tired of the Wagnerian bulk
and apparatus; yet in *Die Liebe der Danae* he falls back in
Act II on very obvious Wotanry, to eke out the character
of the Jupiter of Joseph Gregor's hotch-potch of symbolism
and parody, product of a sort of mythological " Sim-
pliccissimus." When some human sun of sentiment
warms the lay-figured mock classicism of the opera in
general, Strauss warms his genius adequately; and Danae's
aria in the closing act will survive comparison with the
greatest of Strauss's several variations in monologue upon
the theme of the Marschallin over the ages.

So obviously is the old man enjoying himself in *Capriccio*
that none but the solemnest Beckmesser would regard
academically the issue supposedly in the balance of the
libretto's argument: in opera, which is the more important
or influential factor, words or music? From Gluck—and
before him—through Wagner right down to our present
Britten and *Billy Budd*, the problem persists; and maybe
Ruskin made the most illuminating contribution towards
its solution when he argued that though the lover may

freely sing of his lost love the miser cannot sing of his lost
moneybags. But in spite of its title, *Capriccio* and Strauss
have been both subjected to lecture and a caution, simply
because Strauss comes down on the side of his own art,
though in the libretto the Countess is herself unable to
choose between her two lovers, the poet and the musician.
But Strauss relishes the opportunity of playing the part of
his own advocate, so much so that we can only feel sorry for
anybody who lacks the humour, imagination, and sense of
irony and fun fully to enjoy this game Strauss is revelling
in, with all the aces up his sleeve and knowing all the hands.
The issue before the Countess is, as I say, left undecided:
Wort oder Ton, poet or musician? In a monologue
cousined to that of the Marschallin, Madeleine asks herself:
" Willst du zwischen zwei Feuern verbrennen? " and can
the muses not tell her in what way the right end shall be
found to crown opera in a manner not trivial. And exactly
as the nigger-boy enters to bring down the curtain in
Rosenkavalier, the Haushofmeister enters here with his
" Frau Gräfin, das Souper ist serviert," and laughing in the
mirror with an enchanting gesture, Madeleine goes into
the dining-hall, followed by the Haushofmeister, who
mingles admiration and some bewilderment at her gesture.
The libretto of *Capriccio* by Clemens Krauss, is witty and
wise and beautifully patterned; but surely the end was
Strauss's idea? Nobody has excelled him at the art of
giving the finishing touch, the "once-upon-a-time" cadential
flick that lends to comedy some gracious pathos of distance.
Capriccio is not for public show in a large theatre and is
bound to be caviare to the general; it is unmistakably for
the connoisseur, both in the theme discussed and in the
verbal and musical arts by which it is discussed and

caparisoned. Krauss's theatre director, La Roche, has the stature and as much sagacity as the Direktor in the theatre prelude in *Faust* of Goethe. And Strauss fashions an exquisite instrumental texture, discreetly relating recitative to a musical flow and shapeliness with the mellowest craftsmanship. It is almost a chamber opera. How satisfying as art and as relish of the humour and philosophy of age, to listen to *Capriccio* and to contemplate this wonderful Strauss weaving these intricate but naturally and finely spun gossamer webs in the autumn twilight of his long life!

For several years Strauss has had a belittling press in this country in certain quarters, where romanticism has been attacked with a petulant wistfulness, for reasons doubtless as much physiological as æsthetic. *Arabella* was dismissed at its first performance in London nearly twenty years ago as a pale imitation of *Rosenkavalier*. I cannot resist saving my face in this connection by quoting from my notice of this first performance at Covent Garden, printed publicly on 18th May, 1934: "Up to a point *Arabella* is charming enough with instrumentation as stylish and more light-fingered than anything Strauss has ever done before. The tissue is often beautifully woven; there are taste and poise in the orchestra, and plenty of lovely sounds. *Arabella* is proof that Strauss is still the best composer of a Strauss opera . . ."

Action and reaction being equal and opposite, the chances are that criticism will soon go to the length of praising Strauss for virtue not in character. It need not be argued, for it is not necessary so to argue to clinch the fact of his genius, that old age brought to him any new vision or conception of his art. He had no more need than Sir Toby Belch to refine himself finer than he was; he remained the man of the world and a master of all the elements of his craft, a consummate artificer, always responsive to the comedy of manners played in the mirrored drawing-rooms of civilised men and women—women especially. Of much of the weightier or bulkier Strauss we might say that here is perishable stuff; even with *Salome* and *Elektra* the future is uncertain. In the long run criticism conceivably might discover that Strauss, not less than his antipodean Mahler, was a miniaturist too heavily burdened by the elephantine Teuton Zeitgeist. He was at bottom a middle-class sensualist (I use the term without its English Victorian implications); a comedian not even a tragic comedian, but one whose intent was all for our delight. *Der Rosenkavalier* is the perfect opera for all who know what it is to have a savour for leisured living. The work is poised in a period, in spite of mixture of style; with every woman's destiny, which is the passing of time as the sands run out and the wrinkles come in, the ironic informing spirit and *deus ex machina*. Sentiment and costume and mask, power and pastiche and the belch of Ochs, who is Pan blown-out in disguise, ogling through the horse-collar, and knowing the " secret of the bull and lamb." It is doubtful if any composer has enjoyed himself more than Strauss as he made his music.

How much of it will last? For my part I am not interested in the "durability " of Strauss; enough for me that I owe to him many abiding happy experiences. Some of them, I am aware, cannot be lived through again. But what of that? They have happened, and memory holds the ravishing tones. The impressions remain—" Wo war ich schon einmal und war so selig? "

Of Richard Strauss—III

RICHTER AND STRAUSS

IT IS nearly fifty years since Hans Richter conducted in this country or anywhere else, but though his name is seldom mentioned with favour in our newspapers and musical periodicals there is probably a fair number of ageing folk in audiences at Covent Garden and the Hallé Concerts who remember him. I never heard him in charge of a Wagner music-drama; my first impressions of him were received when he conducted the first of all performances of the A flat Symphony of Elgar. These impressions remain, if not as strongly as his broad genial unfolding of the *Meistersinger* Overture, and his thoroughly German and avuncular and gemütlich caressing of the coda of *Till Eulenspiegel*. Nobody to my knowledge has taken the *Meistersinger* Overture at quite the right tempo since Richter, not too fast, not too slow; and in saying this much I do not forget that the Richter tempo in Wagner was not always regarded favourably at Bayreuth.

Memories of Richter have recently been quickened during the visit to Vienna for the Opera's reopening. A sumptuous book, *Wiener Staatsoper*, 1955, has been produced—a Government production and a work of art!—in which Rudolf Kassner describes Richter as " the Bach of

conductors." He was comprehensive, calm—" allum-
fassend, gefasst "—with the smallest gestures or physical
effort. The music of *Gotterdämmerung* flowed out of him
as from a deep inexhaustible source . . . " aus ihm floss
die Musik aus, wie Wasser aus einer Quelle; besser, aus
einem grossen Behälter." " I have heard all the great
conductors since Richter," writes Dr. Kasser, " er war
anders," he was different. This handsome brochure of
the Vienna Opera running to more than a hundred pages,
beautifully made, printed, and illustrated, is not likely ever
to reach these shores in translation; and as it contains so
much to charm and interest music-lovers I feel impelled
to share one or two delicacies with my readers. Tributes
are paid to Strauss in enchanting messages from Jeritza
and Lotte Lehmann. Maria Jeritza was in her day the
most gorgeously handsome of all the singers of the Vienna
Opera; and it was as a manifestation of another dimension
that she appeared one Saturday night in Peter Street, Manchester, in the Free Trade Hall at a Brand Lane Concert.
It was a foggy night, too. Footlights were put on the
platform, probably to create an illusion of warmth and
romance. Jeritza walked on to it like Tosca; she was the
most imperious and majestically seductive of all Toscas,
tall, elegant, yet histrionic. She at once changed the
Brand Lane Concert and the Free Trade Hall into a strange,
fearful habitation far removed from Peter Street. I won-
dered at the time that the Manchester Watch Committee
didn't get to hear of it. And it remains to this day a
mystery to me what Jeritza was doing in Peter Street,
Manchester, at a Brand Lane Concert in November, at the
height of the Vienna season.

Jeritza writes that one day Strauss came to her and said

" Mariandl " (he always called her by this diminutive), " I am writing a marvellous part for you. It'll be your greatest success, better than your Salome, Tosca, Elisabeth." In fact he promised her that she should have the part of the Färberin, the Dyer's Wife, in *Die Frau ohne Schatten*. She fell in love with the part before hearing a note of the music; it obsessed her day and night, so vividly had Strauss described the fascination of it all. Imagine, she proceeds, her despair, desperation and disappointment when after a few weeks Strauss wrote: " Mariandl. I have reconsidered the whole matter. You will sing the Kaiserin (the Princess), not the Färberin." Poor Mariandl!—she was crushed, crestfallen, could not utter a sound: " Ich sass wie versteinert da und konnte keinen Laut hervorbringen." (In the opera *Die Frau ohne Schatten* the Princess sees her husband turned to stone.) Jeritza protested, with all the rebelliousness and audacity of the young. " I will NOT sing the Kaiserin. I WILL sing the Färberin. You promised. You can't possibly go back on your word. My God, what will the people say? " She wept and stormed: we can hear the stamping of her foot. And how did Strauss answer her tantrums? In one of the most endearingly amusing letters ever written by a great composer to a singer: " Mein liebes Mariandl—You are too young and stupid to understand what I have arranged for you. Stop crying and listen to me. I have decided with Hofmannsthal—you must sing the Kaiserin, and I promise you I will revise the part for you immediately." Jeritza, as she tells her story, now laughs at herself as she confesses that at the back of her mind was the question: " Has the Kaiserin more to sing than the Färberin? " Then Strauss writes his little gem of playfulness . . . " Mein liebes Mariandl—Your part of the

Kaiserin is like this: As soon as you come on the stage in in the first act the public will be struck dumb by your appearance: a crown of gold on your blonde head, lace and a blue-white gown sweeping the stage. You don't sing a note, but you will look superb. In the second act you also don't sing at all, but you stand there like a statue, and I'll guarantee, the audience will be turned pale." Jeritza couldn't then see the fun, but after weeping herself nearly sick, she submitted and, as we know, the Kaiserin was one of her best parts. After the first performance Strauss came to her saying: " Now, my dearest Mariandl, hasn't the good Richard been right again? "

On another occasion Jeritza had sung Elsa in *Lohengrin*, with Strauss conducting. After the final curtain he visited her in her dressing-room. " Ah, my child," he said, " you have excelled yourself to-night." Jeritza naturally ascended to a seventh heaven. " But," continued Strauss, " it is a crying sin that you should cover your beautiful legs and ankles with these long dresses. You were made to play in a part wearing trousers." Again Jeritza protested. She was only happy on the stage in a dress with a long train. " You are a silly little thing," said Strauss (to the spectacular Jeritza!) " and you don't understand what I say to you, your old friend. You are the born ' Rosenkavalier.' I tell you, so go to-morrow morning to Professor Foll and begin to study Oktavian." But naturally Jeritza wanted to sing and act the Marschallin. " No, my dear," persisted Strauss, " you will sing Oktavian, and there's no more argument." His accent is really untranslatable. " Du bist ja wahnsinning, nur daran zu denken, du hast ja vorne nix und hinten nix. . . ."

And so it came to pass. Jeritza, after stress and more

tears, became Oktavian and Mariandl in one. Strauss always called her " Mariandl " until the end. Three weeks before his death he wrote to her addressing her as " Mein liebes gutes Mariandl! "

The more one is told of Strauss by artists who worked with him the more one realises how much they not only admired him as a genius but took him to heart as a humane man, for all his show or aspect of coldness on a first acquaintance. He has never been regarded that way in this country: have we, as a people, ever really loved a composer since the death of Sullivan? When Strauss died the English obituary notices were more or less belittling or patronising. The higher criticism still listens to his music suspiciously. His most serious opera, *Die Frau ohne Schatten*, has been described here as evidence of Strauss's spiritual bankruptcy. Even *Rosenkavalier* is turned into musical comedy for English consumption, with Ochs the funny man's part. Lotte Lehmann draws a picture of Strauss the man, in his home at Garmisch:

" Strauss, cold and without sentiment as a conductor, came closer to me when he played the piano, accompanying a song. At the conductor's desk he wore his iron mask; at the piano I have often seen tears in his eyes and felt his warm-hearted surrender to the music. Many times on cosy intimate evenings I have sung his Lieder with him. He loved to try over again old songs, out of his past, and often would his wife Pauline embrace him, also in tears." Pauline, once on a time, was a singer of Strauss's Lieder herself. Lehmann's picture of Strauss at home is no doubt very German, but it is very human and lovable, too.

Of Richard Strauss—IV

STRAUSSIANA

From Munich comes a book which will give immense pleasure to all who are interested in Strauss and owe to him hours of pleasure which can be shared only by mature minds and never by adolescents. It does not add to our knowledge of the music; few if any important new facts are assembled; it is not a biography and it is not the work of one man. Dr. Franz Trenner has gathered together a vast amount of detail, " documentation," *obiter dicta*, and has composed the perfect Strauss anthology or Jahrbuch. He binds memory to memory, episode to episode, in pertinent German, so that we have unfolded before us a great artist's long life; 85 years, and nearly all of them given to music, the creation and the practice of it.

This book (*Richard Strauss: Dokumente Seines Lebens und Schaffens:* C. H. Beck, München) is of a devoted and comprehensive kind which it seems beyond the scope or desire of anybody in this country to produce about an English composer; for it is the consequence of a national and international awareness of Strauss greatness, not merely a specialist tribute from a Straussian school. The English musician feels a certain sense of inferiority as he consults Dr. Trenner's index and finds the name of no English composer; Sir Thomas Beecham and Ernest Newman are mentioned only in connection with Strauss's growing reputation in England. Yet it was Strauss who at the Rhineland Festival in 1902 (or thereabouts) was the first musical genius abroad to hail *Gerontius* as a Meisterwerk.

Such a book as this is not easily produced in England, not even about a Vaughan Williams, mainly because, rightly or wrongly, the world at large still regards England as musically isolated, or at any rate a country in which music remains a secondary art—an impression which our statesmen and " leaders of opinion " do little to counteract. Again, musical life in England remains socially classified, and also it still remains culturally a little aloof, so that a representative English composer might easily spend a lifetime and not come to intimate terms as artist with any contemporary writer or painter of larger than local or at the most national importance. Strauss, of course, achieved international renown before he was in the late thirties of his octogenarian span; naturally he attracted some of the finest minds of the period to his sphere. He was then the " Fortschrittsmann," the " Progressivist." One story about him I cannot find in Dr. Trenner's anthology. At a public dinner he was referred to as the Buddha of music, and in his reply (bored with allusions to his supposed modernity) he said: " I don't know who may be the Buddha of music, but I could tell you who is the Pest . . ." The fascinating exchange of opinions between Strauss and Romain Rolland about the *Domestic* Symphony is given here, summarised from Rolland's book on *Musicians of To-day*; and it is worth recalling if only to appreciate Rolland's acumen in thinking highly at once of a work which to this day is generally underrated. The " programme " matters next to nothing in this symphony; it acted merely as the spur to composition—in Strauss's own words: "Für mich ist das poetische Programm auch nichts weiter als der Formen bildende Anlass zum Ausdruck . . ." Beethoven himself could have said the same of the fifth symphony and the conceptual processes where he went to work. The *Domestic* Symphony contains some of Strauss's ripest and self-contained composition.

Dr. Trenner quotes Pavel Ludikar's evidence about Strauss's views concerning the age and romantic potentialities of the Marschallin. Ludikar sang the part of Ochs in the first Italian production of *Rosenkavalier*. Agostinelli was the Marschallin, and apparently she acted and sang the closing scene of Act I too tragically for Strauss's liking. "Tell her," said Strauss, "she should treat the part as a woman of the world who has had a lover or two before Oktavian, and still will have a few more." The fact is that when Lehmann made the Marschallin lovable the world over—the most beloved woman in all opera—she gave us enough sense of the usages and toll of time on her (without conveying that she was old enough to have closed a romantic heart) to make exquisitely poignant the Marschallin's " Ja! Ja! " at the opera's end, when she and Faninal leave the situation to Oktavian and Sophie; and after Faninal has said something to the effect that youth must have its day. A Marschallin lacking capacity for the backward glance and an appreciation of poetic and pathetic " distance " would certainly not be the Marschallin of Strauss's music. It is, after all, the Marschallin who in the middle of the first act of *Rosenkavalier* sings of the snows of yesteryear and tells how she wakes in the dead of the night and hears time slipping away, so that she must get up and stop the clock.

The general notion of Strauss for many years has been of a man a little too much aware of the price of everything and the value of everything to be truly an artist. His cynicism was merely the sign of that sense of proportion which comes from long contemplative experience. When he heard that Kaiser Wilhelm thought that *Salome* would have a deplorable influence, he replied: " Because of its ' influence ' I could build my home at Garmisch! " (" Von diesem Schaden konnte ich mir die Garmischer Villa bauen! ") Dr. Trenner's book presents Strauss in the round, the worldliness of him a crust, the essence of him supremely civilised, a serious thinker with heart and simplicity, with a culture fine and proud and deepened by tragic irony. The man who in his last year could compose the four last songs especially the nobly resigned and transfigured *Im Abendrot* and the poignant aspiring *Beim Schlafegehen*, who could face the end with all his consciousness steeped in the beauty of the world, obviously was spiritual in the only way that matters. When during the war the American troops sought to take possession of his house at Garmisch, they capitulated when he told them, " I am the composer of *Rosenkavalier*." And Strauss then wrote in his diary: " Total victory of Spirit over raw material! "

At the age of eighty he took a modest view of his life's work. He knew, he wrote, that his symphonic compositions did not touch or reach to the giant range of Beethoven; and he understood well enough his position in music-drama side by side with Wagner . . . (" gegenüber Richard Wagners Ewigkeitswerken "). But he believed that in the history of the creative music of the theatre he would find an honourable place.

Dr. Trenner reproduces Rudolph Hartmann's *Last Visit to*

Strauss, an account of a few hours spent with Strauss on his deathbed a week or so before the end. During conversation Strauss was seized with a short spasm of breathlessness and Hartmann helped him through to a comfortable place on his pillow, but in the movements involved, a button from Hartmann's coat came off and he could not find it. " Stand up," said Strauss, " then it will fall on the floor and you'll find it again . . ." But it needs the German: " Stehen Sie auf, dann fällt er zu Boden und Sie können ihn aufbe- wahren." His last words to Hartmann that day, 29th August, 1949 (he died on 8th September), were: " Yes, I'm getting tired now; but stay just a few more minutes while we talk a little, then I'll go to sleep." Like the end of his own *Don Quixote*!

A Note on Berlioz

THOUGH THE name of Berlioz is constantly appearing in programmes and has been appearing constantly in programmes for more than half a century, he is not known intimately even among avid listeners, as, say, Brahms or Strauss is known. I doubt if the average specialist musician could without the score sit down at short notice and play half a dozen exact quotations from Berlioz, each from a different work. He remains outside the general and cosy habitation of composers whom we have taken into our affections and confidence. Maybe we can say of him that he is frequently outside music, as Felix Feneon said Rimbaud was " outside literature "—not that Berlioz in any way resembles Rimbaud. There appears to ordinary musical susceptibilities a divided appeal in the music of Berlioz, not to say a dichotomy or clash of æsthetic purpose.

We need not at this time of day go into the matter of self-subsistent and " programme " music, except to recall that Berlioz himself objected on principle to music which set out deliberately to describe or imitate phenomena of the external universe. Music was for him really a means of subjective expression; at his best he is as autobiographical as Mahler. He observed the law of music's formal precision and variety of movements with a truly symphonic consideration, yet no less a dramatic composer than Wagner objected to passages in *Romeo* because he thought the music needed the explanation of words to render it intelligible and satisfying qua music. Berlioz himself maintained that " expression is not the sole aim of dramatic music; it would be as maladroit as pedantic to disdain the purely sensuous pleasure which we find in certain effects of melody, harmony, rhythm, or instrumentation, independently of their connection with the painting of the sentiments and passions of the drama."

An epoch that has by habit and experience learned to find musical enjoyment in *Le Sacre du Printemps* of Stravinsky does not need to resort to melodramatic associations or references in order to admire the superb art of musical transformation employed on the " Witches' Dance " of the *Symphonie Fantastique*; and the point I wish to make here is that we have arrived at a stage of musical development in which we might with advantage remove from Berlioz some of the old romantic and " programmatic " labels, and listen to him as a great music-maker who happened to live when one of the composer's pressing problems was the fertilisation of music by drama. The irony is that Berlioz was never so eagerly listened to as by audiences fifty or so years ago—and audiences then were definitely suspicious about programme music. Up to 1903 *La Damnation de Faust* had been played no fewer than one hundred and fifty times at the Concerts Colonne in Paris. The same masterpiece was a hardy annual at the Hallé Concerts, during the days of Charles Hallé; yet the Hallé audiences, or the more venerable members, were outraged when first they heard *Don Quixote*, of Strauss—they protested against Strauss's musical mimicry, the bleating sheep and the windmill. Seldom in Berlioz is the orchestra used to reproduce or suggest sounds and events of the material universe onomatopoeically; as Mr. Newman instructed us years ago, it was Berlioz's error to suppose that the dramatic picture he wished to portray could be achieved by music alone. The very best of Berlioz is subjective expression (I of course am not here referring to Berlioz as an opera composer; his supposed failure in that direction involves no discussion of " absolute " and " programme " æsthetic).

He is always projecting his own emotions and impressions; the point of view of the *Symphonie Fantastique*, of *Harold en Italie*, of *Roméo*, are identical; Berlioz is the commentator, transmuting impressions into subjective emotion which is, in Wagner's term, the stuff of music. Roméo, a withdrawn spectator of the Capulet ball, is the hero of the *Symphonie Fantastique* and also he is Harold, each of them Berlioz. Compare his so-called programme music with Strauss's, which often is unambiguously descriptive in a legitimately musical sense but on the whole much more objective and precise in its dramatic and pictorial references. Until Strauss arrived at his mellow old age and composed the four last songs and the exquisitely valedictory closing scene to *Capriccio*, he wrote no introspective or wholly subjective music. The enigma of Berlioz is not the easier to solve—and the great artists always present us with one— by the alternations or fluctuations in his music from bombast, brass-band stridency, to a restraint in poetic expression which is classical, reminding us that he was a lover of Virgil. The old story is never stale: " You are the composer who writes for five hundred instruments," said the King of Prussia. " Your majesty has been misinformed," replied Berlioz, " I sometimes write for four hundred and fifty."

The March to the Scaffold and all the instrumental rhetoric of the grandiose Berlioz will continued to excite audiences so long as conductors of the brilliance of Beecham, Barbirolli, and Karajan conduct him in his spectacular moods. But it would be to our advantage to lend to Berlioz the ears of our grandfathers, ready to respond to melody as evocative and beautiful as the *Roi de Thule* ballad and the " Romance " from *Faust*. The " Romance "—based on Gretchen's *Meine Ruh'*—is one of the most haunting melodies in existence, with the English horn poignantly poetic; even Wagner in *Tristan* didn't draw from the instrument a beauty more sweetened and softened by sadness than Berlioz breathes from it here. Mephisto's *Voici des Roses* is magical and alluring; Wagner's enchantments during the " Flower " scene in *Parsifal* are banally coy in comparison with these of Berlioz's conjuration. The Hallé audiences of the 1880s—*Roméo* was given to them by Hallé as far back as December 1881—took to heart the love music and the *Rêverie*, undisturbed by the revelry of the Capulets' ball, in which Berlioz lapses into the brassily insistent; but the change to poetic contemplation is heart-catching. And if the *adagio amoroso* is not " pure " music then Verdi and Wagner and Strauss are damned beyond redemption.

The love music of Berlioz is never fleshily or sensuously burdened; there is no arrogance in the passion of it. The music of Dido's death-scene in *Les Troyens* has a pathetic fragility which moved Hamilton Harty to the following exordium; " Most of Dido's final scene is written in low, indistinct accents, as if she were revolving in her own mind all the circle of her weariness and sorrow, and was almost dead to the world and its considerations . . . regarded from another, and I think higher point of view, her end is more touching and more noble than Brünnhilde's." Harty conducted a concert version of *Les Troyens* at a Hallé concert some twenty years ago. He was, like Hallé, an avid admirer of Berlioz. He gave us even too much Berlioz. Manchester, in fact, has a generally all-round Berlioz reputation and culture to sustain; Beecham and Barbirolli have added considerably to the tradition; moreover, one of the best biographical studies of Berlioz, by J. H. Elliot, is the work of a Manchester man.

A Connoisseur Symphony

LATELY I have been refreshing my mind and memory with Mahler's fourth symphony. I shall discuss it not in any mood to make propaganda or to proselytise, or to worship at the shrine of the latest Mumbo-Jumbo of music, which is musicology. I am writing about the fourth symphony entirely for my own pleasure to clarify and make the most of the rare order of delight a constant study of the score gives to me. Also I would like somehow to express my gratitude to the uneasy ghost of Mahler for the enchanted little world he created for us in this " symphony of heavenly life." For once in a while he found fulfilment in this work as a composer and as sensitive human being. It is a symphony which contradicts the general view taken of Mahler; there is little or no frustration in it, no wrestlings with beasts, spiritual or other, no vain emulations of the heroic, no technical miscalculations, no short-circuitings—or only one. Mahler comes by peace and happiness no doubt by what the modern jargon calls escapism; he conjures a realm of child and youth fantasy, a land of cuckoo-cloud and naïve humours. A pastoral symphony to begin with, the fourth modulates through parody of medieval grotesque, through the hush of one of the most ineffable (this is the only word) of music's slow movements, to a simple song finale, in which the birds of the air and a Noah's Ark of animals hurry in excited chatter to the heavenly feast, where the angels bake the bread, and a thousand Jungfrauen dance, Saint Ursula herself laughing, while Saint Peter looks on benignly—he is expressed in a recurrent and delicious modal cadence.

In conception and execution it is one of the most original of all symphonies. It corrects the prevailing mistaken notion of Mahler. He was not bond slave to self-assertion and self-pity; he did not run after orchestral pomp and power for their own sakes. The fourth symphony is miniature in style, with no trombones. The basis of the orchestra is fanciful or intimately expressive string figures and melodies; the wood-wind are used for individual tinting, or for echoes of bird chirpings, lowing of oxen; and the tympani evokes an air and a heaven of jingling bells, with every note, every percussive sound, serving strictly musical and symphonic purpose. The fusion of idea and musical tone and shape is perfect. I know no symphony which is more felicitously realised than this for fresh innocence of melody and subtle thought-processes in the development of the material, everything contributing to the given and very personal poetic conception. The first movement begins by the statement in quick succession of five melodies, no fewer. Several years ago a critic wrote to the effect that the fourth symphony of Mahler could never be popular because, as he asserted, it lacked melody, a remark which reminds me of one of Sir Thomas Beecham's sayings: " You know, my dear fellow, you belong to a fraternity " [meaning the critics] " that has almost a genius for stating what is exactly opposite to the true facts." Every work of art has its defects, I suppose; if only the defects of its qualities. The fault of the fourth symphony, if any there be, is superfluity of tunes. They threaten to overgrow or overcrowd the symphonic outline or trellis.

There is none, or very little, of the familiar Mahlerish wrung-out nostalgic melodies, flavouring of the banal, at least not until we get well into the slow movement, where the inveterate glance-back on the past is expressed yet again in rising aching string phrases followed by an appoggiatura, the Mahler signature-tune. (See Universal Edition, third movement, after cue 2, bar 66–71.) But now the painful tension of string tone is elevated or purified in an orchestral whole, the point of which is melodic and rhythmic invention. The movement opens with a long-phrased song, beautifully punctuated by contrabass pizzicato, the most heart-easing tune since Schubert. This song is developed by variations passing through magical key transformations. A high *poco adagio*, gorgeously divided in string parts, with a still more lovely modulation, leads us to a climax. We hear the bass pizzicato again of the movement's beginning, and now the gates of the child's celestial Kindergarten are opened. But before this sudden access of light and height are achieved, another superb stroke of musical imagination occurs, to which I particularly wish to draw attention. At the passage marked " Andante subito " (cue 11, third movement, Universal Edition) there is a horn call which in itself is a conjuration of genius.

It is not heroic music, not Beethoven. It is not strong-minded or altogether manly; it is not Brahms. It is pure musical fancy and good-heartedness (we do not usually think of goodness of heart in Mahler!) controlled by one of the sharpest intellects which has ever been attracted to music. The reader might assume from my summary of the symphony's " content "—a child's heaven, ginger-bread and birds of paradise—that there is mawkishness in the air, hints of Barrie-esque Never Never Land embarrassments. Not at all. The work is mature; the slow movement is one of Mahler's most contemplative, in its early phrases. The development section of the first movement is as though thematic changes were seen through the Looking Glass; the melodies grow or they diminish, they scuttle underground like white rabbits, they appear now in extension or in shorter shapes, mad hatters and March hares of tunes and rhythms. But, I insist, every note is governed by strict musical purpose, strict symphonic form. At one point only does Mahler find his hands so full, with so many themes to toss about and conjure with, that he is obliged to call a halt and begin again—he gets back to the first subject or theme-group of the first movement only by drastic use of an orchestral cæsura. (Universal Edition. First Movement, cue 18, bar 239.) It is not easy to think of a mind in music of the last hundred or so years more penetrating and more flexible than Mahler's, putting aside the question whether other composers, such as Brahms, Strauss, and Vaughan Williams, for instance, have possessed minds of stronger tissue. We are certainly wrong to believe that Mahler's music perpetually lives on its nerves. Compared with the musical mutations in the first and third movements of this fourth symphony, the " working-out " labours of Brahms are often so much joinery and carpentry; and of course I am not here being rude to Brahms.

The fourth symphony of Mahler is pungent with Upper Austrian air and legend. In the second movement, the scherzo, the spirit of medieval grotesque is played with in a Dance of Death; but the shadows are as though cast by the nursery candle. In the slow movement. the opening of the heavens is a perfect " Transformation Scene," tinsel and all. The finale is for soprano solo, with four strophic sections telling of the heavenly sweetmeats and the wine that costs nothing, where there is no echo of the earth's noise, where to live the heavenly life is apparently to have a jolly good time, all the time. The orchestra is content here with ritornel accompaniments, but the kernel of the symphony is in this movement, as it goes softly away from us, not ending so much as receding from us, after it has warmed the heart with delight and kindliness.

The symphony leaves me more and more astonished at music's miracle; how, out of sounding air, imagination and consummate craftsmanship can weave a world so rare and lovely.

The Genius of Liszt

As ANY music season gathers momentum, the critic resigns himself to the contemplation of programmes sent to him by the agents. They are as repetitive as the calendar, the same composers in the same order. All piano recitals begin with Scarlatti, the same sonata; and nearly every recital is by a pianist, male or female, who seldom resists the lures to destruction in the B minor Sonata of Liszt. Do pianists in bulk know nothing of Liszt except this sonata, the concertos, *La Campanella* (but do many of them know that it is one of the " Etudes d'exécution transcendante d'après Paganini "?) the most ubiquitous of the *Liebesträume* and *Waldesrauschen*? The Liszt Society in London has contributed towards casting some light on the piano music of Liszt's last years, when he was occupied in prophetic experiments in tone chemistry and keyboard spacing. But the average performer nowadays doesn't seem to have heard even of the " Harmonies poétiques et réligieuses," especially the supremely beautiful " Bénediction de Dieu dans la Solitude." Unfortunately the Liszt Society is known only to a few of that public on whose approval the lazy-minded virtuosi confidently depend.

Harm is, of course, done to any artist if claims on his behalf are made which are excessive. If anybody is told he may turn to Liszt for a profound and many-ranged musical satisfaction, he is likely to suffer disappointment. Myself, I find Liszt interesting because of his imperfections and the mixture in him of fineness and rubbish. He is certainly belittled by the general presentation of him as a composer of circus music. Too many fairies crowded round his cradle; and it is difficult to say which were the good and which the evil ones. They lavished on him genius in abundance, also physical powers of rare fascination. He was a prince of men when young, wearing the garments of grace and brilliance; and age brought him something of nobility— Franz Liszt, greatest of piano players, possibly the first to sit sideways to the audience, so that they might enjoy his profile; and not only a magician at his instrument but a composer who discovered a new music for it, leading to worlds not dreamed of, intoxicating, exciting, thunderous in turn; the Liszt of the salon, voluptuary among the countesses, also the man of prayer, and for ever the actor, yet never forgetful of the great Liszt who saw as far ahead in his art as most men and was the progenitor of ideas for more fully realised creators. He was the rudder and good steersman of the foundering ship of Wagner, the guide, philosopher, and friend of all.

He encouraged Mussorgsky and Borodin in a remote age in which Russian music was virtually unknown at large. Somebody once said of Liszt that Wagner was indebted to him for much besides money, sympathy and a wife. Siegmunde and Sieglinde may be discerned in their germ-cells in the *Dante* Symphony, and every tyro is quick to detect resemblances between the main theme of the B minor Sonata and Wotan. None the less, the fact should be gently stressed that we can only argue Liszt's indebtedness to Wagner for seminal musical material in the way that we can argue Shakespeare's debt in Holinshed. Wagner himself wrote to Liszt saying he had unconsciously used a theme by him and Liszt replied " Now at least it will be heard."

Noble in his life, and in his art many times hollow and meretricious—for among the fairies at the cradle was the spirit of cynicism and sentimentality. He played Mephisto to his own Faust; indeed, he was a Faust of music, searching and seeking to renew himself. But the Mephisto in him was not exactly the intellectual force that comes from the spirit of denial, the sincere sceptic. Rather it was a dæmon of melodrama. Who looks for truly hard thinking in Liszt, over a long period, will look long and in vain. At bottom he was the improviser of genius, sending out the flash of illumination to reveal direction to others. His influence on music in the nineteenth century was as strong as anybody else's. He was conscious that music in his day was concerned overmuch with classic procedure; he saw that form in music of the future would need to forge a fresh logic and way of moving from point to point. He did not himself solve the problem of " programme music "; it was left to Richard Strauss to give to a symphonic poem a shaping power which would be none the less symphonic even if it followed the sequences and emotional curve of a poetic idea or " programme." Liszt's symphonic poems remained more or less tied to a classical pattern: slow and quick movements suggesting a sonata contrast and origin. His contribution to the symphonic poem was in a swiftness of gesture, more pointed than with any other of the romantic composers except Berlioz. His most original stroke is the note of " Diablerie " in the *Faust* Symphony.

His trouble was want of reticence, apart from the plain

truth that his brain was not a Beethoven's, a Wagner's or a Chopin's. His music, at bottom, is " décor," theatrical. He must strike an attitude. We are perpetually " discovering " him. Sometimes he seems to foretell the advent of Hollywood in a splash of limelight grandiloquence; he gives us " fade-outs," cavalcades, purple and goldleaf; cascades of tinkling notes and blatant rhythms. Sometimes, alas, he is a sawdust Cæsar. (By the way, how much of his best orchestral music was scored by Raff?)

He was much the child of his age. The new liberalism made for free and inevitably loose and windy speech. Rhetoric ousted epigram. Music was removed from the palaces and put down for all ears to hear in the concert-halls. The appeal to the larger crowd meant a gesture more than life size. It was the age of the rise of the virtuoso everywhere, the orator, the actor-manager, the " poseur." There was virtue at such a time in the *tour de force* of the charlatan. The audacity announced vitality in living and pride in the welter of it. If it is not easy to attend patiently to Liszt to-day, it is partly because we have travelled far from the decoratively heroic. We have persuaded ourselves that we prefer the penny-plain to the twopenny coloured, making virtue of necessity.

Chopin and Pianists

In THIS present time, which gives much on the one hand and takes away as much on the other, we are obliged in the world of music to get used to the idea and fact that no truly great player of Chopin remains with us. The tradition is passing and no wonder; for Chopin was romantic and aristocratic, and where to-day is romance or aristocracy? His music is either weakened by a loose rhythm or by broken melodic wing, or he is given the speed and brilliance of streamlined technique by performers under the influence of the American musical æsthetic—if I may use so strong a term.

The Time Spirit has been at work among pianists and no mistake; among musicians generally, in fact. If romance has not been expelled altogether it has had to conform to a democratic view which insists on a sort of equality in all our reactions of imagination. The inhibitions are terrific. If the artist indulges in efforts at recognisable sentiment or what is called " beauty," he is condemned as "escapist." The average weak-minded practitioner therefore submits to the general dowdiness, levelling of tastes, and uniformity of mental approach. Chopin is endowed with the inhibitions common to a civilisation that lives in the mass. The " virtuosi " play him no doubt with a technical bravura, not to say arrogance, beyond the scope of players of the past.

The hazards risked by a Horowitz or a Rubinstein are the same as the hazards risked by an accomplished airman. Not temperament but engine-trouble will be the cause of accident, if an accident should occur at all in a thousand flights.

Chopin is never brilliant or sentimental. Brilliance suggests display and excess. Chopin is passionate when he is not lyrical, but it is passion of imagination as much as of senses, and always does the style, the poise of manner, tell of breeding. He is fastidious in the expression of feeling, so that the first quality any pianist should bring to his music is keenness of tone and security of rhythm. Fastidiousness and sentimentality cannot go together, as Samuel Langford wrote years ago: " Sentimentality is known by its heaviness and its want of melodic and rhythmical flight." The languor of Chopin never droops. I could even argue that he is a mettlesome composer.

Tempo rubato ? But there is no excuse in the name of this blessed term for the rhythmical delays and shilly-shallyings heard so frequently in Chopin. Obviously his music must not be accelerated or retarded with the slightest abruptness; *tempo rubato* in Chopin means subtle changes of motion and rise and fall of melody, imperceptible as the rise and fall of a fountain in the air; you cannot say at any given moment that it is going up or down or being blown this way or that. Chopin was famous for his treatment of *tempo rubato* when he played his own compositions, but there is no evidence that he could analyse how he got the effect. It was probably a matter of musical instinct.

Berlioz and Charles Hallé arrived independently at the conviction that when Chopin performed his Mazurkas he played four, not three, beats in a bar; then, when the fact

was mentioned, he couldn't believe it. It is reported that
he had his own secret way of controlling an ornamented
melodic passage in the right hand over the harmonics of a
measure controlled by the left—at least, that is the opinion
of those who argue that rubato in Chopin means freedom
for the right hand and discipline for the left; but I have
never so far met two great pianists who agreed on this
point, which is probably a matter to be solved by the sensibility of the individual. In the arts, said Heine, as in
religion, grace matters more than anything else; it makes
all the difference in Chopin between a poetic penetration
and a technical facsimile.

Moriz Rosenthal was one of the most beautiful of
Chopin interpreters. The first notes I ever heard played
by him came on my senses on a lovely September evening
years ago, when I chanced to call in at the Bösendorfer
Salon in Vienna, possibly to inquire about a concert-
ticket. From an adjoining room the opening phrases of
the nobly elegiac C sharp minor Étude, of the Second
Book, came through the twilight, autumnal music and
solitary. I did not know at the time who was the pianist,
but to my breathless questions " Rosenthal " was the
answer.

He came to Manchester towards the end of his long life
and as he touched the keyboard, the hall in which he played
throbbed in the thirteenth Prelude with withdrawn reticent
tone, taking the imaginative ear into the Ivory Tower of
Alfred de Vigny. But in earlier days Rosenthal had, like
Godowsky, done strange things with Chopin. I remember
suffering some restlessness as Rosenthal, towards the close
of the final movement of the B minor Sonata, tried to

establish a resemblance to the main theme during the ascending passage of semiquavers.

Rosenthal, like Chopin himself, was witty and sharp of tongue. To Vienna once came a pianist celebrated for intellect rather than felicity of touch; and he astonished even his admirers by giving a Chopin recital. At the end of it, Rosenthal went round to the artist's room to pay the customary courtesies.

" What do you think of my Chopin? " asked the Great Thinker.

Always suave, Rosenthal replied, " Very interesting. You play him different—yes? "

" I for the first time bring out the philosophy of Chopin," boasted the perspiring pianist.

" Ah, I see! " replied Rosenthal, " Chopin-hauern."

I cannot recall Paderewski's Chopin, but Pachmann played Chopin as nobody else since, in the Waltzes and the Nocturnes; for the larger and stronger Chopin forms he needed a weightier and more significantly pointed harmony. His tone moved light as thistledown; his interpretations were miniature and gem-like. For all his eccentricities of personal behaviour on the piano stool (which I am told he reserved for English audiences), he was a purist of the instrument. " If I played like the rest," he said, " I'd never play at all." Now and again Pachmann's loving pre-occupation with melody in Chopin reminded us of Wagner's gibe that Chopin was a composer for the right hand. Wagner, I take it, never heard the Études, and in any case he would naturally enough find his musical imagination drawn to the Bellini influences in the Nocturnes, which had at least something to do with the melodic rise and fall in " Tristan."

Cortot in his prime avoided prosaic execution in Chopin, with the consequence that certain of his colleagues maintained he had little technique at all. He could play the Etudes with the closest observance of their technical aim and exploration, yet keep them in the world of music and poetry. I know no contemporary pianist capable of this dual achievement; and perhaps it is as well that no contemporary pianist attempts the two books of the Études in one and the same programme. The unequalled gift of Chopin was to breathe magic of music into the strictest exercise or study.

In the Études, as I believe, we find Chopin at his most original and fully realised, mind and sensibility in proportion. The same genius in transformation vitalises every note of the Mazurkas. In each work, in every piece he attempted, Chopin revealed a new aspect of style. No two waltzes are alike, no two études, no two mazurkas. The Mazurkas are belittled if we regard them as national dances. Chopin's " nationalism " was a poetic, not only a patriotic feeling, which flowed into elegy or lamentation of longing, ennobled with pride. Liszt said that to do justice to the Mazurkas a new and great pianist was needed for every one of them, so changeful, so elusive are they. Easier to play than the Waltzes, no doubt; it is the aroma, the mingled wit, fancy, strength of stride, and gesture of regret, that escape most players. Friedman was incomparable in the Mazurkas; he played them as though they were history and geography in piano-tone; and with what affection and reluctance he would take leave of each piece in the postludes which are among Chopin's most endearing touches!

I find myself at the end of a chapter on Chopin, and I

have referred to none of the expanded works, the Ballades, the Sonatas. It is a tribute that much can be said of his slightest compositions. " If I have time," wrote Mozart, " I shall rearrange some of my concertos and shorten them. In Germany we rather like length, but after all, it is better to be short and good."

Brahms and the Piano

No MATTER how diligently we may attend to our critical faculties and try to keep a steady eye on standards, we are bound periodically to suffer reactions which we find it difficult to reconcile with reason. Our taste changes, if only momentarily, as though from some physical metabolism. We turn against a composition as irrationally as a man with a bilious attack against a favourite dish. This is why criticism should as far as possible remain at a distance from clique and fashion, and look suspiciously into the latest " movement." It is not certain that a composer because he writes in a contemporary idiom is better worth listening to to-day, or more likely to bear listening to to-morrow, than, say, Delius, who at the moment is out of fashion.

I confess that lately I have felt a certain weariness while listening to Brahms, or rather to his symphonies. It has struck me, more forcibly than before, that they are here and there mechanical in development and that the material lacks range. For the life of me, I cannot understand why any of the Brahms symphonies should have been accepted in most places as greater than any of Mahler's. Of course we hear too much of the Brahms symphonies; the ear becomes wanting in expectancy as it pursues a furrowed track. The dramatic critic isn't expected to attend twice a month to

Hamlet. Out of my loyalty to Brahms, and as proof of my gratitude to him for many years of pleasure and fortification, I have endeavoured to correct, and find an antidote for this reaction against him. And I have found it in the works of Brahms himself: the piano pieces of opp. 76, 116, 117, 118 and 119.

The development of Brahms as a writer for the pianoforte was peculiar. Four of his first five publications were for solo pianist, and included among these was the superb F minor Sonata, an astonishingly big piece of musical thinking for a youth of nineteen or twenty. He was only twenty-five when he himself played his D minor Concerto at its first performance at Hanover, Joachim conducting, a work as old in the head as the hills and sometimes as sublime. The critics attacked the concerto, and young Brahms wrote to Joachim; " My Concerto has brilliantly and decisively failed," adding, " it is the best thing that can happen to me: it makes one concentrate one's thought and enhances one's courage." Nowadays if a successful composer produces a work which is not unanimously hailed by the press as a masterpiece he rushes into print suggesting that critics should be abolished or, at least, removed.

After Brahms had composed the Paganini variations in 1866 he wrote nothing else for solo piano until in the Eight Capricci and Intermezzi which are collected in op. 76. A transformation in style begins. So far Brahms had honoured the intellect of the piano rather than had wooed the impressionable senses of an instrument which some of us still have the courtesy to think of as a Grande Dame of instruments. The technique in op. 76 reveals so fine a feeling for the keyboard and the blending of its tones that we are stirred delightedly to exclaim, " God bless thee,

Johannes: how thou art translated! " More important, we can get more than a sense of some tightening of cerebral processes at no hurt to nature, blood, sensibility and humours. When we arrive at opp. 116, 117, 118 and 119 we find at times the mental fibre and darkness of contemplation which come to men after middle age. The later piano pieces of Brahms are akin in spirit to some of the poetry of the meditative twilight of Thomas Hardy; we are a long way from the Brahms whom we may occasionally regard as avuncular. Even in the obviously lyrical or playful of these pieces we are aware of an uncompromising masculinity and a more concentrated syntax than we get anywhere else in Brahms.

Let me instance the little Intermezzo of op. 119, the third in C major, " Grazioso e giocoso," which runs its course in a minute or two. It is the most popular composition of the set, but none the less the close thinking—witty thinking—is a characteristic we have not until now expected from Brahms. The verve and ripple of it, the variety of accentuation, the concealed melody, the change to A major and the hide-and-seek of going back to the original starting-place—it is spontaneous creation, with none of the stiffness of compartment formalism which interferes with organic growth in much of Brahms's music in large scale works.

It is easier, naturally, to dispense with elaborate scaffolding when the building is not on a large scale; still, there is a finely woven thought-sequence in these later piano pieces which reveals that Brahms as he grew older was preparing, like every greater artist, to tackle the old problem—how to make form significant in all its parts, seminal and unfolding from within, so that there may be no superfluities, no padding, no manufacture. One of the gravest charges against Brahms is that he was prone to submit to the strait-jacket of sonata form; that he made too much music according to a ground plan not necessarily his own; it seems many times as if he worked to the blue print of the wholesale architect. He certainly wrote an abundance of development sections which are so much professional pad-ding, a kind of technical " marking time " until the main theme or second main theme shall be reached. There is, as we are able to see for ourselves in much music of the present day, an accumulated mass of technical formulæ at hand for composers who have nothing urgent to utter. This fault is not absent, we must admit, from No. 5 of op. 118; for example, I quote the D major Allegretto division of this Romance in F, where a succession of lilting phrases or variations, eked out by ornaments and scales, is sustained by the device of a low note or pedal. It is all very charming, with a suspicion that the composer is tem-porising until he brings back the opening main melody; and he can only negotiate this return by the old trick of repeated trills.

We at once feel a vast difference of organic growth in the F minor Intermezzo of op. 118, which could have come only from a genius at the height of his mental power, with his emotional life in control and matured by philosophy. There was a time when Brahms composed as though too much flesh were on his bones; in this epigrammatic work the brain is taut. The logic discards easy connecting links; it is elliptical. There is not a full-stop in it. It makes the subtlest use of the musical semi-colon. And as the mind of Brahms became more consecutive the heart grew not less warm or full. The supremely beautiful Intermezzo in E flat minor of op. 118, in which Brahms poured out his sorrow at the death of Elizabeth von Herzogenberg, has a truly great tragic intensity and disturbance. When we consider, too, opp. 118 and 119 of Brahms it is possible to think there was a vein of music in him still to be opened: he died maybe, only in his " second " period, and wastefully was not permitted to live to see the world and music with that simple clarification of vision which came to Beethoven in the end.

The Songs of Hugo Wolf

THANKS TO the arts of Schwarzkopf, Fischer-Dieskau, Flora Nielson, Bruce Boyce, Gerald Moore, and Ernest Lush, Hugo Wolf is enjoying a revival at the moment. But it is not likely that his songs will ever be taken to heart in this country. He seldom wrote melodies that straightway enter the ear and remain there simply to be sung or remembered for the way the notes go up and down, melodies self-subsistent. With Schubert or Schumann or Brahms a song can frequently be enjoyed by the musical ear alone; it is a musical conception which absorbs words into the world of tone. A song by Schubert or Schumann or Brahms can be understood and fully appreciated if we know merely the barest outline of what the words are about. If we have grasped the general significance of a song such as the *Sapphische Ode* of Brahms, or of any setting in the *Winterreise* cycle of Schubert, the composer will hold us by his own aural spell.

With Wolf we need most times to comprehend in detail the poem he is setting. Moreover he is frequently penetrating not only the poetry but the psychology of minds and imaginations still alien to normal English ways of emotion and of living. Love is characterised by Wolf with a pathological intensity; his lovers are not related to a social or domestic scene; they come under no influences which are bourgeois or external to themselves. They live on their nerves, or on their intelligences; they are often obsessed

133

romantically, but it is a romanticism with wormwood at the heart. Wolf, like Mahler but in a different way, sniffed the wrath to come in the winds blowing from the Wienerwald. Love in Wolf is a secret, a rapture or pain snatched in an inimical world: *Geh' Geliebter, geh' jetzt*—" Go now beloved, see the dawn is glimmering "—a song of illicit ecstasy but exalted nobly by the beauty and pride of Wolf's transmutation of the scene and the brief stolen happiness. The drop of the voice to the word " dämmert " takes the breath away, as in the Mignon song, *Kennst du das Land*, when the voice descends to the low B flat on the word " glühn." We can see in poetic and musical imagination the glow of the orange in the twilight shadows. The point is that our poetic sense is engaged by Wolf equally with our musical senses. A realisation of the greatness of *Kennst du das Land*—and I am tempted to say it is the most poignantly beautiful of all songs—depends on some acquaintance not only with the strange child-woman Mignon but with the mind of Goethe ever looking to Italy and, while he remained a great poet, catching a glimpse of the shining statues and the glittering hall and the cloud-capped mountain, and ever crying from his heart "Dahin! " " There let us go, O Father! " The song has received criticism on the ground that the music is psychologically not true to the simple innocent Mignon. Goethe, never a protean imagination, poured into the poem his own responses to an idea or conception symbolising ache and yearning for distant and lost enchantment. And Wolf, the most psychologically experienced and sophisticated of all composers—Freudian before Freud—penetrated Goethe's symbolism, and in one great sweep of his imagination created a song in which Mignon, Goethe, and Wolf are indivisible.

There is of course much musical satisfaction to be obtained from " Kennst du das Land " by the listener, who knowing not a word of the poem, attends only by ear. He is, to say, in touch with Wolf only on one dimension. He is, if I may indulge the metaphor, trying to be in love by telephone.

Wolf's creations of pure song, of spontaneous independent melody, are rare. The best of these, possibly, is " Anakreons Grab," a setting of such floating melodic phrases and of such swaying piano responses that the whole of the beauty is yielded up to anybody who knows no more than that the song tells of the resting-place of the old pagan poet Anacreon. But he will miss a wonder and heartbeat of the song if he doesn't understand what the singer is saying in the eleventh and twelfth bars, where the descent of the voice from D to F at the end of the phrase " Es ist Anakreons Ruh "—" 'Tis where Anacreon rests "—is nothing less than a benediction in tone. In a Wolf song the melody and the voice combine to make only one factor in the scheme; the piano is at least as important as the voice. Wolf's piano parts are frequently worked out quasi-symphonically, and a magnificent example of this quasi-symphonic style (he has other ways too!) will be found in " An die Geliebte," one of the Mörike settings. The poem is a sonnet, and Wolf's music keeps strictly to the metre and verse-lengths of the sonnet form. Not one of the fourteen lines repeats the music of any other line; every change in the musical shape, every accentuation, is governed by the sonnet. The first four lines present the poet contemplating his beloved; the second quatrain develops this idea or feeling. Then, in the sestet, the emotional crescendo and consequence of the octet are expressed; and Wolf's music follows the sonnet so closely that we are persuaded to say that it is not so much set to music—it changes or dissolves into music. We are far now from the scene and psychology of *Geh' Geliebter*. *An die Geliebte* is as near to the style of the reverently devout as Wolf well could approach; it even echoes a note of " Wagnerian-Lohengrinian " idealism of sentiment.

No two songs of Wolf are alike in conception or essential tone. It would be incongruous to sing one of his "Spanish" settings in a sequence of his " Italian " settings. When he composes music for Goethe the diction changes, also the weight of harmony. Only the style that is the man links the genius of the Spanish songs to the Eichendorff settings. The Spanish songs are playful, ironic, mystical, passionate; the Eichendorff songs are, for Wolf, quite healthily and sanely objective. Maybe Wolf's genius is revealed at its most magical, and least conscious of its dualism, poetic and musical, in the " Italian " book. Such treasure-trove as the miniatures of " *Ihr seid die Allerschönste,*" " *Und willst du deinen Liebsten sterben sehen,*" " *Heb' auf dein blondes Haupt,*" and " *Sterb' ich, so hüllt, in Blumen* "—these songs, which he composed with four score or so others of the same book in terrific spates of tranced creation (following terrible periods of frozen sterility), are matchless. As we listen to them, sing and play them, and better still, study them alone, our hearts more than ever go out to the dæmon-haunted mortal who gave them to the world, along with " *Geh' Geliebter,*" " *Kennst du das Land*" and " *Fühlt meine Seele.*" It is good to know that Wolf is in the fashion again, if only for a while. He is not, all the same, for the crowds who at a recital must needs make the sound of rushing restless winds as they turn over the pages of the pro-grammes, " following the words."

PART THREE

ABOUT OPERA

The Tragic Sense in Carmen

A NEW recording of *Carmen* from New York refreshes happy memories; I had not heard or seen the opera for twenty years, excepting a recent Covent Garden production, which changed it into a spectacular " musical," the scene outside the bull-ring somehow suggestive of Piccadilly Circus on a hot day, with Eros peculiarly replaced by a crucifix. The recording of *Carmen* is published in this country by H.M.V., played by the R.C.A. Victor Orchestra, with Rise Stevens as Carmen, Jan Peerce as Don José, Lucia Albanese as Micaela, and Robert Merrill as Escamillo. The conductor is Reiner, and seldom have I known the score to sound so clear, so dramatic and suggestive, yet all the time so musical, as under his direction.

I doubt sometimes if the truly musical excellences of *Carmen* are properly appreciated, especially in this country, where it is most times played and sung in entirely the wrong style and spirit. The opera's genius springs from the French lyric tradition, even though originally the dialogue in it was spoken. Recitatives were later added by Guiraud; if I remember well, the beautiful transposition of the Toreador song, played softly as he leaves the inn of Lillas Pastia was one of Guiraud's contributions. The conquest over every musical world by *Carmen* is proof that it is " foolproof "; a bad performance cannot quench the fires, a bad Carmen cannot enter the flames and not become transmuted. Has anybody heard a really satisfactory Carmen since Supervia's? In a long experience of the opera, I can recall no other singer who as much as Supervia got under the skin of the part. I never heard Calvé, of whom Bernard Shaw wrote: " There is no suggestion of any fine quality about Calvé's Carmen, not a spark of honesty, courage, or even the sort of honour supposed to prevail among thieves." Calvé no doubt took her cue largely from the Carmen of Prosper Mérimée; and perhaps Bizet himself was not conscious of the amount of style, poise, and breeding he was giving to his music for her. He was incapable of tasteless touches.

Bizet's Carmen must never be acted or sung in a familiar style, never presented as a common cigarette-girl. She has natural dignity and reserves. Essentially, from almost her first note, she is a tragic figure. When she flaunts Zuniga, with her " La-las," she is merely teasing; there is no sting or menace in her tones; she is " playing." But when she sings the apparently alluring light-hearted " Seguidilla " to Don José, the vocal colour is becoming touched with a menace of fate of which she seems instinctively aware already. It is with the accents and colours of voice that the singer must express the main points in Carmen's psychology. Carmen's music does not call for extraordinary flights of song; it is most times related to dance rhythms and also to a declamation which cunningly borrows at one and the same time the pertinence of words and the sensuous curves of melody. The " Seguidilla " is pure rhythm warmed, as it passes, by Carmen's breath. In the bodeful burdened line of the " Card " song, Carmen reveals the whole heart of herself, her intuitive nature, her inborn unselfconscious tragic dignity. In all the range of opera there is little of finer, swifter, and more moving imaginative musical power than that which Bizet gives us as he contrasts the sportive cutting of the cards of Frasquita and Mercedes against the dark drag of menace in the orchestra as Carmen tells of her own doom. Carmen in this scene is alone with her own presentiments. She is, in fact, one of the loneliest of opera's heroines—which may be a paradoxical view to take of a character generally presented as a wanton gipsy, or as a flirt who is capable of being realised on the stage simply by any confident mezzo-soprano who presses two hands on her hips and sways on her feet as though going through exercises in deportment. Carmen remains apart from the Frasquita-Mercedes-Zuniga group; she is obviously not one of the cigarette-girls, though of them. Her pathetic efforts to amuse Don José with a song " all of her own invention " is ruined by interruption. Her part in the quintet, the major ensemble piece of the work, is formal; nothing that she sings in it comes out of her nature; she merely " makes a five." At the end of all, she no doubt has had her hour with Escamillo, but the shadow that falls over the heat and brilliance of the scene outside the bull-ring is poignant in its hints of a terrible brevity of happiness, as Escamillo sings " Si tu m'aimes," and she responds. The brilliance and pageantry flare out again; and then, Carmen is alone as never before, confronted by Don José.

We must count amongst the ironies of opera's history that the killing of Carmen by Don José was indirectly an inspiration to the " Veristic " or " realistic " school of opera in the nineteenth century, breeding Turiddu and Canio. The finale of " Carmen " is as pitiful as it is tragic,

141

but there is catharsis. The terror and blood are purged. The music of Bizet holds our sympathy for both Carmen and Don José—the instinctive brave girl, faithful after her fashion to the death, and the sadly demented castaway who has lost much for her, after all. The edge of brilliance, by which Bizet can sharpen his music, emphasises the tragic core of the work.

The originality of the musical shaping of the opera has been rather overlooked in our spellbound admiration of the colour and the drama of *Carmen*. It is a reticent opera really, as operas go. Seldom does anybody hold the stage alone in a " big " scene. Micaela's air in the " mountain " scene is gentle enough, surely. The " Toreador " song is as much part of the necessary stage action as the " Habanera." The choruses are also dramatically to the point. And they are separated into individual factors or aspects of the scene or occasion—a boy's chorus, a soldier's chorus and so on. The haunting smugglers' chorus at the beginning of Act III is not a conventional ensemble piece; it paints the night's own colour, and sets the mood of whispering nocturnal movement. The cigarette chorus in Act I, with its floating drowsy enchantment, is somehow premonitory of the Carmen tragedy to come. The orchestra is likewise revealed in its individual tone. A tone texture or weight happens not more than once or twice throughout the score; only the most delicate wood-wind playing is able to convey the poetic allusiveness of the little codas clinching the vocal scenes—for example, the closing bars of the " Habanera " as Carmen makes her escape; and of the " Seguidilla." Even a trumpet is made part of the romantic dramatis personæ.

It was to *Carmen* that Nietzsche turned from Wagner—

though there were deeper forces at work in the minds and temperaments of both men to account for the revulsion. In the score of *Carmen*, Nietzsche claimed to hear or find something of " the light feet of the South, the dance of the stars, the quivering dayshine of the Mediterranean." But Nietzsche was not a reliable music critic, and *Carmen* is really a masterpiece of French lyric opera, with the Spanish colour an affair of surface. Would Bizet have composed a better opera than *Carmen* had he lived beyond thirty-seven? There is no evidence in *Carmen*, or in anything else by Bizet, that had he lived longer he would have developed into a greater and more profound composer. It does not matter. *Carmen* will outlive most operas of its period. As I have listened to the music again, I have been unable to stifle the thought that in no English opera, and in no English song, is a woman revealed who is fascinating, passionate, alluring, romantic and young—and dangerously young.

Verdi's Masterpiece

MANY PEOPLE still alive and in more or less full possession of their faculties will remember a time when the average English or German musician took rather a patronising view of Verdi. Some lines of a verse by Alfred Noyes come back to mind, though I do not promise to be entirely truthful to the original text, as I quote:

> "A barrel-organ's playing somewhere in a London street
> As the sun sinks low,
> Though the music's only Verdi, yet the melody is
> sweet . . ."

"Only Verdi!" That was once the common opinion when I was young and Wagner and German music dominated the scene. The barrel-organs, played by olive-skinned and genuine Italians, who bowed low to the earth at the end of a recital, whether or not you had thrown a coin from the upstairs window and before they went " into the next street," confined their repertory to *Il Trovatore* and *Traviata*. None of us had then heard a bar from *Otello*, and in Italy itself *Falstaff* was scarcely known. Nowadays at most performances at Covent Garden of *Otello* or of *Falstaff* we may be sure that in the foyer during the intervals the high voice of some present-day young leader of thought will be heard saying, " What a relief, my dear, after

Tristan." Though he will be a little late in the day in his reaction, it will no longer appear irrational or uncivilised; for *Otello* as a music drama on the theme of tragic love does not suffer compared with *Tristan*, either in sustained imagination or in musical art symphonically shaped to meet the needs of developing stage action, with voices the chief protagonists. As a fact, in point of musical art applied to visibly changing drama serving the needs of opera, *Otello* is even more marvellously made than *Tristan*. The stage action of *Tristan* moves slowly, prompted by Wagner who was, when he composed the work, a quasi-symphonist before he was an opera dramatist. Verdi, born of opera and breathing the changeable air of it, is swift to the dramatic cue, swifter in *Otello* than ever before, but with no hurt to the old surge and fount of melody, though now the melody has been through a finer filter of mind and imagination. After *Aida* had been produced in December 1871 the public heard no more of Verdi, except the *Requiem Mass* and a new version of " Simon Boccanegra," until sixteen years later; then at the age of seventy-four he gave *Otello* to the world, his masterpiece, I believe, in spite of the miracle of *Falstaff*. I agree with Mr. Francis Toye, author of the best of all biographical studies of Verdi, that it is not " so remarkable that a man of 80 should have written a masterpiece of sparkling wit and mellow wisdom as that a man of 74 should have written the master-piece of intensity and passion that is *Otello*." But we need not set in contrast, for comparison's sake, these two creations of the youngest old man of music since Haydn; in *Otello* and *Falstaff* we have a glory of the moon and another glory of the sun.

There remains to this day a small obstinate body of

English folk who cannot listen to *Otello* because, they say, Shakespeare composed his own music to the play; and they cannot "associate" him with Italian opera and Italian tenors and what not. Once I took a revered and scholarly dramatic critic of *The Manchester Guardian* to a performance of *Otello* and when he heard the tenor (Otello) and the baritone (Iago) baying the moon at the end of Act II, he said to me, in necessarily more than a whisper, "It's a good thing that not many in the audience know their Shakespeare." This duet, by the way, is a sudden act of atavism on Verdi's part, a throwback to the cruder biology or metabolism of *Ernani*. I once referred in a notice of *Otello*, printed in *The Manchester Guardian*, to the "banal duet" which brings down the curtain on Act II. Next day this phrase appeared as the "canal duel between Otello and Iago. . . ." Boïto, greatest of opera librettists, first called his text "Iago," possibly remembering that Rossini had composed an *Otello*. Boïto, himself composer of the opera *Mefistofele*, an impressive work of which nobody seems able to remember a bar of the music, was a true Goethean, so much so that he brings to Iago a semblance of metaphysical awareness to evil as a part of the creative process, a Mephistophelian point of view scarcely applicable to Shakespeare's Iago. Hence the "Credo," which Iago sings in *Otello*; and the music here again is a throwback to a less subtle Verdi. The supremely great Iago music occurs in the scene where Iago describes to Otello the dream of Cassio. The atmosphere of insinuation, of poison voluptuously distilled into the tissue of jealousy, with nocturnal suggestions, sensuous and secret— this is genius, nothing less. The effect of the *dolcissimo* strings is magical when they tell us the dream has ended;

yet they tell us, too, that Iago's poison has entered Otello, ear and brain. Evil is not easily expressed in music, for it is an idea, a moral mode, ethically perceived, not of the stuff of emotion out of which music is made. Verdi was the most vividly plastic of all composers who have written for the theatre. Outside the theatre his music is only half-alive; imagine a concert of Verdi " numbers," given in the manner of a Wagner programme!

The Shakespeare-purist objection to *Otello* is irrelevant. Shakespeare borrowed his plots to compose his music to them; Boïto borrowed from Shakespeare, sometimes translating beautifully to serve Verdi. Shakespeare's *Otello*, in fact, almost inclines to an Italian opera libretto, with arias, ensembles, duets, and the required amount of melodrama thrown in. At no moment does Verdi, while taking the measure of Shakespeare's characters, forget that he has always to be attending to the needs of Italian vocal art and technique; and, for that matter Shakespeare never allowed strictly dramatic considerations to hold up his powers and course as a master of rhetorical speech and the purple patch.

Verdi did not, as old-time critics imagined he did, completely change his style towards the end of his long lifetime. On the face of it, the progression from *Trovatore* or *Rigoletto* to *Otello* involved a scarcely credible metamorphosis or a musical and psychological double-somersault. To the end Verdi retained certain traits of style and expression. He did not eject essentials of his earliest methods, as Wagner had to; there is not a palpable psychological or technical connection between *Rienzi* and *Tristan*, but it is possible to think of phrases from *Stride la Vampa* appearing not much changed in the *Requiem*; and the sudden outburst of Desdemona when she bids farewell to Emilia, so poignant in its context and by contrast, might have ended an aria in *Luisa Miller*. In his musical treatment or portraiture of *Aïda* we can trace the outlines of the purer and more sensitive vocal style and nature of Desdemona. The continuously developed orchestral tissue of *Otello*, as pertinent bar-by-bar as anything in Wagner, did not of course, spring from Wagnerian influence. In fact, Verdi displays in *Otello* all the old vocal opportunism now subtilised, combined with a flowing quasi-symphonic orchestra, not in any way Wagnerian, but comparable to that used by Mozart in his ensemble finales. As an amalgam or synthesis of vocal melody, felicitous and pertinent and powerful instrumentation, with recitative nearly always itself so much potential melody true to character, every note of voice or tone of instrument evocative of the right mood, atmosphere, or movement, *Otello* has not yet been excelled. And there was, to follow, the fine-spun musical wit and fantasy of *Falstaff*—it is an old but constantly staggering story of genius that matured profoundly but never aged, and was inexhaustible until death, after waiting with unusual patience, stepped in.

Return to Vienna

I

ONLY A thoroughbred Englishman could hope to write
about the opening of Vienna's new opera house and not
expose himself to a suspicion of sentimentality. I confess
that for my part I have once or twice been emotionally fairly
bowled over, perhaps in the first place because I declined
to submit to official procedure by deciding not to attend
the formal ceremony this morning.

I anticipated, and rightly, that the speeches, invariably
made on these occasions, would seem longer and more
platitudinous than ever in German. So, while the golden
key was being handed to the director, Dr. Karl Böhm, by
the Minister of Education on the spacious stage in the
presence of all the notabilities, I wandered through
the adjacent Burggarten, a quiet, intimate park, stained
with autumn, a place apart and belonging to the past.
A statue of Grillparzer sits alone in a more secluded
corner.

As the enchantment of atmosphere got to work on me,
and as I emerged from this Vallombrosan arbour to the
gracious main boulevard, and as I stood opposite the Parliament House, with its sumptuous rhetoric of architecture,
winged chariots and prancing steeds against the skyline,

a miracle happened. We have often been told that music lives in Vienna's air, in its stone. Well, I now suddenly heard music floating all around, music from the trees, from the marmoreal signs and symbols surrounding me, music of *The Mastersingers*, then of course the strains of Johann Strauss, *The Blue Danube*—lilting, rising, falling, like the brown leaves from the trees, invisible music, yet coming from different and encompassing directions.

The explanation was simple enough: the reopening ceremony was being broadcast from within the Opera House and was coming to an end as the Vienna Philharmonic played the assemblage out. The fact remains: I had momentarily heard and seen Vienna as music, intangible and wafted about magically. Possibly the microphone and broadcasting have never before approached as near as this to spiritual revelation. For, to be precise and not to mince language, there were happenings yesterday in Vienna that awakened depths of spirit not often touched in the traffic of the public world.

As the privileged people drove last night to the Opera House in cars specially labelled so as to assist scrutiny by a highly ornamental and polite police, crowds of spectators lined the paths and pavements, crowds of the ordinary Viennese folk, unable for a month to afford to go to the opera. (Not until January would the prices of tickets fall to the range of average pockets.) But all Vienna stood for hours watching the happy and favoured few.

It was like a royal occasion in London, almost a coronation. In the crowds stood little girls and boys, already getting the opera into the blood. They were all rewarded, for the whole performance of *Fidelio* was heard by microphone outside the floodlit beflagged palace: it is a palace, nothing less.

The appearance of the Opera House seen from the outside is much the same as the old. It was when I climbed the long rising flights of steps to the balcony on Friday that I had misgivings: would the interior look clinical, according to the modern custom in these things; would the architecture and ornamentation strike a chill to the heart and appear attuned to the tone-row anatomists?

The first glimpse reassured me—the multitudinous passages, the approaches to the centre, the luxurious cloak-rooms, the salons for refreshment as brilliant and as chande-liered as a ballroom, all in white and gold, all designated to lead enharmonically to the auditorium itself, also in cream with delicate gold embellishments, a sort of revised or, if a word may be coined, contemporised baroque, cunningly concealing functional intents and uses: no pillars or obstacles interfering with vision, a clear, perhaps too reveal-ing acoustic, an orchestral pit big enough to accommodate or house instrumentalists in long-legged stretches of comfort. The mingling of opulence, taste, and structural necessity is remarkable.

The new Vienna Opera House is in these times truly a resurrection. Why has it been rebuilt in this beautiful, aristocratic way if not as a symbol of man's aspiration and worship of a lofty thing? There would have been ample justification if Vienna had decided to adapt the rebuilding to a modern economy and to the bare bones of the con-temporary æsthetic and general view of life. Vienna has preferred, in spite of stress and burden, to honour a tradition.

Anybody who feels disappointed with this new temple of

fine art is likely to find paradise equally disappointing. The interior is not as high as Covent Garden's; the gallery is not out of touch. I could myself listen to and see opera very happily from this gallery, where on the opening night, at any rate, one or two white ties and tails could be seen. I am told that the stage covers a space larger than that of the auditorium. There are six movable platforms so that different sets can be got ready more or less simultaneously.

During the performance of *Fidelio*, the distance from the front of the stage to the background, when the prison's courtyard gates were raised showing the surrounding countryside, was apparently so great that the entrance of Pizarro seemed a matter of perspective and persevering pedestrianism. It was perhaps as well that Furtwängler was not conducting: Pizarro might not have reached us at all.

The technical equipment of the new house is extensive and fabulously devised, reducing opera activities in England by comparison to the primitive. Yet a doubt assails me. In the presence of such mechanical scope and perfection none except human aim of the strongest spiritual power is likely to succeed. We can only hope that Karl Böhm and Vienna's tradition will prove equal to bending to imaginative ends the service of a superb machine which could easily turn into a devouring Moloch.

The performance of *Fidelio* was, as it needed to be, devout and musically very serious. The opera was well chosen for the occasion because its theme is essentially ethical. In Leonora, Beethoven transcended the presentation of a woman's character and love: he created a musical symbol of " das ewige Weiblich." Martha Mödl acted eloquently and sang out of her heart: her treatment of Leonora's great aria was heroic in its surmounting of certain technical limitations of her highest register. Irmgard Seefried as Marzelline, brought to the prevailing atmosphere of austerity a delightful piquancy of personal and vocal touch, reminding us that the opera has its relationship to the Singspiel.

The production in the main concentrated on the loftier and more generalised and portentous aspects of the work; perhaps the " Gold " aria of Rocco was left out as likely to be an unnecessary and additional reminder of the uses and abuses of filthy lucre. And Pizarro's aria was sung out of place, on his entry before the arrival of the letter, thus making it more or less meaningless verbally and dramatically.

The hero of the evening was the Vienna Philharmonic. The playing was superb, effortless, each instrumentalist an artist but seemingly an inseparable part of the whole. But the tone at times became a little larger than the lifesize of action on the stage. Maybe the orchestral pit can be lowered; or perhaps my seat in the balcony received excessive vibrations of tone. I will reserve emphatic judgment on the house's acoustics until after later performances.

Meanwhile, it is not easy continually to fix attention on the opera in the Opera House because of the opera that is always going on in Vienna outside in the streets and manorial coffee-houses. The other evening a taxi-driver taking me to Sacher's restaurant was obliged to diverge from the usual route: some function at the Opera, a dress rehearsal, involved special traffic arrangements. The taxi-driver argued with the police and got his way, a short cut.

He assured me he was the only taxi-driver in Vienna

capable of getting me to Sacher's that night for hours. He also explained that right of way was that night reserved for " die wichtigen Leute " (the really important people). By the way, the waiters in Vienna's coffee-houses and restaurants are polite and solicitous as ever: the lower the bow the larger the tip.

II

Since Sunday we have been enjoying a two-day pause in this festival of opera while the rehearsals—the final rehearsals—of Strauss's *Die Frau ohne Schatten* are taking place. Rehearsals have been in progress since May. For forty-eight hours we have found time to attend to the ordinary and habitual opera of Vienna's life and existence in the changing scenes of the coffee-houses, the spacious streets and boulevards surrounded by the elaborate architecture of a past which seems now to have built not for a day but for all time.

On Sunday afternoon a crowd gathered on the main avenue of the Opera, the Opernring, to watch a policeman directing the traffic. He wore a musical comedy military uniform and white gloves. The traffic was not busier than it is in the Mall in London any Sunday afternoon, but his gestures and swoopings of the body, his genuflexions and struttings conjured before the imagination the dizzy whirl and speed and sense of inevitable catastrophe of a thousand speedways and Brooklands. His rapid contortions of arms, as many apparently as of an Indian god, created the illusion of slow motion in the traffic itself. He was obviously conscious of his audience; I almost expected applause and an encore. When there was a complete lull and no automobile was adjacent he scanned the horizon and blew a whistle, hungry and anxious for more traffic.

Opposite the Opera an underground passage has been made to cross the street. A subway not as extensive as the one in Piccadilly Circus, it was officially opened on Saturday, and thousands of Viennese turned out to ride down the small escalator. The subway is highly decorative with, of course, a café, the most important and necessary feature. A Viennese cannot very well be expected to travel underground even for only thirty or forty yards without the knowledge that a café is not far away.

The traditional coffee-houses of Vienna, large, nearly, as the smokeroom of a London club, are as ever numerous and cheek by jowl. Seldom are they full. I am writing this article in one of them, supplied with the morning's newspapers. If I wish I can remain here all day, under no obligation to call for another cup of coffee.

The performance on Sunday of *Don Giovanni* was broadcast, so that the crowds unable to get tickets could hear the singing and also the playing of the Vienna Philharmonic Orchestra. The music came out of the floodlit building as though from a gigantic stone musical box, and was wafted on the air to remote, empty dark streets. At the corner of one of these streets a woman was selling roasted chestnuts from a brazier of burning tinder. In the glow of it two old Jews crouched, following the broadcast performance with the score. They were lost to the world and from time to time they warmed their hands at the brazier's slow fire.

The actual performance had certain disappointments. *Don Giovanni* lends itself to all the contemporary arts of plastic suggestive stagecraft. We naturally expected that opportunity would be seized extravagantly to exploit the new opera house's comprehensive and protean technique of production. But the first act remained set in the same scene; at one side of the stage the house of Donna Anna, at the other the house of Don Giovanni with staircases curving from them, making a sort of bridge in the middle distance, the background suggesting the roofs and towers of a Spanish city. This setting served for the killing of the Commandatore and for Don Giovanni's ball.

The more the drop curtain fell to rise again the more the picture and pattern remained the same. Here, I thought, was an example of baroque "mit Sparsamkeit"—the baroque with parsimony. Perhaps it is a good sign that the modern Moloch of the theatre is already being worshipped with a certain fear and proportion at the Vienna Opera. The singing was excellent, if not always as distinguished as the costly occasion demanded.

George London as Don Giovanni is scarcely an aristocrat in passion or in vocal timbre. Lisa della Casa, always a lovely singer and lovely to look at, is not of the right tragic stature for Donna Anna. The Donna Elvira of Jurinac and the Zerlina of Seefried, together with that matchless orchestra, reminded us that the evening really was the second production in the new phase of the Vienna Opera's history, a phase already advertised the world over. The Vienna Philharmonic is still the hero of the festival. Other orchestras probably contain instrumentalists as clever and of a more brilliant virtuoso efficiency, but none excels it for unity, in which skill is instinctively put to the service of style, the composer's style. The playing is never intrusive, never comes between us and the music.

On Saturday morning the orchestra performed at the opening ceremony; in the evening it played *Fidelio* and afterwards appeared at the midnight ball organised by the Philharmonic Orchestra; next morning it was ready for Bruno Walter in the Konzertsaal and a programme of Mozart and Mahler (the fourth symphony); and then, on the evening of the same day, enchanted us in *Don Giovanni*. At the present the orchestra is rehearsing, as I have said, Strauss's *Woman Without a Shadow* and also the ninth symphony of Bruckner, which Bruno Walter conducts on Sunday morning. A love of labour.

III

During the first week of the renaissance of the Vienna Opera the great theatre has been closed on no fewer than three evenings, including Saturday, because of final rehearsals for *Don Giovanni*, *Die Frau ohne Schatten* and *Aïda*. But whether the opera house be closed or not, there is plenty in Vienna to satisfy the appetite for pleasure, artistic and other.

Situated in the most beautiful place on the city's main boulevard, opposite the university and next to the loveliest little garden imaginable, is the stately Burgtheater, built in white, crinkled stone, and at first glance almost as big as Buckingham Palace. It has, like the Opera, recently been restored after war damage, and was reopened a few weeks ago—an event which from other cities might have been trumpeted far and wide, for the Burgtheater of Vienna has a tradition in Europe not less honourable if not as venerable as that of the Comédie Française. On Saturday night every seat was occupied for a performance of Goethe's *Tasso*, a play entirely untheatrical, with no visible action and little psychological excitement. The characters talk in limpid blank verse, or rather they instruct one another in philosophy and homely wisdom. It is a didactic play, dealing entirely with things of the mind, the spirit, taste, and conscience. There is not a moment's appeal to any worldly view of life and the theatre, let alone to a modern view. Yet this crowded audience attended to Goethe in absorbed silence, and the young people in the standing places applauded favourite speeches as though listening to arias sung by famous tenors.

I almost expected an encore after the storm of hand-clapping which greeted the end of Leonore's speech to Antonio, with its charmingly womanly " So, Antonio, hat man für ihn das ganze Jahr zu sorgen." A murmur of appreciation was heard in the auditorium when the lines were spoken to the effect that talent is formed in solitude but character in the tumult of the world. " Es bildet ein Talent sich in der Stille, sich ein Charakter in dem Strom der Welt." It is always a surprise to an Englishman, even if he is acquainted with Goethe, to be reminded that this famous and great platitude, which might well have appeared in a conversation with Eckermann, comes trippingly from the mouth of the Princess Leonore, who is surely one of the most adorable bluestockings in literature.

This Burgtheater production of *Tasso* was set in scenes of Alma Tadema and Winterhalter statuary, columns and portraiture, with ornamental terraces, blue sky, golden sunlit interiors, extremely elegant and antique. The play, which is supposedly evocative of Tasso's Italy, is most agreeably Weimarisch. I could not imagine an audience in London listening intently to a play with no stimulation to the senses, a play essentially didactic, concerned mainly about principles of conduct and poetic ways of living, all treated with a deliberate neo-classicism of diction and poise. A certain naïveté is needed in order to get into this world nowadays: and perhaps a certain naïveté is needed at the base of civilisation. We could in London undoubtedly profit in the theatre from a little of this seriousness and simple faith among audiences, if only as a kind of solvent in a mixture of extremes of sophistication and triviality.

As a contrast to *Tasso* there is a production at the Volksoper (a sort of Sadler's Wells in Vienna) of Leo Fall's operetta *Madame Pompadour*. I went to this in a mood of agreeable anticipation, because I remembered the enchanting treatment of the same piece in London years ago, a Cochran production if I am not wrong, with Evelyn Laye a delightful Pompadour. I also remembered the fine musical style in which Vienna once presented operettas by Lehár and Oscar Straus.

Frankly, the Volksoper performance of Fall's engaging little work was a surprising disappointment; it was noisy and even vulgar. The first scene looked like a night club of the period after Hollywood had finished with it. The chorus was strident, clapping hands to the music's down beats, supposedly indicative of high spirits. The singing of the principals was loud and usually hopeful of applause at the end of each number. An orchestra lacking lightness and variety of touch did far less than justice to Leo Fall's score; it sounded rather thin and tawdry, but really it is not. Vienna is on the whole so devoted to tradition that it is sad that the graciousness and whipped-cream carefree gaiety seem to have been temporarily removed from the Lehár-Fall school by later and less insinuating influences. Changes in the popular taste are usually significant of changes of social outlook, manners, and character: Vienna has not altogether escaped the levelling and sometimes cheapening influences of our period.

On Monday the production of *Die Meistersinger* at the Opera was efficient and spacious with great distances to be travelled by the singers, especially in Nuremberg, steps coming down from high to the workshop of Sachs. The adipose prima donna of old could never have coped with them. Again the orchestra was superb, in spite of prosaic conducting by Reiner. Apparently the revived Vienna Opera now possesses everything except a guiding mind and spirit of genius. The *Meistersinger* performance was disappointingly lacking in imagination and nuance. Sincerity is not enough: in fact, without sensitiveness and poetry, sincerity can end in heaviness. Schöffler as Sachs sang the Flieder monologue more or less at the audience. Irmgard Seefried's charmingly coquettish Evchen might have danced out of *Fledermaus*. No other artist was outstanding.

One danger, a handicap to the Vienna Opera's immediate future, could easily come from want of a truly critical press and also, from want of self-criticism in Vienna in general. There is a hint of provincialism in the city's air of musical complacency. One of the most famous of Vienna's music critics discussing this performance of *Die Meistersinger* is not at all backward in informing his readers that the production is the work of his own son, and proceeds to praise it without a suspicion of a blush. Yet I leave Vienna with sorrow and pleasure enough to last a life out. I shall miss the Wiener Philharmoniker, the Vienna taxicab-drivers, the warm, comfortable coffee-houses, the great sweep of the boulevard past the Parliament Houses, the old-world graciousness of the Burggarten, and the pigeons. And I am pretty sure that the pigeons will miss me; nobody else in Vienna seemed to feed them.

IV

In 1875 Wagner arrived in Vienna to conduct the State Opera. Hugo Wolf was then a student at the Conservatoire, in his sixteenth year, and not far removed from poverty. He described in a letter how he went to see and hear the Meister:

It was Tannhäuser . . . I took up my place at a quarter past two, although the opera only began at half past six. There was such a frightful scrimmage that I was worried about myself. I wanted to back out, but it was impossible, for no one near me would make way. So nothing remained for me to do except stay in my place. At last the door was opened, the whole crowd pushed their way inside, and it was fortunate that I was drawn into the middle, for if I had got to the side I should have been crushed against the wall. But I was richly compensated for my mortal anxiety. I got my good old place in the gallery . . .

Eighty years after this memorable happening in the short life of Hugo Wolf, I myself went to Vienna and I walked up a spacious staircase at the first night of the reopening of the State Opera in November 1955. I was admitted to a seat in a box, after showing a ticket priced at a sum which would easily have kept young Wolf alive for nearly half a year. As I ascended the staircase, with elegance and luxury all round, I thought of all the greatness enshrined in this building, the men who had been in charge of it—Richter, Mahler, Weingartner, Schalk, Bruno

163

Walter, Strauss, Clemens Krauss. And when Karl Böhm, the man chosen to govern and guide the resurrected Staatsoper, took his place at the conductor's desk, and as the great distinguished audience rose to welcome him, with Bruno Walter and the Vienna Philharmonic leading the applause, I, for the only time in my life, envied another man. " This," I said to myself, " is Böhm's finest hour. He has attained to a power and glory far beyond any dreams which could possibly have visited him when he was a young student. Now might he chant his Nunc Dimittis."

Less than half a year after the night of Böhm's apotheosis, the following statement and comments appeared in a Munich newspaper:

Dr. Karl Böhm, the director of the Vienna Opera, has resigned. From August 31 next he will be guest conductor only. The differences between the Ministry of Education (who insisted that Böhm be solely active at the Opera for seven to eight months a year) and the conductor (who wanted to maintain his extensive activity abroad . . .) could not be reconciled.

Böhm absented himself from Vienna and when he returned he was hissed by the audiences in the "standing-places" and the gallery; for while he had been away some of the performances drooped to routine and hastily improvised standards. Böhm might conceivably argue that he had successfully launched the new Opera in Vienna during the months of November and January. But the fact is that while he was launching it the prices of admission remained luxuriously high. The average Viennese music-lover did not object that only the people with money,

mainly visitors, could be present for the glamorous in-
augural periods; if they could afford to pay through the
nose, very well: all was grist to the mill. Obviously Böhm
chose to absent himself from felicity at a tactlessly wrong
moment, the moment of the ordinary man's opportunity.

To a handsome book produced to celebrate the Opera's
reopening, Dr. Böhm contributed an article in which he
stressed the importance of a permanent ensemble at any
great opera house. " I can announce with pride and
pleasure that we have for the next three years made secure
a first-class ensemble for Vienna."

The world is open at the present time for rather uncon-
scientious exploitation by the musical " stars." From
north, south, east and west they are attracted by material
rewards hard to resist. The 'plane is really an enemy to
style and continuity of tradition in the opera houses of our
period. Once upon a time, a conductor or a singer regarded
that the ambition of a lifetime had been fulfilled the day on
which he was engaged as permanent member of the company of a historic opera house; to be one of the Vienna
State Opera was to be among the chosen few. To-day
much more money can be earned by singers and conductors
by appearing here and there and everywhere as " guests,"
birds of passage, flying by night. An opera director in
Munich " produces " *Zauberflöte* in his own theatre and
in Rome, both in the same week. The director of the
Berlin Philharmonic Orchestra, recently appointed, is
scarcely seen oftener now in Berlin than when he appeared
there at concerts " as guest." Presumably the only permanent factor in the new arrangement is the salary guaran-
teed to him by the Berlin Philharmonic.

The crowds in the galleries and standing-place in Vienna

should be congratulated that they forcibly, if unmusically, expressed themselves against Dr. Böhm's precipitate withdrawal from a scene which for ordinary opera-goers had not yet got through its first act. If a director of an opera does not consider himself essential to a permanent ensemble, can we blame singers not less famous than Dr. Böhm if they too fall to temptations from other quarters? Most of us, were we appointed to an office as honourable and responsible as that of Director of the Vienna Opera, would devote the rest of our lives to a proud and jealous service, working or watching night by night; we would hardly take leave or our eyes from a single performance or rehearsal, whether in Vienna or Covent Garden, at least, not during the first year of our appointment. Or wouldn't we?

In December 1907 Gustav Mahler wrote a valedictory letter to the Vienna Opera; he had dedicated himself to it for ten years, transforming it to the finest in the world. (Between whiles, during his holidays, he composed his greatest symphonies, and *Das Lied von der Erde*.) Here is part of Mahler's letter of farewell:

The hour has come which brings our common work to an end. I take my leave from the workshop which I have come to love. I dreamed of rich and complete work, and instead of this I leave behind fragments—unfinished. [After ten years of genius!] It is not for me to judge what my work has given to those to whom it was dedicated. Yet at this moment I can say for myself that I was sincere and my aim was high. . . . In the throng of battle, in the heat of the moment, you and I were sometimes hurt or hit by error. But once a work was achieved, a problem was solved; we felt fully rewarded, even without obvious signs of success. All of us have travelled a long way, and with us the opera house for which we have worked.

On 19th September, 1897, Hugo Wolf, now thirty-seven, joined his friend Hellmer at their table in the restaurant in Vienna, " Zum braunen Hirschen." Wolf, agitated and hungry, consumed his chop in torn shreds. Hellmer, though used to Wolf's moods, was alarmed. When Wolf said to him in a confidential whisper, " I have become Director of the Vienna Opera," Wolf's brain had snapped. At the moment of the collapse of his finely but precariously woven mind and consciousness one idea was left to obsess him, one ideal—Director of the Vienna Opera.

The moral of my tale?—what you will.

Words and Music in Opera

THE BRIEFEST study of the history of the development of musical forms encourages the sense of irony, a sense consoling to the ageing critic, who, if he is worth his salt at all, is at bottom a Mephistophelian. In recent years we have witnessed the reaction against the Wagner idea or æsthetic of opera based on a quasi-symphonic orchestra. We have witnessed, also, the passing of the prima donna and indeed, the passing from opera altogether of the virtuoso vocalist. It is the strange and possibly humorous fact that, for an authentic production of *Wozzeck* solo voices as great as Friedrich Schorr's or Lehmann's, or Olzewska's, to go no farther back in time, would be an impediment, not to say an embarrassment. Wagner argued with a Teutonic logic all his own that in opera music should act as the means but not as the end; the end in view, he maintained, should be drama. But as he was a composer of genius, he could not help in spite of his theories using his dramatic material as so much fuel for such an extravagant orchestral conflagration of music as the theatre has ever known. The crowning irony is that the Wagnerian opera æsthetic is to-day being employed by the contemporary anti-Wagnerians, who are concentrating the main interest of their operas in stage action and words, using music as not much more than an accompaniment or commentary on the turn of the dramatic screw. In other words, they are giving us operas in which music is a means to a dramatic end.

In the second part of Goethe's *Faust* Mephisto returns to Faust's old study, and there he once more puts on Faust's fur mantle; " Once more am I the Principal " (I quote from Bayard Taylor's indispensable if prosaic translation). And he is told by Baccalareus " of the school new founded," that " This is Youth's noblest calling and most fit! The world was not, ere I created it . . ." And when he has finished and departed Mephisto says:

> Go hence, magnificent Original!—
> What grief on thee would insight cast!
> Who can think wise or stupid things at all
> That were not thought already in the Past?

The " new " opera æsthetic is really a reversion to primitive type and structure. Its emphasis on words and dramatic interest recalls the theory and practice in vogue at the close of the sixteenth century in the house of Giovanni Bardi. The reaction then, as now, was against the domination of music over the rights of words and poetry. But the course of opera has usually gone contrary to a rational conception of libretti and stage action. The greatest operas to this day are those which live mainly and sometimes wholly by the opportunities they offer for free-flowing music-making, and for an uninhibited display of a voice that really can sing. I am not reactionary enough to argue that a sensible libretto is not preferable to one that is non-sensical. But I do believe that Wagner was right to insist that there is certain " stuff " of music, a certain kind of dramatic subject and order-pattern of words, upon which

169

music will readily feed. I believe he was right, too, to think that a libretto should deal rather with types of feeling embodied in the dramatis personæ than with highly individualised characters; and that a libretto is no use for a musical setting if it depends on plot and circumstances needing close verbal explanation. Music cannot argue or serve the purposes of verbal exposition. Again I must quote Ruskin, who though he knew little about opera, went to the root of the matter when he said that the lover may sing of his lost beloved, but the miser may not sing of his lost money-bags. The statement goes too far, but it points to the limits beyond which a composer will go at his peril when he is searching for words and subjects good and fruitful for musical treatment.

Most times it is fatal to an opera's chances of musical survival if the libretto has been written by an accredited man of letters. Hofmannsthal served Strauss's art magnificently because he was a poet with musical intuitions and taste. Even Hofmannsthal would have missed many operatic chances, even in *Rosenkavalier*, had Strauss not guided him, with all his vast experience, along the right lines. If the words in a libretto are excellent enough in themselves as dialogue and drama, they don't need music, and in fact, are wasted on music. It is perhaps true at bottom, at very bottom, that what is too silly for speech may conveniently and even pleasantly be sung. Walter Pater—out of date at the moment—thought that the condition of all the arts " aspired to music." At the present and more egalitarian time the determination of each of the arts seems to be to invade the territory of the other. At any rate, the day is at hand, obviously, when dramatic critics will need to accompany music critics at first nights at the opera. Clear enunciation of words will be demanded from the singers even more urgently than good voices. And any efficient orchestra containing musicians quick at reading a restless, peripatetic score will be chosen, rather than the Vienna Philharmonic Orchestra, to play the music. After all, the Vienna Philharmonic Orchestra in *Wozzeck* is a positive distraction: the " tone " itself obscures the intentions, psychological and other, of librettist and composer alike.

" In der Beschränkung zeigt sich erst der Meister "— " within his limitations the Master reveals himself," to quote again from Goethe, whom we neglect at our peril these days. Decadences and disease begin in the arts, as in the social order itself, when structure and function lose strict relationship. Opera is not only a musical form; it is a form of vocal music. Wagner himself had to compromise his symphonic orchestral procedure and give the singers scope by using the forms and pattern of vocal music concerted and solo. The finest operas of the best of contemporary opera composers—Benjamin Britten—are exactly those which encourage the virtuosity and vanity of the solo vocalist. Though it is necessary that the composer should set words to a kind of orchestration which does not make it impossible for us to hear them as they are sung, he is not aiming at clearness of orchestral texture simply that we may catch every verbal nuance. He aims at giving the singer material and opportunity for song. It is no criticism to ask of an opera singer: " Will no one tell me what she sings? " The question is, can she sing in musical numbers?

Of British Opera

It is, perhaps, a great comfort that at the present moment English opera is springing up around us with an almost tropical profusion. There is scarcely a contemporary English composer who is able to sit down at will and not write an opera. Britten, Walton, Tippett, Berkeley: everybody's doing it, they are all at their operatic exercises. Yet it is a fact that outside London the majority of English people have little or no knowledge of or interest in opera; it is still possible for a man and woman to live years in a large English town or city and hardly ever hear and see a performance of *Tristan*, *Falstaff*, *Zauberflöte*, *Rosenkavalier*. Outside of London there is no opera house and no theatre possessing the technique or the atmosphere of an opera house. In short there is no national tradition of opera in England to this day, no feeling for it. The average Englishman is not in passionate need of any of the arts, opera least of all.

We have nowadays not more but fewer English opera singers than we could boast of in the period of the Beecham régime. There are no English equals at the moment of Frank Mullings, Robert Radford, Walter Widdop, Agnes Nichols, Kirkby Lunn, Miriam Licette, Norman Allin (the best English Gurnemanz, the best English Ochs), Frederic Austin, Heddle Nash, Robert Parker (the best English

Wotan; none of the Germans of to-day is better). Without aid from Australia it would not be easy in 1957 to produce *Rosenkavalier* or *Die Walküre* with a company of English-speaking artists. Apparently we can as a nation give birth to opera composers but not to singers or actors of opera, or really instinctive and natural producers of opera.

Is it certain that our composers really are writing opera, and not adapting to words and a more or less dramatic text musical forms and musical ideas which, though far from negligible qua music, are not essentially operatic? Opera can take many shapes and modes of musical style and emotion, but it begins from song, from the voice as protagonist. Opera is, in fact, heightened and elaborated song. It is a particularly curious aspect of the present activity of our composers in the realm of opera that, while they are busy grappling with the most difficult of all forms of music and art, turning out opera one down t'other come on, there is not a dozen contemporary English songs that are convincing or memorable or fit to survive comparison with a French, German, or Russian group at a recital. There is virtue of a modest order in small and successful beginnings. Beethoven waited long, grappled with doubts, sought high and low for the right librettist, before he could bring himself to the task of composing *Fidelio*. Wagner at the rise of his fame as opera composer ceased writing music at all for years while he " overhauled the catechism," and worked out a new æsthetic of opera. In the Strauss-Hofmannsthal letters we may read of the theoretical or intellectual labours the two men went through to arrive at some fulfilment of their conceptions; and here we have two experienced masters on the job, each the product of an opera soil well tilled, each born to breathe the air and tradition of opera in his cradle.

If we consider the operas of masters bred in lands where opera is as much part of the national way of life and entertainment as cricket and novel reading are in England, we are bound to confess that all of them had to suffer frustrations, pass through much sore trial and error, before they could compose an opera really worth while. Even though blessed by genius, with opera technique and procedure a daily habit and routine, few composers have produced a first or even a second or third opera which has not soon seemed immature, mere 'prentice work. Who wishes to hear early Wagner to-day or early Verdi? except the fashionable intelligentsia who, if it is "the thing" to say so, are ready to argue that *Traviata* is a greater opera than *Tristan*. Who nowadays really wants to hear Strauss's *Guntram* or *Feuersnot*?—yet both works are, considered in relation to the period in which they first appeared, imposing enough.

The moral is obvious. My cautionary tale is told in the hope that it might restore critical proportion in this country. Let our composers receive all the sensible encouragement in the world as they get down to the hard work of laying (once again) foundations of English opera. But if genius finds it a long and arduous occupation to write opera in an atmosphere which is opera's element, what are the odds still against the appearance for some time to come of an English opera likely to be accepted universally as a masterpiece? My point is that if recent critical judgment is to be taken seriously in this country it is now as easy—Benjamin Britten having shown the way—to turn out operas as regularly and as much after the manner born as in the older times English composers turned out oratorio. But Britten happens to have a touch of genius, and it is for genius to say " I lead—follow who can! "

Our busy opera composers certainly must be encouraged. And criticism will help them by keeping its head and balance. For my own part I have never yet heard an English opera which has disturbed my feeling that opera is not an art or way of making music that comes by nature to English people. I am not sure that the contemporary activity in the production of English opera is not a cult. Our national form of vocal and choral music is probably still the oratorio. The finest English composition for voices and orchestra—and the most dramatic—is Walton's *Belshazzar's Feast*. No English opera so far written fulfils as convincingly as *Gerontius* the English synthesis of words and music, the English way of joining voice and orchestra with a tale to be told. *The Mass of Life* of Delius is another example of the tendency of English vocal music to take its rise from a traditional and oratorical source. " Oratorio? " asks the nearest young man in the foyer at Covent Garden. " Parry? Or even Elgar? Dear me! " But what if this long historical musical tendency of the English should lead in time to a Bach, or to a Stravinsky capable of another *Symphony of Psalms*? I am no doubt suggesting reactionary doctrine. I have never agreed, all the same, that it is necessary that English music should, for health and con-science' sake, virtually drill itself into opera. Much as I wallow in opera at its best, I do not regard great activity in opera as a sure sign that a nation is musical. I have never regarded the Italians as a musical people, taking them by and large. So, while it is satisfying to know that contemporary English composers are taking up the task, begun by Stanford, Delius, Holbrooke, Boughton, Ethel Smyth—to name a few—of producing a recognisably English corpus of opera, it will be as well to keep in mind the uses of the dramatic cantata and oratorio as means of extending and deepening the English musical consciousness. One or two songs as good as any of Strauss's last four would be excellent to be going on with.

*   *   *   *   *

It is not often that a composer's first opera turns out a permanent masterpiece, not even if it is the work of a writer of opera born and bred in a land in which for generations opera and the habit and technique of opera have been part of the day-by-day environment and air. If William Walton's *Troilus and Cressida* stays the course for a decade, and lives that long up to its present reputation, the ghosts of Wagner, Strauss, Puccini, to name a few, will look on with admiration, and perhaps with envy. But Walton has had opera in his musical bones and blood for years. *Belshazzar's Feast* is charged with dramatic power and instinct for " atmosphere " and " scene." The light touch of comedy, of swiftly-changing characterisation, is in *Façade*; there is a rich vein of brooding solitary melody in the viola concerto. There are the urge and sweep of pomp and pageantry in the superb *Crown Imperial* march; and in his film music Walton has demonstrated gifts in the way of fitting evocative tunes to visible action.

He has so far lacked only one truly operatic essential; lyrical melody of a feminine flavour, or to be downright, of erotic suggestiveness. Perhaps opera has grown out of original sin. There are no passionate lovers in any contemporary opera known to me, certainly not in Hindemith

176

or Stravinsky. And by passionate lovers I mean a man and a woman who love passionately. Even in *Wozzeck* there are eroticism and a hint of the fragility and beauty of sex. English opera has so far veered away from romantic love as experienced unsentimentally by the protagonists and depicted with appreciative irony—as in *Rosenkavalier*, or with tragic acceptance, as in *Tristan* or *Pelléas*. Once on a time, when patriots in this country were crying out desperately for a school of English opera, it was suggested that Elgar should write one, instead of wasting his time on oratorio—oratorio of the *Gerontius* order, presumably. But Elgar was incapable of expressing in music more than a hint of woman engaged in earthly love. He actually set his *Falstaff* in a minor key and moralised about Falstaff's misspent years. And his women in *Falstaff*—" my God, what women! " as Robert Louis Stevenson said of Shaw's. Langford wrote much to the point about Elgar's women: " Do they muster up an ounce of beauty between them? If he holds them virtuous, so much the more is he bound to have made them beautiful, and not a mere bevy of cackling laughter. . . . Whoever before attempted to describe woman without some continuance of melody? " Britten made a masterpiece out of the libretto of *Peter Grimes* because the interest and drama of it is concentrated in the clash of Grimes—and his " exercises "—and the sea-and-wind-and-fog-swept borough. The love of Ellen is maternal; she is a spinster really, whose best music is inspired by an art of embroidery. We need not review the tragic heroines of opera—the Salomes, Isoldes, Elektras, Violettas, Carmens—to realise how much the characterisation of the temperament and physical being of woman is opera's essential function; let us think (with enchantment and delight!) only of Suzanna, Despina, the two heroines of *Cosi*, Zerlina, the Marschallin, Sophie, Oktavian, Mimi, Manon; to know them has made opera and all its recurrent stupidities and artificialities well worth while.

In the opera of Delius, *A Village Romeo and Juliet*, is contained some of the most beautiful love music in existence, but it is not erotic, not even theatrical. It is the music of young love, love awakening and about to lose innocence. Delius sets the melody of these ill-starred children against a background of his own musical sensibility, against a harmonic tone and colour which tell of his acute awareness of the brevity of the kind of love he is presenting. The opera has failed to win a place in opera repertory anywhere because of its want of obvious visual action and plot and character appeal. Delius composed a dream opera; like his *Mass of Life*, it is not for extroverts; it is all inward-looking, or rather inward-feeling. I do not mean that it is introspective or concerned with abstractions. Delius's music is intensely human and passionate; but it is as though all passion and sense have been drawn into and through Delius's fine-spun imagination, and changed to poetry. There is no prose in it; it is all vibrations, vibrations of happiness, ecstasy, foreboding, pity, loneliness, resignation.

The main defects of English opera so far have arisen because of want of experience in the technique of composing with stage action always in mind. Good music in itself will not make an opera. A learned English musical scholar once confessed that he could not listen with patience to Puccini for the reason that Puccini lacked counterpoint. As an example of academic English opera at its musical best and theatrically weakest we might refer to Gustav Holst's *At The Boar's Head* which is based on the tavern scenes from Shakespeare's *Henry IV*. We are expected to get the smack and flavour of Falstaff and Mistress Quickly in a score founded on airs from Playford's *Dancing Master*, set to or elaborated by brilliant and manifold counterpoint. But the opera is an interesting and valuable contribution, because Holst skilfully tackles the problem of a sustained recitative which moves as swiftly as the spoken word, with a certain appositeness and lightness of touch. But the music remains a thing apart from the flesh and blood of the characters. Another instance of academically composed opera is Vaughan Williams's *The Pilgrim's Progress*, often extremely beautiful qua music. It has been called by a wit, " the poor man's *Parsifal*." Much of the music written in English opera sounds better in the concert-hall than in the theatre. None of Verdi's music sounds better in the concert-hall than it does in the opera house.

After trial and error, English opera is gaining identity and some confidence of touch and intention. We owe much to the pioneers who, because they were pioneers, were destined never to arrive anywhere near the promised land. What would we think now of Ethel Smyth's *The Wreckers*? It was admired in its day by good judges here and in Germany. I imagine it is, or was, the kind of opera Brahms might have written. He avoided opera; and Beethoven found the task of composing his only opera often a burden and frustration. He conquered an alien medium only because he could not help composing great music to a theme not consistently belonging to opera.

In our pride and enthusiasm for British opera to-day, and for Benjamin Britten and William Walton, we must remember the spade-work of the pioneers. It is certainly a far-cry from Sullivan's *Ivanhoe* and Mackenzie's *Colomba* to *Peter Grimes* and *Troilus and Cressida*. And we have still to go a long way and work hard before we create in these isles a *Meistersinger*, an *Aïda*, or even a *La Bohème*.

Let's Make an Opera

THERE IS also the theme of opera to consider, the subject; does it provide material for music? A lover may sing of his lost love, as I think we have already been told, but the miser may not sing of his lost money-bags. This is perhaps to overstate the case against non-poetic or non-romantic opera; but we are here very close to sound æsthetic doctrine. Music is still, even after contemporary composers have handled it, an art of emotional or picturesque expression. The poet or librettist should make his opera-text musical in the patterns or sequences by which the action is carried on. Action on the stage, circumstances of plot, the tempo of words, the rise and fall of the feelings of the characters, and the nature of the feelings, gay or tragic—the librettist must attend to these factors with the musician's ear governing transition and modulation, avoiding, if possible, any abruptness that upsets musical continuity and balance of mood; and, on the other hand, avoiding stilted " situations " cramping to music—which is essentially an art of motion, in time and not in space. The opera librettist will also cut down to a minimum all explanatory dialogue. Music cannot deal with factual talk except by accentuation, which isn't artistically necessary, or by recitative, which is plainly a musical evasion.

Britten's recitative in *Billy Budd* is most times redundant;

and wearisome, not through any fault of his own but because the text contains lines that don't encourage musical invention, such as "Don't you answer an officer back. You take care, I've my eye on you." "Silence! I believe that is all you require, your honour." "Ay, at Spithead the men may have had their grievances, but the Nore—what had we there?" And so on.

Wagner absorbs entirely into the world of music the conversation—prose colloquial dialogue—between Sachs and Beckmesser in Act III of *Meistersinger* (*Die Tinte noch nass* and the rest); he was free to do so for the reason that the rhythm of the talk, the byplay of verbal aptness, flows on the current of the Wagnerian orchestra and its "endless" melody; and, incidentally, the words and the music were more or less simultaneously born in the mind of the same man. Strauss can cope with a scene of small-talk between Sophie and Oktavian in Act II of *Rosenkavalier* and not drop from a musical, not to say lyrical, plan. He too maintains melodic and quasi-symphonic continuity in the orchestra. Britten's orchestra in *Billy Budd* is not continuously symphonic or melodic; the texture of it cannot serve as a kind of trellis on which the vocal growths may hang, or climb, or blossom. There are, sad to say, few vocal or melodic plants in the score at all. We all know what Britten is capable of in *Les Illuminations*, when his musical imagination is feeding on the words of a poet. As I say, the text of *Billy Budd* is not a constant source of musical inspiration. Britten is frequently obliged to resort to "incidental music," ingeniously contrived if rather fussily onomatopœic bar after bar. What with the garrulous orchestration and the talk on the stage, no wonder many of us were temporarily overwhelmed when at the end of

Act III, we heard a succession of slow-moving chords, warm and imaginatively disconnected. Though they went on too long, they brought to some of us a sense of oasis, with visions of Sarastro and a heart-warming feeling of humanity and pity. So, in the " ballad " of *Billy Budd*— Britten here has escaped from the prose particularity of the text; here is the stuff of great music for him and he has seized on it.

" Let's make an opera " by all means, so long as fidelity to the medium of expression is observed. *Peter Grimes* is an opera, sure enough, and a masterpiece. It keeps to the main rules. A liberty was taken in *Billy Budd* when opera was deprived of women's voices, and very skilfully does Britten repair the violation. But it is simply not possible to make an opera largely out of an orchestral running-commentary on a stage action which contains little development of character, with much vocal recitative plastered on top of instrumentation—no doubt resourceful and fascinating to musicians—harmonies in evocative position, etchings in colours that flash suddenly, every device in Britten's superb equipment used economically, with a sense of the theatre rare among English composers. But still we don't make an opera. A play or a film with background music, yes!—the formula is here in convincing guise. But for the purposes of opera, voices must sing music that differentiates one character from another and at the same time satisfies the ear; or, as in Debussy's *Pelléas*, a speech-song is used that draws breath from a text pervaded with poetry, so that recitative enters the dimension of music.

I have read reviews of *Billy Budd* which have scarcely mentioned the vocal writing in it; apparently an opera can be put together by so many " conflicting harmonies,"

" thematic allusions," and " cross references " in the
orchestra.   It is as though I were to describe a beautiful
lady thus: her swan-neck, her tapered fingers, her poise,
and the liquefaction of her clothes; then, when asked what
about her face, I replied: " Face?   Faces are no longer
worn by beautiful ladies in the best places nowadays."   Up
to the moment of writing three major English composers
have trusted distinguished men of letters to write opera-
librettos for them.   Eugene Goossens turned to Arnold
Bennett.   Bliss to Priestley, and now Britten to E. M.
Forster and Eric Crozier.   Another melancholy instance of
the wisdom in the old saying that what is too silly to be
spoken may very well be sung.

PART FOUR

TRADITION AND
EXPERIMENT

" Contemporary " Music

ONE OF our national industries at least, or amongst them, is working at full pressure, so much so that output seems sometimes to run ahead of power of production. All over the country new seams are being opened in our fields of composition. Symphonies and even operas are to be had for the picking and hauling. There is a formula available, and it is all the easier to handle, since the reaction against " romanticism " made it unnecessary and unfashionable for a composer to depend largely on a melody which average intelligent and civilised people would recognise as a melody. It is to-day possible to put together a large-scale work in terms of the attraction to or repulsion from a tonal centre, jig-sawing your material into rhythmical patterns, or by working-out mathematically (or arithmetically) inversions, diminutions, expansions, and so forth, of a germ-theme of new notes which anybody could pick out on a piano. The industry is stimulated also by the knowledge that no individual experience of emotion or spirit is deemed now-adays essential to the making of music; on the contrary, anything of the sort is regarded suspiciously by contemporary criticism, which is content to discuss and estimate a work in terms of the formula by which it has in all its parts been assembled.

It is not the first time in music's history that the pioneers

have had all the roads " up " and have run here and there
happily inspired by the delusion that every step forward is
a sign of progress. " Nicht jeder Vorschritt ist ein Fort-
schritt "; it is an old tale indeed, reminding me of G. K.
Chesterton's army, which " advanced in all directions."
Activity and prodigality are not necessarily signs of the
presence of creative genius, but they get ready the atmosphere and the soil for it. The condition of British music at
the moment is healthy, and if the energy may at times
appear related less to æsthetics than to a national love of
exercise and athletics, let us be patient and hope for the
best. There is for our guidance the example of the lady
who from girlhood upward attended the Sunday morning
concerts in Vienna every week. In the same seat she sat,
first with her mother and father, then with her fiancé, soon
after with her husband, who was brilliant in his "Imperial"
uniform. Then, later, she was there, in the same seat,
deep in mourning. The war was over, and Franz Josef
and the old glory had departed. But music remained, and
in spite of the roll of the years she came every Sunday to
the concerts just the same, though owing to the wear of
time her face was sad if tranquil, her hair snow white, and
she was obliged to listen with an ear-trumpet. None the
less, music as ever made her eyes glisten and she would
murmur, as she sat alone, " Schön—ach Gott, schön! "
One Sunday the programme began with the " Unfinished "
Symphony of Schubert. At the close, tears of joy were in
her eyes. " Ach Gott, schön, schön! " The next in the
programme was Five Orchestral Pieces by Schönberg; and
nobody had warned the old lady about them, and she did
not read the newspapers diligently. Still, when the conductor was ready to begin them, up to her ear went the

trumpet, and the habit of a lifetime brought the look of heavenly anticipation on her face as the Schönberg pieces began. But after a few bars her expression changed to perplexity. She withdrew the trumpet from her ear and blew down it vigorously. She gave the " new " music the benefit of the doubt, and we must all try to extend to the latest modes and fashions of it the same gentle and kindly tolerance.

Critically, of course, it is as well to be reasonably on guard. The plain facts of history prove that seldom has the great and abiding composer been a technical innovator. The genius who has something to say and is consumed by a creative dæmon needs a language at hand, an established organised language which he has learned, as he learns his daily speech, instinctively because it is in general use; he needs for expression a vocabulary already steeped in " meaning," in association-values, so that he can convey his ideas to others. If he is truly a great man he is not satisfied to spend himself making an alphabet or trying experiments. There are wise words to my present purpose in Ernest Newman's *A Musical Critic's Holiday*. It is a law " that no genius of the first rank uses anything like the full theoretically possible resources of his time. It is sheer ignorance on the part of modern journalism to call a contemporary composer a reactionary because he refuses to avail himself of all these theoretic new resources. He is obeying a sound instinct; he knows that if he is to express himself with perfect freedom he must not diverge into the speculative." Mr. Newman quotes a passage from an essay of Stanford where it is pointed out that in the introduction to the third act of *Tristan* Wagner experimented with the whole-tone scale (bars 6 to 10), " and drew his pen through it, as was to be expected from a composer whose every work proves the writer to have had the pure scale inbred in him."

The composer with something to say is not free to be drawn into a technical or stylistic sidetrack of empiricism. He must, as far as means of expression go, remain in a known and comprehensible world; he cannot take part in exploring the possibilities of a new language, expanding the alphabet, the grammar, the parts of speech, and at the same time compose a masterpiece. For the statue is, in a way, in the block before the act of creation actively begins; in other words, the conception is implicit in the material the artist uses, so that he subdues his hand to the colours of it. Philipp Emanuel Bach was the " progressive "; his father Johann Sebastian was the conservative who adapted to his needs the current forms and technical rationale. Philipp Emanuel ventured along new paths, and where is he now? The contemporary pioneers—and as pioneers they will take honourable places in the books of musicology —are right to sustain their adventurings by the belief that they are composing for posterity. Let them conveniently reject from their minds the notion that the advent of genius often gives an entirely fresh twist to a " movement " in music, or to any other art. Even the boy is not father of the man if he is creative and therefore under the inexorable obligation to shed skins. What is the relation, blood or æsthetic, of *Rienzi* to *Tristan*?

The plea in this chapter is for patience on the part of the public with the innovators, and modesty on the part of the innovators and their propagandists as to their value as makers of music. I cannot recall the time when we have not boasted great or important British composers. I have seen them come and go, names as illustrious as those of

Britten, Walton, Rubbra, Fricker, Rawsthorne, Bliss to-day; and now they repose alphabetically in the mausoleum of the musical dictionaries. Yet they were highly esteemed by critical intelligences just as acute and, in relation to their particular cultural habitat, just as well informed and sophisticated as the lions of the reviewers of the moment. To these our present reviewers perhaps one word of protest will be permitted. Some of us are tired of the technical inventory they are continually giving us of a new or un-familiar composition. We know all about the formula. Schönberg and his atonalism, the subject lately of much learned technical exposition, has been in the public view these forty years; since the time when *Punch* sighed, " O, for the good old tunes of Strauss and Debussy! " Forty years ago Debussy was not altogether easy listening for the average attender of concerts, but he is accepted to-day by thousands, and so, too, is Béla Bartók.

The old " romantic " æsthetic is obviously no longer a working principle in the criticism of new works; we are told that contemporary music is a thing in itself and should be examined and appreciated qua music. This is to play with words. What the average intelligent man and woman wants the music critic to write about is something of the content of a work as well as of its technical " patterns " (that blessed word). It is not enough that a composer should have given a " shape " to this or that kind of mat-erial, atonal, polytonal and the rest. What æsthetically has he done with it; what has he, in musical terms, said of importance to the imagination of others? " From the heart to the heart "; so Beethoven spoke of his own lines of communication; but this is old-fashioned and reactionary language in the extreme.

Revolt and Tradition

THE RECENT concerts of contemporary German music, heard in the Third Programme, reveal an even more acute state of disintegration than is at once perceptible in composition to-day everywhere. At any cost young composers seem determined to prove they are contemporary; " if there's no future for us," we can imagine them saying, " then let us at least live in the present—and for heaven's sake let us forget the past." To echo romantic cadences or harmony is, apparently, to lapse into barbarism. The ironical fact pointed out by history is that the great composers have seldom paid tribute to the Time Spirit, have gone their ways indifferent to the ideologies of the hour, have not worried at the threat that the latest young critic might regard a work as likely to " date." There is no hint of the contemporary scene in Mozart, for example; no matter what may be said of the *Figaro* of Beaumarchais and its relation to or reflection of the French Revolution, Mozart's music, like all his music—*Don Giovanni, Cosi,* the symphonies, the G minor Quintet—is as indifferent to the demands of the Zeitgeist as the novels of Jane Austen. The hints of a later and more tragic harmony sounded in *Don Giovanni,* a music which foreshadows the creative disruption which was Beethoven's most seminal contribution, have nothing to do with ideologies, or the ebb and flow of external events. They came from an inevitable and strictly musical development, the consequence of the evolution of traditional forms acting and reacting to musical genius working from within, from its own coil of imagination. Wagner, a revolutionary in his day compared with whom Berg and Hindemith and Schönberg must be regarded as timid bourgeoisie tentatively dipping cold feet into the advancing tides; Wagner, for all his theories of the " Art Work of the Future," the " Zukunftsmusik," based his masterpieces on myth, his idea being that music can deal, in opera, only with broad types of human nature and emotion and consciousness, not with circumstances and conceptions needing historical context and explanation. Beethoven himself, the iconoclast who was the real cause of all the wrath to come, composed out of a spiritual belief. If he did begin a symphony not with a melody but with a knocking at the door as forbidding as the knocking in *Macbeth*, he was always willing to turn his vision inward and compose tunes which are only more seriously grounded in tone and feeling than Haydn's because he was the more serious man of the two. But overmuch is made of the Promethean Beethoven; he wrote as a full man, with humour, geniality, and solemnity in proportion. There is no symphony in existence that honours pure musical art more proudly and strictly than the *Pastoral* symphony.

The critics nowadays make a terrible fuss if they think a work of art is " dated." You will hear them, any Sunday evening, talking Ibsen out of existence because in 1957 the departure from the house of the next Nora is no longer of much economic or dramatic significance, and certainly not an event in the theatre calling for a portentous banging of a door. But in the world of imagination nothing dates;

we might as well object to the ghost in *Hamlet*, as to the exit of Nora, on grounds of topical " truth." If any play, by Ibsen or anybody else, possesses imaginative power of conviction time and space cannot touch it; it is the most prosaic sort of criticism that condemns a work of art mainly because it continues to hold the mirror up to a period. In music it is not of course easy to point out where a composition is dating; for music cannot really express or convey ideologies or concepts capable of verbal contradiction or approval. Yet there has been an attempt to render a mode of feeling obsolete for the purposes of musical composition; at any rate quite a number of anti-romantic critics are satisfied that romanticism is a form of outmoded emotional expression. Certain styles, certain technical formulæ, become in time associated with certain ways of conveying modes of artistic feeling and conception. Every classic, said Stendhal, was a romantic in his day. The danger in all the arts at the present time is the label, the fashion, the drive of the self-conscious schools (for never has the creative artist been rendered by events as self-conscious of his processes as to-day). The critics praise and damn from contemporary and often æsthetically irrelevant points of view. It is the " psychology," the " pathology," the " criticism of life " that make Alban Berg's *Wozzeck* fashionable in post-Freudian circles; the fact is overlooked that Berg's music at its best is as firmly rooted in the soil or soils of the romantic Mahler, Wagner, and Schönberg, as Wagner was rooted in Weber. Only the second-rate composers have had time to pick and choose their ways of expression or their subject-matter; only the second-rate composers have been so free from the sway of tradition as to go to work saying in advance: " I shall react against romanticism, avoid excessive chromaticism, and take care I don't fall under the influence of a dated school or subject-matter."

The proper genius is in the possession of his dæmon—and the dæmon usually breathes the informing fires of tradition. No composer so far has preoccupied himself with " new forms," " new idioms," and at the same time given the world a masterpiece. John Sebastian was the old fogy; Philipp Emanuel was the innovator who appealed to the avant garde!

Obviously the language of music must change with the everlasting unravelling of the stuff of consciousness. The critics will be the last to discover the music that achieves the next integration, and relates to basic continuous growth the new shoots and plants from the fundamental earth-tone. And the less of a rational critic the composer is himself the better for his powers of inspiration. The truly great man will find himself standing apart the more he remains with his forebears.

The Pioneer's Dusty Path

AT AN annual conference of the Incorporated Society of Musicians, Mr. Ernest Bradbury, music-critic of the *Yorkshire Post*, undertook or threatened to sing quotations from Schönberg throughout the lunch interval, to demonstrate that atonal music can achieve melody. The idea of a vocal music critic is unusual. I have heard of all sorts of vocal curiosities—a singing policeman, a singing Irish terrier, a singing barber, a singing tenor; but I have not as a rule expected any burst of song from a music critic except from the bathroom and as a matter of quite unpremeditated art. In passing, assuming that amongst my colleagues there are really a few natural-born singers how would we suit each of them to parts in opera; which, say, would be the unmistakable Hans Sachs, which the Papageno, which the Loge, which the Klingsor? There would be no lack of convincing Beckmessers.

Authentic Schönberg, which means music by him coming after *Verklärte Nacht* and *Erwartung*—authentic atonalism, and the tone-row technique derived from it, have not yet produced music appealing to average intelligent and educated listeners who have passed beyond the years of æsthetic adolescence. This kind of composition has been, in different phases of development or arrangement, before the public some thirty years. There is no mystery about

196

it; at any rate deductions from the basic formula do not
go beyond the comprehension of an ordinarily perceptive
mathematical understanding. But so far, though the
system has attracted an increasing number of contemporary
professional and amateur musicians, it remains esoteric and
apart from the main stream of general musical appreciation.
It is still a close corporation, almost a conspiracy. Would
sometimes it were a conspiracy of silence. As Mr. Frank
Howes pointed out the other day, atonalism or the serial
technique which satisfies "the impulse of construction," very
much and naturally becomes the fashion in a disintegrating
period socially, spiritually, and æsthetically. It is easier to
construct, to build or add together with factors which can
be grasped intellectually and ordered in their sequence by
logic, than it is to create, or cause to grow in a traditional
soil from seeds of imagination. In other and simpler words,
it is easier to be a logician or a mechanic than a poet. The
notion of a composer as poet is nowadays old-fashioned.
Music criticism seldom nowadays tries—even tries, for the
effort is hard and most times doomed to vain failure—to
find out if a new composition is " saying " anything of
importance to us as thinking and experiencing beings.
Contemporary music criticism ends mainly in technical
description and analysis. The sterility of it, taking it by
and large, is perhaps excusable. For who can tell whether
composers using atonalism and the tone-row technique are
indeed saying anything at all? The " language " of
atonalism and the serial method is not yet formulated into
symbolical significance; it has not yet acquired "meanings"
or " associations." Nobody is in a position to claim of a
work composed to this formula or system that it is great,
good, indifferent, or bad, as a work of art or as a well-

composed work of music. It is almost an impertinence for anybody not a specialist student to discuss experiments in atonalism, to discuss them strictly as laboratory investigators. And to judge or estimate atonal and tone-row compositions as music, with æsthetic verdicts merely implied, is effrontery. By what standard is a critic able to decide that a new work in this latest school is well and truly put together, considered strictly as atonalism or tone-row technique? And by what standard does he rank it in relation to music as we have known music in our different lifetimes? It is perhaps as well that Mr. Bradbury undertook to sing atonally; for if a music critic must on occasion, and under severe provocation, burst into song the composer had better be Schönberg than, say, Mozart. We won't be aware overmuch if he should sing out of pitch or " off key."

I am all in favour of the tonal and atonal pioneers; good luck to them. We are not living through the first upheaval of the elements from which so mysteriously emerges the singing spheres of music. Some day a genius will relate the " new " language to the " old "; he will find a bridge-passage. The dry or dusty road of the pioneer is for the young and the ingenious, or for those mortals who have been born without the need to mature imaginatively or philosophically. My own personal reluctance to spend much more time with atonalism and the rest than already I have spent is that I have not unlimited years before me now and, more important, experiments of any kind bore me; they do not put into vibration the sense of life that I have developed in a pretty long and arduous experience, human and æsthetic. It is not possible even for a Schönberg to compose a work that means anything to a grown mind while he is working in a musical formula or language not yet spoken by anybody instinctively, and not yet known in its parts of speech well enough to be grasped immediately. Technique, said Wagner, is a matter for the composer's private study and discussion; the public should never hear of it. The musical public at the present time hears of little that is not technical from the multitudinous verbal exponents of the art. It is of course much less difficult to describe and analyse a composition than it is to give an account of it as it has passed through your mind as human being and musician. In the first instance little is needed except some knowledge of the technical set-up. But to try to understand the composition as the composer conceived it calls for the insight which comes, alas, only to few of us, after an accumulation of years and work which in retrospect cause the spirit to quail and the flesh to falter.

There is a danger, much in evidence at the moment, that contemporary critics are inclined to dismiss a new composition as of small account if it does not, directly or indirectly, admit a debt to the " latest " influences. William Walton's *Troilus and Cressida* has come under the suspicion of the most gifted of our younger critics on the grounds that it reveals a " reactionary " technical tendency. To call a work " reactionary " or " romantic " is, in 1957, apparently a death sentence. We are here face to face with judgments which are really political. The Victorians we are told, were incapable of looking at any work of art, books, music, or pictures, except as moralists. To-day we are, as a people, scarcely more capable than our fathers and grandfathers were to respond to a work of art æsthetically; we have replaced moral with social, psychological, or quasi-political judgments. " The modern dread of beauty," wrote Ivor Brown a few months ago, " is a queer form of cowardice." The best moments in *Troilus and Cressida* are proof that Walton is able to compose, in a style recognisably traditional and as recognisably his own, passages as memorable as any in any opera written since *Turandot*. And that, my young friends, is high praise, praise likely soon to be confirmed by opinion in countries not less musical and not less operatically sophisticated than England, whether the critics there can sing Schönberg or not, before, during, or after lunch.

Relative Values

It is a melancholy thought that human nature, the more it changes the more it remains the same. We live by habit. We actually make a virtue of our chains and grooves; we heartily hail one another: " Good old George, always the same! " We like to know where we are with people and things, especially when we are dealing with anybody as shifty as a music critic. The public is at once suspicious of him if he changes his mind and expresses in January 1957 an opinion different from one he published in October 1915. He is accused—and rightly so—of inconsistency.

I am certain, therefore, to be thoroughly misunderstood during the course of the present chapter. Useless for me to assure the reader that I won't be saying half of what he will insist I am saying; he will charge me with flat and open apostasy the moment he gets partially through the following sentences. I have recently been interested in a certain modification of my response to, or rather, my dependence on music. Once on a time, and not long ago, I would often wonder how I would choose, if the choice were thrust on me, between blindness and deafness; or, to narrow the issue strictly to an æsthetic dilemma, whether I would prefer to be cut off from books or music. I fancy that to-day I could arrive reasonably soon, and more or less painlessly, at a decision. Life is not conceivable to me at this stage without books, and without the lasting satisfaction of reading them in bed alone, while the world sleeps.

I have heard nearly all the music I shall ever come to understand; and it is in varying ways drawn into my consciousness for good and all. Music is a fixed art compared to literature. The masterpieces of music are marvellous as the planets are marvellous and the starry universe. And they are as static; they do not acquire fresh significances as we deepen in experience. (The musician who here jumps up and says he "Finds something" in a Beethoven score every time he hears him performed is out of order.) Books deal directly with life; the writer's material are the words we use in our everyday existence. Literature is open to new imputations (to draw on Samuel Alexander's word) as we extend and develop in imagination and sense of physical and super-physical being. It is, in a word, co-extensive with life, ranging from the sublime to the comic, from Dante to Dickens, from the Book of Job to Mr. Pooter. The sense of inward and poetic and spiritual perception to which Bach can appeal is not beyond the scope of a Milton, who also is equal to filling the mind with a musical satisfaction. But music is usually silly or ineffectual whenever it tries to be funny. We all know the gurglings of bassons—and why should the poor bassoon perpetually have to bear the cross of facetiousness? Tchaikovski thought the instrument tragic enough for the beginning of the *Pathétique* Symphony. And we all know the giggles aroused in a concert audience by the supposedly "humorous" formulæ of music. No series of notes or harmonies or arrangements of tone patterns can produce an epigram. The "ideas" of music are not concepts grasped by the ordinary intelligence; the stark truth is that the world of music, though miraculous and for certain of our moods precious and indispensable, is, compared to the world inhabited by Shakespeare, Tolstoy, Goethe, Shaw, Proust and P. G. Wodehouse, limited.

Music at its best and most realised is, as the ancients regarded it, a " divine " harmony, an art of numbers. To live wholly in music a man is obliged to deny many moods and needs; it is—again I speak of music at its best—something much too fine and good for human nature's daily food. Whenever music tries to appeal to the average man and woman, it compromises its unique part, vacates its citadel of the absolute, and becomes an imitation of other " human-all-too-human " arts and phenomena. It then gives us picturesque or programme music and opera. Contemporary composers have in fact protested against music's compromise with everyday appetite and the urge of most of us to seek in the arts for sublimation of the ego. They have endeavoured to expel " emotion," " Romanticism," and the rest. In a world no longer naïve, no longer able to believe in a spiritual absolute, these composers have looked back into the temples of " classic form," only to find so many deserted shrines. So they have fallen back on reactions to " expression," or on parody and satire, to state in tone a general maladjustment. But to express states of mind essentially critical, words are necessary. You can't be a Swift, a Voltaire, a Shaw in music.

Music, I find, is demanded largely by my better self. Alas, he doesn't visit me constantly; my exalted moments, those that place me " beyoud these voices," don't occur every day. The paradox is that while for myself music becomes increasingly the art of a superterrestrial felicity, causing me to turn now and then almost in relief to the more tangible and earthy stuffs of literature—the paradox here is that week by week a larger public flocks to concerts. Music has become part of the ordinary " set-up " of entertainment. A public not altogether literate, or at any rate a public which would diffidently and perhaps reluctantly enter the presence of Dante, Milton, Goethe, Browning, Henry James, and Matthew Arnold, can apparently get at once into touch with, and feel quite at home in, the minds of Bach, Beethoven and Brahms. I don't believe it. It is the SIGHT of the instruments that holds sway, the visual as well as the aural sensations. Also, and perhaps most important of all, a concert satisfies the aggravated gregarious instincts of our period; we are not left alone with the Masters! And as the first appeal of music is to the sense of sight and of ear—always two very popular senses—we are not called on for any sort of austere collaboration, or to be frank, for any abnormal act of cerebration, to open up lines of communication to entertainment at a concert.

Musicians themselves are not, as a class or fraternity, people of unusual intelligence, or of unusual experience of living. If anybody admitted ignorance of literature, we should certainly think the worse of him as a civilised being. But nobody would think much the worse of, say a Henry James or a Bertrand Russell if he were to confess to a general ignorance of music—" no ear for it." We should regret a deficiency in these great men; we might look on it as a regrettable drawback, like colour blindness or even deafness, but not as a definite and crippling sign of undeveloped intelligence or consciousness.

Our enjoyment of music is much more a matter of responses of nerve and sensation than we are willing to believe. It may, as a matter of irony, become some day thought to be strange that music, considered once the " heavenly " introspective art, the art by which spirit speaks to spirit, is really for the extroverts, the people who like to get their æsthetic pleasures in a crowd from vibrations directly and physiologically experienced in the first place. Music is made from material that is without reference to, or " meaning " in, the visible universe. Until a new set of association-values or synonyms has been established, contemporary composers are bound to fall back considerably on abstract patterns. And if great lasting music is a perfection of abstract patterns, then the frost working on a window-pane or a lawn will beat Schönberg and the rest any winter morning. Many years ago, George Leach, a great special correspondent of the *Manchester Guardian*, entered Samuel Langford's room late on Thursday evening. Langford was engaged upon his Hallé concert notice. " Excuse me, Langford," said Leach, " but I've been across to the Free Trade Hall, to-night, my first Hallé concert for years, and though I wouldn't wish to influence your own judgment in any way I must say that in my opinion—for what it is worth—the Fifth Symphony of Beethoven isn't what it was. . . ."

A law of diminishing returns threatens our regard, as the years pass, for all but the very best music. For the greatest music our devotion increases. Sometimes, I, for my part, feel I have heard too much music; but I have not listened to it for as many hours in a lifetime as I have read my books. In spite of George Leach, the Fifth Symphony remains as good as ever it was, even if it remains in C minor. None the less, as one who has had his fill of the delights of the visible universe, it is more and more to books I give my attention, as I look for the wisdom and humour that illumines experience word by word, and breeds, word by word, more awareness to life, and more literature in proportion. Still, to change a phrase of Doctor Johnson, charitably used in an entirely different situation and context: " Music is a very fine thing."

Music and Literature

FROM THE Library of Congress I have received a reprint of an address called " Words into Music," delivered on behalf of the Louis Charles Elson Memorial Fund, by Jacques Barzun, Professor of History at Columbia University, and author of the monumental study of Berlioz published a year or two ago. Professor Barzun's address is a valuable contribution to the æsthetic of musical criticism; more than that, to the æsthetic of music itself, as far as music is a means of widening and deepening consciousness of life, and worth the while of men such as Beethoven, Bach, Wagner, and the rest of those composers who outgrew and have outgrown adolescence.

Professor Barzun deals with a familiar enough problem which is much in the air just now; are there valid connections between music and words or only accidental associations? . . . Is it possible to describe music in ordinary prose, or is technical language indispensable? He answers the question in an affirmative arrived at after a brilliant and acutely logical exposition. I have myself argued in these pages to the same end. Music is a language; so as Beethoven, Bach, and the rest have in music lived and worked as temporal and spiritual beings, exactly as Shakespeare and Dante lived and worked in their particular media, it is permissible and natural for the music critic to write about

music exactly as the literary critic writes about poetry—
that is, he is free at any time to refer to matters which
technically and formally are extraneous. The reaction to
romanticism, a sensible distaste of bogus poetising by
writers not musically minded, has encouraged the view
which is to-day fashionable: " Words are words. They
mean 'something definite, therefore the literary critic dealing
with a poem has something to ' go upon.' But notes
signify nothing to the intelligence. The music critic should
keep to his subject, tell us how sound is organised, developed,
and so forth: he can't discuss ' meanings.' He should
avoid ' literature.' "

As a fact, words in themselves mean nothing as " literature." The dictionary is not even readable. Words achieve
literature only after they have been arranged in a certain
context by imagination. A celebrated author telegraphed
to his publisher: " What offer for 100,000 words? "; the
publisher telegraphed back: " Which words and in what
order? " Do musical notes really mean anything? They
sure don't, as some of Professor Barzun's students might
affirm. But how many words in any spoken language
" mean " anything, except from long association with
objects and feelings with which, in the beginning, they had
no intrinsic connection and, indeed, became in countless
cases associated by habit, convention, and chance? I
remember when the German word " Tod " seemed silly
to me as a name for Death; until then it had suggested
to me a lively and very great jockey. After I had
learned a little German, " O Tod " seemed a much more
beautiful and expressive word than " Death " in the
phrase of Ecclesiastes set by Brahms in his *Four Serious
Songs*.

The language of music has likewise, by law of association, acquired " meaning." But the notes which the composer puts together are no more fruitfully to be discussed in terms of abstract patterns—" qua music "—than Shakespeare's nouns and adjectives and inverted stresses are to be discussed with profit to literary criticism. Here is the joke of the current controversy about the " impossibility " of writing about music in ordinary prose; it is precisely the " objective " critic, the one that insists that " only the music matters "—he is the chaser of the futile, the insubstantial, and the irrelevant. The critic who, by using his imagination while he has worked habitually in the stuff and material of music, and has found an extensive scale of association-values in notes and in the tone characteristics of different composers—he is always likely to get his teeth into something pertinent to the work under discussion. " Ah, but," comes the retort of the metaphysically uninformed, " he'll not be writing about music, only about himself as he heard it! " What does the critic of a book, poem, or play tell us about that is not inextricably bound up with his sensations while reading Shakespeare, or seeing a play by him? Knowledge and experience of Shakespeare's language, imagery, conventions, patterns, and the sound of his voice, enable the literary or dramatic critic to get on the right " wave-length " and translate to us as much as he has " picked up " of the things uttered from another dimension.

" The music critic must," says Professor Barzun, " like the critic of literature, translate one kind of experience into another. To do so he must use words, for they are the most general medium of communication. And he is entitled to translate music into words because all the arts concern themselves with one central subject-matter, which is the stream of impressions, named and unnamed, that human beings call their life."

The current insistence on " music as music " is foolish and dangerous to our approach and interpretation of the greatest composers. Is the *St. Matthew Passion* greater as art (" greater " is an ineffectual word in this context, but the reader of sense will know what I mean), than the *Well-Tempered Clavier?* Most of us would agree that it is. But it contains nothing " greater " qua music than you'll find in the " Forty-Eight." And it is not from association with the Scriptural text that the *St. Matthew Passion* obtains its tremendous significance. Stainer, though long associated with words as portentous as those set by Bach, remains as musically trivial and dull as ever. To the *St. Matthew Passion* and the B minor Mass, Bach brings all his range of musical art, but now he is applying it to a theme extraneous to music: in a word he is applying it to " literature."

Music criticism is, of course, still in infancy. The jargon and pedantry of the present are not more edifying and are certainly less entertaining than the picturesque mode of writing which discovered moonlights in sonatas and Fate knocking at the door. The chances are that Beethoven also heard the beginning of the C minor Symphony that way. I have never heard any great composer talk of music qua music; all in my experience have spoken of it exactly as any educated layman talks of books or plays or poetry or life in terms of a general imagination.

" The goal for the critic to keep in mind is that of significance "; this is one of Professor Barzun's most forceful points. It is a barren pedantry that insists on a technical account of the " organisation " and the " pattern."

Organisation and pattern may be found assembled *in excelsis* in a vast amount of Max Reger's output. In Reger, in fact, is music qua music to be appreciated at its most uncompromising. Most of it is null and void for all that. Richard Strauss once dismissed Mahler's symphonies as " literature." It was a peculiar remark to come from a composer who wrote most of his best music on a literary basis; still, it was a compliment, if Strauss had only known it. Besides, I fancy that before long we shall most of us be finding just as much music qua music in Mahler as there is in Strauss—enriched by " mere literature."

Music and " Meaning "

A CORRESPONDENT fourteen years old asks, " How should I listen to music? Should I feel anything, or see pictures? My teacher tells me that music means nothing but the notes." Out of the mouths of babes. The teacher, of course, is wrong æsthetically and metaphysically. He is mistaken if he imagines he has broken free of his skin of sensation and penetrated to the Thing-in-Itself, the *Ding an Sich*. When somebody asked Beethoven to explain the " meaning " of the *Appassionata* Sonata (or was it the *Waldstein*?—but I pray that readers will regard the question as entirely rhetorical. I can look it up myself), he said, " Read *The Tempest*." It is the composers themselves who have usually described their music by poetic or even prosaic allusions and metaphors. Only the pedants and the contemporary Patternists (my convenient label for those who talk of music mainly in terms of its technical make-up or rationale) have denied that music can, or should be as expressive of ordinary life and emotion as any play by Shakespeare or poem by Leopardi or sermon by a Dean Inge.

The meaning of music, we need hardly remind ourselves, cannot be put into words; for that matter, the " meaning " of a poem cannot be conveyed except in the words and rhythms chosen by the poet for a special purpose. But we are not at all shy of discussing poetry; critics have produced literature while writing about it, around it, and, as they say, interpreting it. As poetry and literature are made out of the materials of everyday speech, it is easier than it is with music to catch the drift of the "meaning" of a poem, no matter how subtle its overtones. Music does not seem to address itself to the same centre of our consciousness by which we receive our impression from literature; and we cannot use the language of music in our day-to-day social intercourse.

How, then, may we talk of music and not fall into nonsensical irrelevances? Most of us are weary of the sort of writing about music that refers to sunsets and tragic broodings and grapplings with the soul, yet are obliged to try to describe impressions received from music in language and terms used generally to describe or define ideas, feelings and events that we have experienced in the tangible everyday world.

Obviously, it is absurd to listen to Beethoven as an "objective pattern," and to attend to him as if he were a sort of monstrous spider spinning a web of tone by instinct. Music is no more "abstract" than poetry; it is a language in and through which composers have expressed themselves, their conceptions and visions of the world, precisely as Shakespeare, Goethe, Dante, Cervantes and Lewis Carroll have expressed theirs. (And, by the way, when a Richard Strauss composes a *Don Quixote* he is not trying to say all over again in music what Cervantes has said once and for all in words; Strauss is conveying through his own medium his own imaginative experiences, and the pleasure he has had from them, while reading Cervantes.)

213

There is no music worth while that is, in the familiar jargon, " absolute " or " abstract." It is all expressive in the most particular sense. Once on a time John Sebastian Bach was held before the young as the Great Self-Sufficient, Pure and Undefiled by Pictorialism, presumably because he wrote an amount of fugue. Bach, as we are soon able to see if we look for ourselves, was persistently seeking to inflame our imaginations with dramatic and pictorial suggestions; his music is as alive with " motifs " as Wagner's.

It is the language of music that is abstract, or removed-from-life, not necessarily the imaginative content. But we need to learn it, exactly as we need to learn the language of poetry, along with the conventions and procedure—epic, lyric, ballade, sonnet and so on. There is nothing imaginative that music cannot express which other arts can express. It simply takes everything into its own world, as poetry does. The difference between " absolute " and " programme " music is most times one of form: " absolute " and " programme " music are not different because of absence of human argument or expression in the one and the presence of such argument or expression in the other. Let us be short with anybody who tells us there are certain things music may deal with and certain things it may not. As well might a critic of poetry object to epics and insist on nothing but " pure " sonnets as a musician narrow the boundaries of the art to so many " patterns."

There is also another hoary objection. " Ah, yes; but we know what words mean; we can look them up in the dictionary. But music is mere sound, and no note has a fixed meaning." Has any word a fixed meaning, if it comes to that? Are they the same in behaviour if used by a poet,

a lawyer, a politician, a lover, and say the next pedestrian?
Only onomatopœia has meaning requiring no "explanation," or (it amounts to the same) "programme."
"Whoosh!" "Bang!" "Flop!" may fairly be described
as "absolute" language. Words in general have acquired
their meaning by association. "Death" suggests nothing
to a Chinese who does not know English. The chord of
the ninth speaks volumes when we have heard *Tristan* often
enough, whether we recognise it under its technical
name or not; and it is not necessary to know how the
chord is classified in the dictionary of music any more
than it is necessary to know that "incarnadine" is
adjective or transitive verb when we hear spoken the
music of

> . . . rather,
> The multitudinous seas incarnadine,
> Making the green one red.

It is for want of significant material that so many contemporary composers appeal only to our interest in the
technique of music-making. They are in large part using
a vocabulary and syntax not yet steeped in association-
value; consequently their productions have little "meaning." Music, like poetry and literature, draws inspiration
from the same source; it comes from experience by mind
and spirit, put into transfiguring forms which enable us,
in the words of Dr. Johnson, "to enjoy or to endure life."
Music, of course, should be well composed as music, but
this is not enough. And it is not enough to listen to it
strictly as music. More than in any other art, style in music
amounts to the man himself. "I should compose," said
Verdi, "with utter confidence a subject that set my blood

going even though it were condemned by all other artists as anti-musical." We would all do well to listen to music with Verdi's words in mind, remembering at the same time the remark of Harry Zelzer, a Chicago impresario: " Good music isn't nearly so bad as it sounds."

Music and Nature

To THIS day we are told that music is wrong, almost wicked, to try to express anything except itself: music is, so the canon goes, " self-contained," an art of absolute form. Even Beethoven was nervous about getting across the Law, and he assured the world that the " Pastoral " symphony is " more feeling than painting ": but none the less imitated bird calls with as much realism as Strauss imitated the hanging of Till Eulenspiegel. It is indeed, as " natural " for music to imitate or indicate sounds of the everyday world as to weave a pattern, in fact more so. Rustling leaves and the ripple of water and waves are easily suggested by rhythm: nearly every minor composer once on a time succumbed to the temptation to write a piece called " Jet d'eau " or " The Rustle of Spring." I go so far as to say that it is in the nature of music to be " programmatic," to suggest concrete happenings and emotion, and that it is only in its advanced and sophisticated stage that music aims at abstract design. A sonata is a sign of a long period of cultivation in the art of music; it is not a form implicit in music from the beginning. We might argue—and why not?—that it is not the composers of programme-music who are unfaithful to music but the so-called absolutists.

Few composers as a fact have written absolute music:

that is, music which sets out to avoid reference to the phenomenal universe and is satisfied to create a sort of architecture or tapestry or arabesque of tone. At any rate, no composer of genius has been content to write like some musical spider, spinning a web of sound lacking human significance. Music is a language and a way of interpreting man's imaginative and spiritual experience, his subjective and objective impressions, things seen and things felt. Bach, as we all know, composed not only fugues; he also employed vivid and pointed pictorialism in his *Passion* music.

As I say, it is the most natural thing in the world for music to convey to our imagination the motion of waves and the ebb and flow of the sea. But it is not enough for a composer merely to make a noise like water; he must add poetry. He must not attempt photography, or end at onomatopœia, or act as a kind of microphone. He must add personal vision to his view of objective reality. And curiously enough, all the best sea music composed so far has come from land-lubbers. The most vivid sea pictures have been written by men who have lived mainly on the Continent of Europe, in cities; sedentary men who probably trembled at a Channel crossing. In England, this island surrounded by water and rained on most days in a year, this England whence emanated Drake and Captain Cook and a deathless race of sea-dogs—we have usually resorted to hornpipes when it has come to the expression of the sea in music, or to sea shanties which are or were as apt in a Chelsea penthouse as in the fo'c'sle. Until Britten made the sea sweep through *Peter Grimes* like an active force of fate, we could boast of little music fit to put against the seascapes of the land-locked foreigners. There is the lovely song by Elgar,

Where Corals Lie, Sea Drift of Delius, *Tintagel* of Arnold Bax, and the *Sea* Symphony of Vaughan Williams. *Sea Drift*, like the Vaughan Williams work, is really a human music-drama set against a background of the sea as an imagined presence or atmosphere. *Portsmouth Point* of William Walton is not about the sea but rather it is a musical equivalent, so to say, of Rowlandson's print, depicting a scene on the waterfront; an animated roaring throng in a tumult and confusion of masts and sails of waiting ships, and labourers carrying bales or rolling barrels, and officers bidding farewell to sad-sighing ladies; clothes on the line and wind and sky. The music, like the picture, is disorderly yet keenly etched, untidy and voluble yet concentrated. And the sea is brought in largely by a parody of a hornpipe!

One of the first, if not the first, pieces of sea music was the *Fingals Cave* Overture of Mendelssohn, admired by Wagner, who had no use for Mendelssohn as a whole. It remains magical in its evocations. It not only gives us seascape; from the trumpets and the woodwind of the middle section we hear calls and cadences which seem to catch the spirit of Wordsworth's

> . . . breaking the silence of the seas
> Among the farthest Hebrides.

In the fine tone-poem *Tintagel*, Bax gets his effect of surge of sea and sense of distance by borrowing something of Mendelssohn's formula, blending it brilliantly with devices drawn from *La Mer* of Debussy; but of course Bax makes the work entirely his own and throws in one of the best and most beautifully curved melodies in all the music of our time.

219

After his North Sea passage, Wagner never forgot the sea or the menace and sweep of rushing waters. The Rhine flows through the *Ring*, and in *Tristan* the sea beats wearily at the base of the cliffs on which stands Tristan's castle, where he is dying and waiting for Isolde. The music is marvellous as an expression of a sea which by alchemy of imagination rises and falls in accord with Tristan's pain and fever and deferred hopes. The ascending strings tell us that Kurvenal, Tristan's man-servant, is gazing over the sea to the horizon, looking for the ship bringing Isolde. And they tell us that he finds nothing. The miracle is that Wagner adapted to this scene and atmosphere themes born for an entirely different purpose—as settings for Mathilde Wesendonck's song *Im Treibhaus*. I can never hope to get over or get accustomed to the astonishment of realising or believing in this musical metamorphosis.

Of all sea music, though, Debussy's *La Mer* is the most wonderful. This work has wrongly been described as descriptive, " Impressionistic," and in other terms borrowed from painting. But it is not just a picture of the sea. I would dare to call it a re-creation in music of the sea itself felt and experienced by as sensitively poetic a mind as music has known, with the mythology of the sea the inspiration, not only the sights and sounds of it. It is a living sea, a world of sea, complete in itself, an iridescent habitation of delight; dolphins at play, waves in rainbow foam, sun and vast stretches of sky, wind and sea-horses, and the sound of Triton's horn. What brass writing! The orchestration appears to come unbidden from the instruments. It is immediately and rapturously swift in every note, with every note alive, a pulsation. If I am not mistaken, Debussy composed it all in a hotel at Eastbourne.

The genius of *Peter Grimes* is in the sea music from the first phrase of the prelude; it is a vision in tone. The call of the gulls, the bitter tang of the air; then the drama is pervaded by sea and the spirit that shapes those who live near it, and are of it. Music can indeed suffer a sea-change, into something rich and strange.

What is a Banal Tune?

ARISING FROM articles written to commemorate Sibelius's ninetieth birthday, a revered and distinguished English composer wrote to me to ask: " Why is the tune in *Finlandia* so often termed banal? I love it for its forthright sincerity and inspiration. For years I have held the belief that the inevitable tune—like *Finlandia's*—becomes the ' obvious ' and ' commonplace ' tune if constantly repeated, simply because people get to know it too well. Does the fault lie in the music or with the listener? "

It is a question that takes us to the heart of things; in other words, it is a poser. What is a bad or banal tune; are the badness and banality implicit in the notes themselves, the way the notes go, or are the badness and banality acquired by association, by the notes getting into dubious company? Is the quality or characteristic which makes a good melody demonstrable to musical intelligence or science? Richard Strauss described Mozart's melodies as " Platonic ideas," not to be grasped by the reason, but so essentially " divine " that they are to be " intuitively perceived only by the emotions "; untrammelled by any mundane form, the Mozartean melody is the " Thing-in-Itself " (*Ding an Sich*). It hovers like Plato's Eros between heaven and earth, between mortality and immortality, set free from the will. It is the deepest perception of artistic fancy and of the subconscious into the uttermost secrets, into the realm of the ' Prototypes'." All of which is very resonant, especially in German, but hardly lands us anywhere, especially if we remember that a certain respected English music critic has said that Mozart is not strictly a great melodist. By this extraordinary statement, on the face of it, he probably intended to say that many Mozart melodies are instrumental in style and symphonic in function; at any rate he must have meant something other than the bare words of the indictment.

Clearly we cannot define the power that informs and generates a production of genius. We cannot even say why for some of us, certain tunes stay in the mind for ever, heard once or twice, while other and more deeply expressive ones don't. On paper we are able to analyse certain melodic properties; some tunes, for instance, can take flight for a distance—not too far—on the wing of their own notes; that is to say they are not entirely dependent on harmony. There are many such melodies in Berlioz. Other tunes, and very famous ones, are very much derived from the harmony which seems only to support them. But formal analysis in the abstract won't explain rare essences. A really awkwardly composed melody may plausibly be exposed in its creaking parts almost by a visual diagram. Take, as an example the song written especially for Santley by Gounod and put into *Faust*—" Dio possente ": in English, " Even bravest hearts may swell. In the moment of farewell; quiet home I leave behind." Usually the song is so bellowed over the footlights, at the operative words, that we are bound to think that the home will be much quieter in future. Here is a melody which soon meanders into a sticky state of bogus modulation: it is a broken-backed melody. And the use of this phrase reminds me that another distinguished critic—Mr. Blom, I think—has called the *Preislied* a broken-backed melody. The *Preislied* is certainly not a model of balanced phrases intended by Wagner to convey that it was " durchkomponiert," put together symmetrically in a fastidious school. It was written to suggest free and natural improvisation conceived in a dream. Mr. Blom's point no doubt is that the artifices in the syntax of the *Preislied* do indeed hint of conscious and not unpremeditated art. For my own part I have sometimes considered Beckmesser's Prize Song the more promising composition of the two, in its first few phrases, until Sachs rather pedantically corrects it, not so much as a musician than as a prosodist. The redemption of the *Preislied*, if it is ever in need of redemption, comes at the end, when Wagner brings to it warm and marvellously sequential choral harmonies.

Familiarity will breed contempt now and again with the greatest music. It is ourselves, though, that suffer the variations of taste and reception. Then there is the fact that for causes deeply psychological most of us are destined for a lifetime to remain allergic to certain kinds of tunes and composers. The music critic tries to rationalise inexplicable " dislikes," only to get no closer to the cause of them. There are tunes which affect me as an unpleasant odour affects my nostrils, or as a colour, agreeable to most eyes, displeases my own. Some law of association probably is the determining factor. Do highbrow critics consider the melody of *Finlandia* banal because so often has it been heard in this country played by brass bands in our municipal parks? Do critics and musicians here and there feel that the melody which begins the adagio of Mahler's ninth

symphony is a banal one because it calls back to their
memories the most familiar of the settings of *Abide with
Me*? My composer-correspondent is not far wrong when
he says that a good tune can come to sound commonplace if repeated overmuch, especially if it is heard most
times in the wrong place and company. To this day, many
sensitive musical ears are not happy with the *Requiem* of
Verdi, the melodies reminding them in a religious context
of La Scala and Italian opera singers. Mahler set himself
deliberately at times to compose banal melodies for his
symphonies to express the common traffic and earthliness
of the world as a contrast to the spiritual or elevated parts
of his music. A striking example of this Mahlerisch
" banality " occurs in the second symphony, where at the
Last Trump the rabble of the earth march to judgment.
Mahler's trouble was that he was prone to lapse into
banality while intent on originality and loftiness of melody.
But here, you see, I am begging the question. How do
I know that Mahler is at times deliberately banal, and
how should he himself know, if banality cannot be demonstrated and defined? Rhythm and tempo are perhaps as
decisive a factor as any other in our discussion. By changing
the pace of his Adagietto in his fifth symphony, Mahler
makes a parody of it in the finale. By shortening the notes
of the main melody of the Mastersingers, Wagner repre-
sents the apprentices and tells us that Jack's as good as his
master. We all know what can happen to a melody if some
sentimentally indulgent conductor drags the time and
weakens the phrases.

When we come to think of it, all the tunes and music we
usually call vulgar or banal come from the nineteenth-
century, an age near enough to us to cause reactions of

taste but not far enough back in time to seem " period," with the mists of distance lending enchantment to the view. We do not find vulgarity in Bach, Haydn, Mozart: the passing of the years has transformed familiarity into classicism or the antique. In this country a reliable prophylactic against the suspicion of vulgarity, which I recommend to all aspiring composers, is counterpoint. Nobody ever recoils from counterpoint, strict or free, for fear that it might be common. A celebrated English professor of music once told me he couldn't possibly listen to Puccini: " he is so much wanting in contrapuntal interest." I hadn't the courage to remind him that *Butterfly* begins with at least a dash or suspicion of a fugue. Perhaps Strauss was right. The great tune is perceived " intuitively." From long experience of listening to all sorts of music, we develop the faculty to feel in a sequence of notes the calibre of the mind behind them. And from the way the melody is treated we can get to grasp the composer's power of sustained musical thinking. It is as well if we bear in mind that melody is not the be-all and end-all of a major composition. The first movement of the *Eroica* Symphony grows from the simplest arrangement of the chord of E flat. Maybe, as Tennyson said, with a different intention, " plenty corrupts the melody."

Composer and Public

It was once a favourite trick amongst playwrights and novelists to put into the mouths of servants or working men some phrase which revealed a culture not in those days associated with what was called the artisan or lower-class. Shaw makes Straker, the chauffeur in *Man and Superman*, call his employer John Tanner to order on a matter of quotation from Beaumarchais. More than a hundred years earlier than Shaw, the barber Partridge appeared in *Tom Jones* (a man's novel which can be read once a year in a long lifetime); Partridge talks dog-Latin " non si male nunc et olim sic erit, I was born and bred a barber." In recent years a Greek slave in W. P. Crozier's only novel finishes or rounds off a quotation by his master: " You may not know it, but our national poet Virgil actually says with regard to one's past sufferings—' that it gives pleasure to recollect them.' Yes, sir, I remember the passage. . . ."

It is fairly certain that before long we shall all musically seem much the same and equal in the eyes of Providence. Any morning Sir John Barbirolli may find himself put right by *his* chauffeur about Béla Bartók. In the near future, the butler (if any such office shall continue socially to exist) will be as sceptical of the household gramophone library as of the wine-cellar. " I cannot confidently recommend, sir, Shostakovich, so soon after dinner. He is, if I may say, rather low. Perhaps a little Ravel? "

The other morning I heard a youth, who in other times than the present might well have been a butcher's boy, and he was whistling a tune from Bach. He had learned it of course from the radio; and that he was able to whistle Bach would be regarded by many as a sign of " progress." Whether he knew it was Bach he was whistling is perhaps conjectural: for my part if I were a boy again I'm sure I would get more pleasure out of Leslie Stuart than from a Brandenburg Concerto: more profit too, possibly, and easier to whistle. Thirty or so years ago, music was not easy to come by except after some training and searching. I remember when the names of Wagner and Strauss were as much an essential part of intellectual conversation and intercourse as to-day are those of Schönberg and Proust. In a world that knew neither of wireless nor the gramophone, even a young student of music might be lucky if he heard the same Brahms symphony twice in a year, unless he chanced to live in London. Nowadays he can, if he wish, hear any Brahms symphony oftener in a year than Brahms himself publicly heard a work of his own in all his lifetime.

Does easy hearing lead to imaginative listening? The question is nearly rhetorical. Music is becoming part of the general means of entertaining the public. Naturally there is a risk of the lowering of standards of taste, and of a weakening of subtlety and originality amongst the makers of music. A symphony of Mozart was the flower of a certain order of civilisation. Will the composer of to-morrow write, consciously or unconsciously, for a large and mainly uninformed audience? (And " information " is not enough to produce the sensitive audiences which are the composer's environment.) The Time-Spirit, the " atmosphere " of the period, has usually set the style and the æsthetic. There are signs in contemporary music of the disintegration which is proceeding in the world around us. The part—the theory, the *rationale*—is valued beyond the whole. Not what Schönberg is saying is the question; not what he is trying to convey to us as a genius who has had experience of the spirit beyond the reach of common clay. No. Let us rather praise, or at least analyse, his technique of expression! To turn from the life around us, and to seek in the arts another mode of being, of consciousness, is supposedly " escapism," though, as Mr. A. A. Milne says, I do not know why realism in a novel is so much admired when realism in a picture is condemned as mere photography.

There are gleams of hope. The ear of the average listener at a concert or in a dance palace, or at a musical show, is obviously quicker and more sophisticated than in years when Debussy was considered difficult to follow, and when Paul Rubens was the Jerome Kern or Rodgers of his day. A growing awareness to what is and what is not a *cliché* or dreadful platitude in music may in time get into our skins, and become an acquired characteristic in the human race—if in 1957 I may use language as Lamarckian as this. So that in another decade people may " take to " Schönberg as readily and happily as those of us brought up on Mozart and Beethoven took to Strauss. I doubt it; but as Pooh-Bah says, " a man might try." Obviously the composer of these times cannot hope for inspiration by turning to schools and idioms which have been, so to say, worked-out. But there is no need to leave a soil and take refuge in abstract thinking. A soil will survive many " turnings."

In his thoughtful book, *Greatness in Music*, Alfred

Einstein maintains that since Beethoven musicians have written operas and symphonies that are never performed; they have composed out of touch with a public. The idea that an artist should dwell in solitude, praying for or waiting on " inspiration " (with a woman somewhere to attract or ignite the divine spark) was a romantic fiction of the nineteenth century. Whoever has tried to create at all, even on the smallest scale, knows well that " inspiration " will come only by hard work, directed to an end objectively desirable; in other words, the job is best done when the creator knows somebody wants it besides himself. There are signs that composers to-day, for all the jargon written about their methods, are returning to an earlier status. Until the advent of the romantics, the music-maker was, like the architect, painter, dancing-master, sculptor, and story-teller, part of the social service. We have all heard of the answer of Brahms to the soulful lady who asked him how it happened that he could write such " beautiful slow movements." " The publishers like them that way," he said. And the publishers may be trusted in the long run to see to it that composers do not run too far ahead of the public's general knowledge in the way of extreme technical experiment. The announcement that Queen Elizabeth was to have a Coronation Opera by one of our leading composers was another sign of health and changing times. A job of work to be done! In circumstances as functional, Shakespeare wrote *The Merry Wives of Windsor*, not his masterpiece, true, but not the least popular of all that he produced.

Content and Technique

As A critic approaches a birthday which is past the meridian of life he might be excused if he more and more looks within himself to overhaul his own standards and values, forgetting momentarily the current cant about objectivity. I find it hard enough to make a rational account of my own tastes and opinions, as they change with one's developing (or retrogressing) mind and temperament—quite hard enough, without the addition of worrying how and why other people think as they do. Though a man should try to keep in touch with fresh ideas relevant to his special study, his first duty and pleasure is to remain true to his tested personal experience. In youth and early manhood we uaturally put a lot of faith in abstract reasoning, which is a very good and necessary thing in a metaphysician, a scientist, a lawyer even. The arts will not reveal their essential secrets to examination by logic; in music especially, knowledge and fine thinking will go no deeper than the surface, unless directed by feeling and imagination. Most criticism at the present time is descriptive (in Kant's sense of the word) or it is analytical. " Mein Kind," wrote Goethe, " Ich hab' es klug gemacht; Ich habe nie über das Denken gedacht." This was the wisest and most modern man of letters, warning against the dangers of thinking about thinking.

231

It is more than forty years since I wrote my first article on music, or, at any rate, since an article on music of mine appeared in print. It dealt with the compositions of Granville Bantock and maintained that Bantock was a derivative composer, that he had been quick to get his ear to the ground and, during a dark period of music in England, had echoed strange and haunting sounds wafted from afar, echoes of Strauss, odours and reflected iridescences from Rimsky-Korsakov. At this time (1912) many authoritative music critics in England thought more highly of Bantock than they did of Elgar; Bantock was the more eclectic, more in the current stream, while Elgar continued with his devoted labours in oratorio and in symphony of obviously nineteenth century lineage. Where is Bantock to-day, where stands his music? Some of it should have died hereafter; I fancy we could still listen without boredom to *The Pierrot of the Minute* Overture, if only to admire the Straussian string technique. There are surely moments in *Omar Khayyám* worth while even yet and equal to stimulating the sort of curiosity and sense of grandeur experienced by students who visit the Assyrian and Egyptian rooms in our best museums. In a stuffy period of our music, Bantock made a brave adventurous gesture, so much so that critics who believed that all art should be progressive, like science and morals, regarded him as forward-looking, contemporary and not a bourgeois epigone smugly arm-chaired in tradition.

Since 1912 and the years of the Bantock-Elgar conjunction of methods, I have guarded myself against the pressure of fashionable opinion. Nothing a critic can say out of all his store of folly is sillier than to dub a work once hailed as a masterpiece as " dated " and, for that reason mainly, no longer of value. If a work, once highly esteemed, falls into decay and neglect it is because of some failure of vitality within the structure and the imaginative content, not because the theme or subject of it has no longer a topical significance, or one which fails to touch a contemporary spot of psychology or behaviour. As I write this article I have tried to remember when " modernity " or the new was first thought of as a necessary quality or factor in music —I mean modernity or newness in the technical means of expression. In my youth we erred at the extreme; we distrusted technical experiment which we did not understand. The critics, I suppose, must needs fix their attention on uncommon technical procedure; for it is easier to analyse by study from the outside than to pierce with the eye of imagination to the heart of the matter.

The attitude of criticism to music, in this country, has changed so much in a lifetime that the subject dealt with might not be music at all (as I was brought up to conceive of music), but another art altogether, one related to mathematics or the Pythagorean " numbers." Imagine a contemporary criticism worded as follows:

" It is generally regarded as a ' faith ' symphony. One may say the same, in a sense, of all those many great works of music which arrive at a feeling of satisfaction within themselves, and which, for want of other programme, are regarded chiefly for their moral tone. Yet music probably has no other work in which this problem of moral philosophy is so plainly, persistently, and laboriously set forth. We have said that the texture of the symphony is heavy; and it seems also true that it is chosen more for purpose than delight. If we dislike a too obviously moral and purposeful work we may well dislike this one. If we like it we must be well reconciled to the dominance of moral purpose in music."

Thus wrote Langford of the César Franck symphony; old-fashioned now, as much in what he tells us of his ideas and feelings about music as in its diction—heavens, the man writes of music as though it were literature, and as though a symphony were a living man's testament and view of existence! Texture is related by Langford to a spiritual plan; he does not discuss it just as music. I am myself all in favour of trying to " see the object as in itself it really is," provided the object is approached from a proper, relevant, and æsthetic point of view. Nobody dislikes more than I the sort of writing on music which goes round a work, suffuses it in a glow of irrelevant " poetic " or " literary " images, with all the familiar woolly " associations "—fate knocking at doors, Finnish landscapes in Sibelius, and all the rest. We must, as elderly and growing critics, listen to the music, find out if it is platitudinous or not in its way of expression (originality is harder to define and not always a virtue) and if it sounds well and musical in experienced ears. Then, having considered the language of a composer and learned its syntax, the main question arises: What, in terms of music, is the composer saying, and is it worth saying at all?

In the long run, the principal concern of the critic is with style, the style that is the man's spiritual signature. Anybody can analyse technique; technical analysis needs only knowledge which any intelligent musician may acquire. To know and to penetrate imaginatively different styles calls for wide poetic perception. With certain narrow æsthetic susceptibilities styles can be mutually exclusive. A critic might easily expound the style of, say, Bach, and yet find the spirit and outlook of his music alien to his own way of musical thinking and living. Maybe the critic's hardest job is to distinguish between made and creative music, between new technically arresting music, and music that has grown naturally from deep-planted roots.

Fabricated Music

EVIDENCE IS gathering that contemporary composers are not satisfied with the reception given them by the critics. The trouble apparently is not that we, the critics, do not study their works or write about them frequently but that we hesitate to discuss them in a way that will persuade the general public to pay to listen. (Would the critics remain tolerant if they, too, had to pay?) Contemporary music of course is a silly term, but it will serve a shorthand use for the purpose of this article; and I define it, fairly I think, as the sort not readily understood by an ear capable of attending intelligently to a Beethoven quartet or to the sixth symphony of Vaughan Williams or to the Viola Concerto of William Walton—a sort of music in which a normally educated ear often seeks in vain for a recognisable and singable melody.

A point baffling to myself—and I do not know that it has so far been considered in print—is that several composers of this "contemporary" music are still young men, not out of the thirties. How have they so early in life come to think and conceive in idioms and accents which break away from nearly all that was in the air during their teens? Is this "new music"—the latest "new music"—an inherited trait or faculty? Are the arteries hardening of those of us who are of middle-age and beyond? Were musicians born only a few decades ago endowed with different ways of musical understanding and perception from those considered natural at the time? Or is much contemporary music the consequence of deliberate and half-mathematical study and practice?

I am inclined to think that these questions go to the root of the matter. There is little in contemporary music which is not clear to the trained critic; the technical formula, indeed, is becoming almost dated. Our reluctance to ask the general musical public to work at it as conscientiously as the critics have worked at it is because after all the trouble involved little has been found on which heart, imagination, and sense of delight can seize. It is fabricated music, and as such it can be admired. Let us not despise fabrication. An aeroplane is a triumph of man's inventive powers. So is the latest symphony by Mr. X. Never mind. But an aeroplane is not—dare it be said nowadays?—as lovely in life and curve as the white owl sweeping. My own experience is that too much of the new music does not improve on acquaintance; it remains boring, ungracious, un-humorous, and unimaginative, even after the strangeness of method and vocabulary have worn off. If a man talks to me in Choctaw and I am not familiar with the language I am not at liberty to say he is being commonplace and tedious. But after I have gone to the pains to learn Choctaw, only to realise he talks platitudes, I am entitled to some of the satisfaction that comes of a free expression of opinion. I do not believe that the bulk of this music is written from impulses of art or æsthetic feeling; it is the product of experiment or empiricism.

No responsible critic will discourage experiments, though he might be tempted to suggest that they should be performed in private, in the laboratory so to say. Obviously, music could at no time continue along furrowed paths. Let anybody sit down and try to compose anything, from a prelude to a symphony; he will at once feel hemmed in by the old procedure. He will seek escape from echoes, from old association-values, and especially from the pull of a fixed tonal centre. He will try not to " Compose from memory " (as Moriz Rosenthal said Pfitzner did).

Atonalism and the like are not perversity and wilful conceit of intellectuals. There are signs of a drift from a tonal centre in Gesualdo, who died round about 1613. Atonalism and the rest are an inevitable development but not virtues in themselves; they should be regarded as development, which implies organic context.

Music is bound to renew itself, reshape its vocabulary like other languages, out of its own roots. The next great composer will take what he needs from the accumulated technical formulæ at hand; but he will take it instinctively and merge it into the everyday dictionary. All language grows that way. He will not consciously set himself to compose in a given " school," or fear to derive from a period which has immediately preceded his own, whether it be as " romantic " as his grandmother. In no period of music history have composers been so eager to break from the past as at the present time; in fact, our period as a whole is running away as though in panic from the past.

Many of the young lions of the moment imagine that to be contemporary they need only use the latest tricks of the trade. New discoveries get old-fashioned quickly enough; what keeps an art alive is the idea expressed. Composers who have mouldered in their graves these many years are more vital, more powerful in influence to-day, than Schönberg, Stravinsky and Hindemith. Mahler, called a " romantic " by people who would probably call Vesuvius or the Red Sea romantic, is a greater musical influence than any of these three contemporary forces. Mahler kept to the soil, which is always ready to receive a new seed of genius. The mistake of the " moderns," taking them by and large, is that they have left the soil and are trying to rear their plants in a theoretical vacuum. They are in the grip of system. What would the latest symphonist, grappling with a tone-row or a pyramid of superimposed fourths, do with a lovely C major melody if one suddenly occurred to him? The system would be obliged to reject it; it would not " fit in." I could name at least one or two contemporary composers who would be none the worse for twelve months' solitary confinement in the key of C major.

It is not true that contemporary music is not encouraged. Never has it been so easy as now for a new work to obtain performance. The other evening a symphony of Racine Fricker was heard twice in the same programme, a piece of good fortune which escaped Schubert. Swift recognition is expected as a matter of corsue by the merely talented. After finishing *Lohengrin* Wagner composed no more music for six years. He put himself to school again to learn a " new " music, a " new " technique. Even Wagner, arch-egoist, was content to wait. Can any of us quite see a contemporary Young Master, on the crest of a wave of fame, likewise absenting himself from publicity awhile?

239

PART FIVE

ENGLISH MUSIC

What do the English People Really Sing To-day?

Any vocalist about to give a recital in this country must be ready to look in the face a question which, awkward for years, time does not seek to solve: " What about an English group?" The singer, does not, himself or herself, really want to include an " English group " in the programme; it has its convenience as a means of modulating the concert to an end, but nobody in his heart insists on an " English group." The critics often leave the hall before it begins, though to be fair, they do their best in general terms day by day to argue the public into the belief that English music at the present time is the best in the world, even if nobody outside England seems urgently in haste to hear it.

The truth is hard to deny; it is hard to make a transition at a vocal recital from Schubert, Schumann, Brahms, Wolf, Ravel and Fauré to English song. Perhaps the best way out was the audacity of the warbling soprano of other years who told us that her heart was like a singing bird. Here, at any rate, was a flourish and unmistakable cue for the processional delivery to the platform of the flowers. If instrumentalists are at hand the problem can be solved, with no lowering of the temperature, by a performance of the *Wenlock Edge* cycle of Vaughan Williams, which I am heretical enough to think will outlast one or two of his later and more ubiquitous productions. His song *Silent Noon*, too, could be trusted to follow after a Brahms group and sustain the mood of *Feldeinsamkeit*. *Les Illuminations* of Benjamin Britten is a work not properly to be classified as song; the genius of this cycle—and Britten has written nothing more convincingly original or more spontaneously generated—consists of a dramatic and picturesque mingling of speech-song, recitative, declamation, and string texture. The four songs for voice and violin of Gustav Holst should be rescued from neglect, for they are finely wrought and touched with a mystical emotion, but they are not for public use; they inhabit a sanctuary of music. And much the same may be said of Gerald Finzi's fine settings of Thomas Traherne called *Dies Natalis*.

It is strange that with our rich national dowry of lyric verse our music-makers have for more than three hundred years contributed little to the repertory of singers who, after Schubert, Wolf, Moussorgsky, and Debussy, do not wish a recital to suffer anticlimax. No English composer has done for Shakespeare and Keats what Wolf and Debussy have done for Goethe and Mallarmé, or, indeed what Schubert has done for Shakespeare. There are the charming Shakespeare songs of Roger Quilter; they are polished in manner and gracious in a style which, without belittlement to the composer, may be described as drawing-room lyric de luxe. Nothing in music could trip more sweetly than Quilter's *O Mistress Mine*; and there is a haunting melody and refrain in his *Come away Death*, though it has not the intense tragic melancholy of Sibelius's setting of the same poem. Quilter's best song is *Now sleeps the crimson petal*;

elegance and a cultured Tennysonian ardour are one and indivisible in words, vocal caress, and the piano's gentle harmonies. But Quilter no more than Parry escapes from refined art to feeling the natural Shakespearean pulse.

As far as I am able to remember at the moment, Ivor Gurney is the only English composer I could attend to immediately after listening to, say, Schubert's *Die schöne Müllerin*—and possibly George Butterworth; but certainly neither would do to follow the *Winterreise* cycle. The Michelangelo songs of Britten might find a central place in the programme of the vocalist temporarily forgetful of Wolf. We seem as a people much happier composing communally than in the flush of personal lyric utterance. Our choral music and our part-songs are excellent and un-inhibited enough. I suppose it is because our composers lack the gift of a personal lyricism that no English opera has so far gained a permanent place in the repertory alongside *Meistersinger*, *Figaro*, *Traviata*, *Carmen* and *Butterfly*. Even *Peter Grimes* is no longer in regular demand at Covent Garden or Sadler's Wells; yet no other English opera has been so well launched and applauded here and in other countries.

The trouble is lack of music that springs to life only if it is sung well and truly sung. There are melodies in Vaughan Williams's *Hugh the Drover*, but not of the kind to be savoured in cities and theatres at large. Elgar, who could compose instrumentally and chorally with a splendid flavour of melodic richness and salience, wrote songs which on the whole are as insignificant, not to say as puerile, as those of Sibelius in the lump. Frank Mullings, a great English artist among tenors, once on a time persuaded us that Bantock's *Ferishtah's Fancies*—based on Browning—

were tolerable to the ear that had recently attended to one of Wolf's *Cophtisches* songs; but the rare imaginative persuasiveness of Mullings led us astray. Bantock's *Ferishtah's Fancies*, like his *Sappho* songs and his *Omar Khayyám*, are Brummagem—though let it be added, the best sorts of Brummagem. Warlock, Butterworth, Gurney; Stanford, Parry, Somervell—they are light or medium-weights. Were I myself a singer, an audible not an inaudible baritone, I might take courage and finish my recital by some of the Heine and Verlaine settings of Bernard van Dieren, not exactly an " English group," though it might be possible to argue as much Englishness on behalf of van Dieren as on behalf of Joseph Conrad. Something should certainly be done to restore from limbo the music, especially the songs, of this gifted Dutchman who for so long contributed to a vital period in our musical history by living, writing and talking among us.

But vocalists in general are as lazy-minded as pianists: they do not explore much that is not taught them in the routine of their teachers. I have, in a lifetime, not heard half a dozen " professional " vocalists tackle in public the great and glorious " Geh' Geliebter " of Hugo Wolf. Perhaps it is as well; to get to the heart of this song a woman singer needs the combined gifts and allurements of Delilah, Cleopatra, Isolde, and Juliet. I have not heard Wolf's *Kennst du das Land* sung to an audience since, four or five years ago, a girl student at the Royal Manchester College of Music coped creditably with it. How many of our concert vocalists could briefly describe Mignon psychologically and approach Wolf, as he himself approached this supremely beautiful Lied, from the point of view and through the imaginative eye and mind of Goethe?

It is hard to say what the English sing nowadays of songs made in England. Even the popular tunes are flavoured from America. The old music-halls were night by night resonant and bronchial with the refrains of Lauder, *I do like to be beside the seaside*, and John Crook's "catchy" airs composed for Albert Chevalier. The melodies of Leslie Stuart, to the present time, may be heard whenever communal singing is called for in Bermondsey, Brisbane, Camberwell, or Colombo. Stuart's octet in *Florodora* is not only lilting and lively but most artfully patterned, with the key-changes of a musician of fancy. In recent years only Noel Coward's *Bitter Sweet* has contributed something of permanent pleasure to the ordinary non-musical English ear. The American " musicals "—they deserve no better name—are brilliantly orchestrated but after their two years' seasons who dares to sing the tunes in them? Where are the descendants not of Purcell, Arne, Dibdin, but of Lionel Monckton, Sydney Jones, and Paul Rubens? What do the English people really sing to-day? Do they feel there isn't much for them to sing or to sing about?

Period Music

In a presidential lecture to the English Association, Mr. A. L. Rowse consoled his audience by the remark that if " writing is not at a high peak at the moment, English painting is enjoying a more creative period than it has had since the eighteenth century, and English music than at any time since the Elizabethans." I am not competent to discuss this optimistic view about English painting, but I certainly do not share Mr. Rowse's opinion of contemporary English music—and I take it that by " contemporary " he means music by composers not writing in a style or idiom of yesterday or the day before.

I seem to recall several occasions in the brief life that here has been my portion when a certain school of English muscians or critics has hailed the passing moment and, like Faust, called out " Verweile doch! " " Delay, thou art so fair! " There was a definite renaissance when I was a boy, led by Parry, Stanford, William Wallace, Ethel Smyth, and others whose names are now forgotten.

It is not enough to smile at these names; in their period they received recognition from criticism and scholarship which were, in relation to the current taste and culture, equally as authoritative as any we can boast at the present. We flatter ourselves if we think that because there has been

" change " since those days we have inevitably " advanced." Time alone discovers the masterpieces. Contemporary readers will possibly be surprised to learn that Ethel Smyth's opera *The Wreckers* was once thought of as highly, here and in Germany, by a few first-class musical minds, as *Peter Grimes* is thought of to-day, no doubt by larger numbers. *Peter Grimes* has moments of genius, and *The Wreckers* perhaps ends at the point of talent: I am not sure, though, that the difference between the two works is not a matter of degree rather than of kind or category.

History is a terrible leveller. With sad frequency I have seen English composers come and go, a procession of them caught up in the sun of favour and fashion for a moment, only to pass into dusty oblivion. We may resign ourselves to the certainty that in half a century from the 1950s several names now famous and rendered public will have become as remote as those of Granville Bantock and Josef Holbrooke, if indeed they should survive as long. Bantock and Holbrooke came after Parry and Stanford, and were looked upon as an advance guard. A certain critic of experience and renown, not less intelligent and informed than Mr. Britten himself or Dr. Stein, maintained that Bantock, not Elgar, was the really important composer, the one who was opening a new chapter in English music. Three decades ago of flying time, Rutland Boughton at Glastonbury seemed to many musicians and men of letters to loom as significantly and permanently as Mr. Britten looms at Aldeburgh.

Between 1900 and 1914 the following additions were made to English music: The first and second symphonies of Elgar; the Violin Concerto of Elgar; *Falstaff* of Elgar;

Delius's *Sea Drift, The Mass of Life, Brigg Fair* and *Appalachia*; Holst's *Rig Veda* Hymns and his opera *Savitri; The Planets* came in 1917. During this same brief span Frank Bridge and Eugene Goossens wrote chamber music not less worth while than any written in this country since. Let us be fair. The contemporary composer has enjoyed advertisement and help seldom shared in the past by those who were lucky to hear a new work adequately performed once a year, and received no propaganda or conveyance across the Continent of Europe by an Arts Council. The list of compositions above suggests a renaissance in itself. " But," it will certainly be argued, " Elgar and Delius are ' dated,' the one a complacent Edwardian, the other a romantic to the point of escapism." The critical test of music in the 1950s apparently insists not so much on æsthetic values as on values psychological, political, ideological and topical. If a work does not express certain " reactions " of the moment it is dismissed as of no consequence. The fact is that it is just those composers who submit to the Time Spirit and are drawn into a contemporary " movement " that are the first to perish. Besides, none of us who hailed Elgar as a master was aware that he was speaking for a " complacent " and " opulent " epoch; in fact we thought that we lived in not untroubled times, and that the Income Tax was excessive, and our heaven not entirely unshadowed by war clouds. We thought we heard the note of menace, some prophecy of the wrath to come, in the slow movement of the E flat Symphony.

What body of composition have the contemporaries to put against the fourteen years output enumerated above? There is also the despised 1920s, thence to the outbreak of the second war. Walton produced *Belshazzar's Feast* in 1931, the viola concerto in 1929, the symphony in 1935. I do not regard Walton as contemporary either in technique or origins or point of view. He is a Georgian. Between the two wars, Bax produced his symphonies and the best of his piano music, and no English composer has written for the instrument with more than his distinction. Not the least valuable of Vaughan Williams's contribution was given in the 1920s—the *London* and the *Pastoral* symphonies. Bernard van Dieren was actively with us; Ireland, too, was not without honour.

So much for comparisons of periods supposedly " creative." For interpretative talent we are in no position at all to patronise other years. Our orchestras probably play with a finish of technique not general when rehearsals were not as many. But where are the advancing conductors to follow in the succession of Beecham, Harty, Barbirolli, Heward, Sargent, Boult? We have " discovered " only one truly great singer since the war, and her name was Kathleen Ferrier. Covent Garden is more or less dependent on an Australian soprano for a performance of *Rosenkavalier*; and two of the best tenor voices in England are those also of Australians.

Music is in a turbulent melting-pot; we are in a stage of experiment as vital as exciting. The experiments are often done in public. It is difficult in a disintegrating external scene to produce integrated art, difficult to turn the soil and sow the seed at the same time. In such circumstances a certain inferiority is bound to be felt, hence the efforts made by the contemporaries to assert themselves. These efforts need not go to the length of forgetfulness of past endeavours and performances. If efforts and protests go beyond the bounds of tolerance, the retort might easily take the extreme form of the only joke I have heard for months from a B.B.C. comedian: " Your trouble," said a psycho-analyst to a patient, " is not an inferiority complex. You are inferior! "

The English and Music

IT MIGHT well seem during any festival or holiday, movable or fixed, that we English try as a people to eject music for the time being from our public life. We make an exception at Christmas on behalf of Handel and the *Messiah*, for these belong to ritual; we also give licence to the Third Programme, which, we realise, needs constant culture as the salamander needs the sun. It is as though the nation were unanimously saying: " Let us be merry for a while. Begone, dull care. Avaunt melancholy. For God's sake let's close all concert rooms and the like! " And so our concert halls become strangely silent, and the piano tuner may repose briefly in the bosom of his family.

We do not dismiss theatre or any other form of national entertainment from our jovial and relaxed holidays. It is certain that, given a box office demand for it, any concert promoter would quickly organise a performance even of a Mahler symphony on Boxing Night. Nobody suggests that it is only fair that the outside right or centre forward of the Arsenal or Rotherham United should be allowed to rest at Christmas and refresh himself. There would be protests from millions if holiday times in these isles were shared by actors and sportsmen in large numbers. Literature, actually, is freely dispensed at Christmas.

These considerations, which come to me in an idle

period for the critic, merely confirm a lifetime's suspicions that we are not truly musical, for all our contemporary interest and activity in music; I mean that music is not for the English a necessary way of life, a passionate and persistent craving. We do not need music, as we need books, theatres, art galleries and sport, to enlarge our national vision and give scope for the expression of our essential selves. No civilised Englishman really thinks the worse of another if this other should happen to know little or nothing about music. Our opinion of Charles Lamb as a man with a fine and well-stocked mind does not suffer when we remember that he could not tell the difference between "God Save the King" and "Pop Goes the Weasel." Nobody would feel that T. S. Eliot, say, was revealing a serious defect in his culture if he admitted ignorance of the "posthumous" quartets of Beethoven. But what should we think of a celebrated composer or conductor for whom Shakespeare was only a name, and a sonnet any sort of verse-form? What, indeed, do we think of such? Only in recent years has music been regarded as a desirable part of an Englishman's education, and to this day it is seldom that anybody meets a person in this country who is musical in the sense that most mature-minded English people are well read.

Music is not a language that we English speak from our hearts. We have learnt it, mostly by ear. (Samuel Butler said that to learn music by ear was the only way; and maybe he was right.) The trouble is that unless the ear picks it up in a land where music is in the air, native and natural, the result will most likely be music with a foreign accent. Elgar maintained that in order to compose all a man needed to do was to "take it from the air," freely and for the asking. And Elgar himself, for all the great English-ness of his blood and breeding, made his music sound European. Cecil Gray was no doubt outrageous to write, " When Elgar has rendered unto César the things that are César's and unto Brahms the things that are Brahm's little remains . . ." but we can appreciate his point.

The foreigner who listens superficially to *Gerontius*, and is not aware of the Elgar " secret," the English mixture of reticent romanticism and extrovert lane-striding energy, thinks he hears much of *Parsifal* and *Amfortas* in the music. George Moore, an Irishman, shamefully described *Gerontius* as " holy water in a German beer barrel." If Elgar, the only English composer who for half a century has been regarded as " great," did not speak music as a language entirely his own and native, then in what direction and to whom dare we turn to-day to find a composer who without eclecticism talks to us of contemporary things in tones and idioms that touch the heart as well as the minds of average intelligent English people?

We possess cultivated composers enough. I am occasionally told by colleagues that at the present time English composers are " leading the world." The break-up of the European musical tradition has certainly given us a chance of a lifetime. Whether it is being seized by a genuinely creative opportunism none of us is in a position to say. The first proof of genius is far beyond discernment of the fashionable moment. No English composition of stature written fifty years ago has survived to the present hour except one or two by Elgar; and by survive I mean that the work is in the general repertory and still means much in the consciousness of the nation.

If to-morrow we had to seek in music for consolation and

balm for a national sorrow we should scarcely turn to Britten, or Rubbra, or Rawsthorne, or Lennox Berkeley, or Bliss, or Walton, or even to Vaughan Williams. The people, not just the musically minded of us, would yet again fill their hearts with the " Nimrod " movement from the *Enigma* Variations; and if the occasion were one of sudden excess of normal national pride only the music of the second symphony of Elgar would swell in proportion to the bosom of the nation or march with the right stride. In spite of what we are so often told nowadays about music as an art *sui generis*, a thing in itself, a matter of abstract patterns, the fact remains that every lasting composition has had an appeal to the patriotic or ethical or romantic senses of people of all creeds and classes, whether the work be the *Missa Solemnis* or a Chopin mazurka.

From the " modern " point of view of music as a fine art, as a craft and highly specialised form of æstheticism, English music to-day is as satisfactory as any in the world. But, as in poetry, the composing artist finds himself withdrawn from his fellow-men, unless they happen to belong to his " period " or " style." There is a gulf between the contemporary composer and the ordinarily civilised concert-goer. The fact of the many performances given of the sixth symphony of Vaughan Williams is scarcely relevant to our argument (if argument it be); Vaughan Williams is to be described a contemporary composer only because, happily, he is still alive as an Englishman. His roots are even deeper in the past than Elgar's. The average cultivated music-lover—and I count myself one of them—frankly does not listen to contemporary music except for reasons of duty, curiosity, or under social pressure from certain quarters.

The old argument to the effect that composers have
" always " been neglected or despised by the public until
dead is out of date and, anyhow, is not true. Masterpieces
of music have needed to wait long for recognition for causes
no longer persisting; once on a time a new work was lucky
if it received two public performances in a year, or if it got
into the print of a published score. The B.B.C. has considerably changed all that! I doubt if an " Unfinished "
symphony is to-day lying unknown in anybody's desk.
Few of the " neglected " compositions of the past did not
have their qualities appreciated by the few musicians who
chanced to obtain access to the score and to available performances of it. The public at the present time, like the
the public always and for ever, is right to ask for something
in music of the common touch, some recognisable melody
and a rhythm to which a normal two-legged man and woman
may dance. He and she are not interested in " abstract
patterns." If it comes to abstract patterns at all, the
ordinary English man and woman will find them any
winter morning, created invisibly, and without public
announcement, by frost—patterns surpassing in " objective " or " formal " beauty any invention of the human
intellect.

If it is true that English composers are now "leading"
the music of the world, the dominance is probably technical
and " stylistic " in an age not essentially musical psychologically or in its modes of living. We have invariably
boasted of our important composers—Bantock, Holbrooke,
Frank Bridge, Goossens, Havergal Brian, Bax and Ireland,
in addition to Elgar and Delius and Holst, each of them as
highly esteemed in his day as the proudest of our latest
lions; moreover, esteemed by a public not yet under the

severe tutorial eye of an Arts Council. We have usually been good assimilators in music. The evolution of music as an art, the biology of its seminal forms, would have taken much the same course and shape if no English composition had been written these last hundred years.

We have produced no Berlioz, no Chopin, no Debussy, no Schönberg, no Stravinsky—I allude to the Stravinsky of *Le Sacre*. We have reaped rather than sown. We have made " progress " since the dark ages of the 1900s in ratio to the cultural development of music generally throughout the world. But we have opened no new paths. We have been versatile and industrious. No English composer has exactly wielded his pen " with the easy grace of a nobleman " —as Sir Walter Scott said of Byron. So perhaps, after all, it is permissible if in seasons of holiday most of us, our composers included, choose for a while to give music, and ourselves, a rest.

Contemporary English

THE FIRST performance in London some months ago of
Edmund Rubbra's Viola Concerto emphasised again the
admirable culture and skill which are the mark of music-
making nowadays. No contemporary composer is illiterate
or unsophisticated; they can all easily avoid the pitfalls into
which Delius sometimes flopped; none is likely to commit
Elgar's recurrent banalities. Once on a time we used to
speak of the Arts and of the Fine Arts. This was our
pompous way of distinguishing between products of imagination and products of craftsmanship. I do not wish to
suggest that Rubbra is without imagination; I shall
presently try to argue that he is a man with significant
things to say. But the Viola Concerto is impressive mainly
for its finely organised shapes and the sense it conveys to
us of loving and absorbed handicraft. It is a sort of musical
furniture or design in bronze or a tapestry in tone, almost
aspiring to the functional. You could almost walk round
it or sit on it.

A viola concerto, from the style of the instrument, is
best if it refrains from stress of emotion or any show of
rhetoric. Rubbra composes for the viola with the respect
due to the viola; also he cleverly encourages its less inhibited
moods. He is always a thoughtful composer who seldom
employs the materials of his art so as to attract us sensu-

ously; or rather he does not directly and consciously appeal to ear and to the nervous system. He has gradually made his position in our music by works innocent of the least show of virtuosity. He has stated that one of his aims is " trying to bring the contrapuntal texture of the Elizabethan into the wider instrumental forms "; and indeed he seemed at one time to overdo counterpoint. In his symphonies, especially the fifth, the essential Rubbra is unfolded, a fine contemplative spirit and also a lovable man, one not given to familiarity. It is a silly and superficial thing to say of Rubbra that he is archaic and deficient of deep feeling. As far back as the 1930s I heard Rubbra's setting of John Donne's *Hymne to God the Father*, sung by the Fleet Street Choir; and I described it as a " beautiful and personal piece of choral writing conveying something of the mingling of passion and austerity in Donne." This notice was, I think, one of the first written appreciatively or substantially of Rubbra; I mention this fact now because I am from time to time accused of lack of interest in contemporary music. After my first hearing of *Peter Grimes* I wrote that parts of it had a power not to be accounted for in terms of talent; genius was present. And because I did not say genius was omnipresent, hard words came to me from the Britten zealots. Criticism is much too generous in its treatment of new English music; dramatic critics chastise plays (or at any rate they find fault with them) which have involved just as much creative thought in their production as goes into the average symphony or concerto. Arthur Benjamin's new opera, *A Tale of Two Cities*, broadcast in the Third Programme, was manifestly a skilfully-composed affair, even at a first radio hearing. On the strength of a wireless transmission, one of our best critics described it as a " masterpiece " of dramatic composition, adding that in that line Mr. Benjamin is as much a genius as Puccini.

It is difficult to get to the dramatic point of the music of an opera if it is not seen on the stage and heard in the theatre, for clearly the value and relevance of a dramatic point can only be appreciated by recognition of correspondence between voice and orchestra, and action and situation. The music of *A Tale of Two Cities* sounded to me dexterously controlled and—if I may invent a term—dexterously sequenced. The instrumentation was busy, varied in colour and character, always obviously making allusions which it is to be hoped will be theatrically apt in the theatre and not distracting. There was a lack of vocal melody; and here the trouble was that the composer was without doubt trying to write melody of a very " singable " order. But some injustice is bound to be done to any composer if anything like a dogmatic opinion is formed of his opera after a radio performance, with much of the singing as meaningless and uncomfortable as, in opera, only English singing can be.

When I consider the contemporary scene of English music and the help and encouragement given to our composers by Arts Councils and the B.B.C., and the rest, though I welcome the change to a more amenable atmosphere than of old, I am bound to remember the young " lions " of my youth, when Havergal Brian and Eugene Goossens were our heroes and leaders. We imagined we were as " progressive " then as the latest tone-row Leftist. Havergal Brian and Goossens were once regarded by the best critics, none of them less intelligent and experienced than the best critics of 1957, much as Rubbra, Rawsthorne, Britten, Berkeley, and others are regarded now. Havergal Brian has composed two operas at least, and a symphony called *The Gothic*, as long as one by Mahler; Goossens has also composed two operas in addition to a considerable body of chamber music, much of it excellent. It is not always the contemporary composer who most needs " encouragement " and performance; if he is any good at all he usually gets " into the fashion." The tragedy, often enough, is in the neglect, mainly through change of fashion, of the composer who was contemporary yesterday.

Words and Music

Humphrey Searle's setting of Dr. Edith Sitwell's *The Shadow of Cain* revives once more the thousand-year-old question: how far can music be mated to poetry without damage to one or the other? The emphasis should, in this argument, be put on self-contained poetry, not words deliberately written for music. Dr. Sitwell's free rhythms and verbal imagery certainly reach towards some overtones sounding beyond our ordinary diction; it was through some unconscious reaction to her impulses and aspirations that in a notice of the performance of the work I lapsed into parody . . . " takes us beyond metaphysics . . . uses words in a way that transcends logic of reason . . ." " In a way," in that context, is delicious.

Not every great composer has boldly faced the fact that poetry and music, words and tones in their own metrical measurements, obey different laws of accentuation and motion; also they appeal to different faculties of our consciousness. Indeed Handel—for one in a hundred—boldly turned his back on the problem and bent and twisted words to suit the specific patterns of music as he conceived it. " Rejoice, rejoice, re-jo-oi-oi . . ." and so on. Even Purcell, whose subtilisation of recitative was one of the most important contributions made by an English composer to the organic development of vocal music, was oblivious to verbal deportment and sequence when a musical pattern seized hold of him . . . " And mine eyes have seen . . . And mine eyes have seen." But he was writing for the church here, not dramatically.

Burlesque has long enjoyed itself with the repetitions of words and suspended " action " in opera, as a composer has attended to a purely musical or instrumental shape or " period." " Let's away, away, away "—and it takes the chorus a hundred bars to get off the stage, one half to the left, the other to the right, for opera choruses never all go the same way home. These artificialities, or rather let us fairly call them overdone conventions, were partly the consequence of the fact that composers remained obsessed or engrossed with patterns and procedure derived from instrumental music even when they came to the entirely different job of writing music to suit actions and emotions related to the stage, and the goings-on of visible people. It would of course be received to-day as a sign of a mental aberration or of wilfully apeing a " period," if Benjamin Britten were to rearrange the text of a libretto so that the words followed a self-contained balanced musical pattern, with a Da Capo, and all the rest . . . " I am an old man o-o-old man, who has, who has experienced, experienced much . . ." The wedding of true minds among musicians and poets admits of impediments yet. New patterns of music yet remain to be organised to do justice in equal proportion to the appeal of words and to vocal and instrumental tone and identity.

The reaction from the dominance of musical pattern in opera has swung so far that unless it is halted I can foresee the passing of the beautiful voice from opera altogether. The pull of dramatic interest threatens the citadel of the opera composer's essential genius, the genius by which he is able to fertilise drama by music, the genius whereby he can take drama into the world of his own, the world of music, and hold sway there, a benevolent despot under no constitution but that of which the laws of music are the basis. In an opera such as *Wozzeck* an entirely musical voice might well be a positive hindrance, an interfering anodyne or catharsis long before we needed any soothing or purging at all. Even a truly musical orchestra, with, say the golden-voiced strings of the Vienna Philharmonic, might seem irrelevant in Alban Berg's masterpiece. I am not of course in any way casting a reflection against *Wozzeck*, a work of genius in its own style and direction; but the direction is away from the *rationale* of opera as cultivated from Gluck to Strauss. We might even argue that *Wozzeck* harks back in its emphasis on the importance of words and drama to the theories formulated towards the close of the sixteenth century in the house of Giovanni Bardi: the reaction then, as now, was against the domination of musical patterns over the rights of words and poetry. The ideal setting of music to word happens when each seems born of the other; and from this point of view *Wozzeck* is certainly an exemplar. At any rate, it is not easy to think of the music of *Wozzeck* as having existence apart from the libretto.

Much the same may be said of much of Debussy's *Pelléas et Mélisande*. The choice of words for music, by any librettist, depends on the subject or theme to be expressed. Berg writes notes to many words in *Wozzeck* which no more call for music than a medical treatise reproduced in next week's *Lancet*. For centuries the opera composer's worry was to find a way of transition in a

libretto from dialogue necessary to explain plot and circumstance to the periods of full-phrased song. It was also a
problem for the librettist to design a text in which explanation and non-musical words and "situations" would be
reduced to a minimum, to an essential "musical stuff," to
use Wagner's term. The contemporary easy solution, as
I see it, has been to reverse the terms of the problem, so
that the librettist reduces to a minimum the needs of the
composer to cope with lyrical moods and situations which
demand melody and continuous music—and won't be
denied. Declamation, backed up by orchestration and all
the tricks of the "musical background" trade, is easier to
invent than song, or those song-speech phrases which, as
in the monologues of Hans Sachs, go half-way to meet free
and encompassing sweeps and curves and risings and falls
of orchestral tone.

Mr. Humphrey Searle's task with Dr. Edith Sitwell's
poem was not as difficult as that of the opera composers;
he was not expected to match his music word for word,
but to create an atmosphere. Apart from the poem his
ingenious score would have little except a technical interest;
and to say this much is not a complaint, only a statement of
fact. Dr. Sitwell's poem invited music only incidentally;
its appeal is partly ethical—dependent on our reactions to
the atomic bomb and Hiroshima, and partly, even mainly,
to our responses to the imagery of words. Music gets in
the way of recited poetry—if the poetry is too good, or too
good in long stretches.

PART SIX

CRITICISING THE CRITICS

Criticism with Humour

ONE OF the several shortcomings of contemporary musical criticism (which at the moment is having a rough time, especially from its practitioners) is a plentiful lack of humour and an excess of solemnity. Beckmesser is winning with ease. It is still possible to come upon music criticism of this kind: " In Blank's Quartet op. 293b three motifs of entirely different character are opposed to each other in the first three bars; yet they are related to each other through some formal device or another, such as inversion, augmentation . . ." And so on. We might confidently have hoped this stuff would years ago have been slain for ever by the ridicule of Bernard Shaw. He exposed the jargon of musical analysis by applying it to dramatic criticism: " Shakespeare, dispensing with the customary exordium, announces his subject at once in the infinitive, in which mood it is presently repeated after a short connecting passage, in which, brief as it is, we recognise the alternative and negative forms on which so much of the significance of the repetition depends. . . ."

" Some development of the first theme follows, and then an episode in the tonic minor——" it is with us yet, still with us. It is as though a dramatic critic were to discuss Shakespeare not indeed in terms of grammar and syntax but were to reduce him to philology. It is nowadays no

longer possible to go to music criticism expectant of Runciman's gusto of the old *Saturday Review*. He wrote of a
new tenor from Bayreuth this way: " As for the new
Siegfried, I thought little of him. For the most part he
stood about the vast Covent Garden stage like a block of
wood, with his mouth wide open, until the moment came
for him to sing, when he promptly shut it." There is in no
criticism of the present the urbanity of " Max " and
Walkley, the 1912-Cockburn-port-mellow garrulity of
Saintsbury, the donnish dry sherry wit of Tovey, the
shillelagh layings-about of Runciman, the authoritative
querulous enthusiasm of Agate. There would be a shock,
perceptible and national, if a music critic, dealing with some
darling of the moment, began a notice, as Newman began
one about the greatest tenor of his period, with a spacious
preliminary generalisation, a sort of clearing of the ground
before going into action: " The higher the voice, the lower
the intellect." The austere intensity of the search for
objective truth has not blunted the wit of our greatest
writer on music, else he could not have envisaged and
justified the " brave new world " in which music-critics,
at Mr. Newman's time of life, will be performing a more
valuable musical and public service by staying at home
listening to the Third Programme than by going out on
a cold night to a real concert.

A large public avidly turned to Newman, Runciman,
Agate, Langford, Johnstone, Baughan—to name a few—
because these writers saw to it that enjoyment of criticism
began at home. There is no need for the latter-day solemnity. Even Mr. Newman in recent years has seemed
troubled at the thought that the history of music criticism
is one of the fallibility of human judgment; error succeedeth

unto error, prejudice and folly one and indivisible, knowledge a will-o'-the-wisp in the darkening of counsels. It is natural vanity in man, especially if he has laboured hard in scholarship, to seek " to see the object as in itself it really is "; and no harm is done so long as a writer doesn't get on to stilts to look for the Thing-in-Itself. But why should music criticism, more than any other activity of man's mind, tremble to contemplate mortal relativity and proneness to want of settled opinion on any subject for any length of time? And why this fear of how silly a contemporary judgment may look in the eyes of posterity? There is no evidence at all that posterity will be wiser or more intelligent than the best and the worst of us of 1957.

I am not, myself, depressed in the least should argument against the futility of criticism be put to me in the familiar way: " If six of you listen to the same work or the same performance the result will be six more or less different reports." What of it; and who, anyhow, hath believed our report? There would surely be reason for acute depression, and much dullness would ensue, if every critic agreed in the main on any work of genius.

The critic's responsibility is not such a burden that he need wear a long face perpetually and not " enjoy a frisk " now and then. Nobody will be a penny the worse if he pronounces the most unjust verdict; he is not sentencing anybody to death. He will write his best and amuse his readers (and that primarily is what he is paid for) if he brings to his technical and cultural equipment some occasional flippancy or a willingness to laugh at himself. It is long since I personally got a good laugh out of any writing on music. Even descriptions of an opera libretto are now

271

expressed in grave and rational language. " She is still in this melancholy mood when Hans comes in." . . . " Norina rings the bell for the servants and demands that the whole of the domestic establishment be brought before her." I preferred dear old Herr Fr. Charley, who decades ago produced in Leipzig a book of opera synopses for the benefit of English and American visitors to Germany. Mr. Robert Elkin the other year edited a new edition of Herr Charley's masterpiece; but it omitted one or two of the author's finest prose passages, notably the following graphic account of what happens in Ambroise Thomas's *Mignon*—I quote from memory, for alas! my " original " copy of Herr. Fr. Charley's *Opera Glass* has long since been lost by or stolen from me. Herr Charley wrote his English vividly and comprehensively, thus:

Mignon, Akt. 1. Seen. 1. Courting Yard Olde In. Modtly crowde gahthered for rejoigings. Townsmen and Travaillers. Enter Troup with Philine, dazling coquette. And her fiend Laerte. Also old anged Minstrel Lothario, strike sombre tune. Extracted of misfortune be roometh for seek of dauhghter Sperata. Band of Gypsys dance. Young maid nameth Mignon is make to perform by strong bullied stick of grasping Leader Brack of Wiskerth. Wilhelm Meister forward sprang gasping wiskerth villan of the neck outward where it brake nearly. " Let go her! " Wilhelm shouth. And villan paled to obeyness.

Where is the critic who would not increase his public and his value to the community if he could in a notice emulate Herr Charley's evocative prose and describe some

" Conduktor gasping wiskert neck of Tennor where it brake nearly." How apt and poignant, in the context, is the phrase " Townsmen and Travaillers." Oh, Charley, thou shouldst be living at this dry-and-dustily pedantic hour!

The Objective Ear

SOME CURIOSITY has been stirred by the fact that recently a famous orchestra played twice within twenty-four hours in the same hall and received high praise at the first concert and some drastic criticism at the other. There would be no occasion for surprise at such discrepancies of opinion in a world not metaphysically uneducated. There remains yet a body of public opinion which regards a concert performance as a thing in itself easily located in time and space and as easily to be objectively contemplated as Mr. Micawber contemplated the nail in the wall. The general public's attitude to the critic is entertainingly paradoxical. Most time he is regarded with the healthy suspicion which is rightly the portion and desert of all experts; but if ever he contradicts himself he is assailed as though he had contravened holy writ. For all the discipline he goes through, and the check he keeps on his personal predilections, no critic can hope always to escape from his skin; besides, purely physical let alone psychological causes can at times unseat reason; the wrong place in the hall, or the wrong hall. Years ago certain subscribers to back seats at the Berlin Philharmonic Concerts complained that they could not hear Furtwängler's pianissimi. "They should buy more expensive tickets," he said.

One night a critic will be dealing with some work he

knows backwards and loves; he will now tend to listen hypercritically. Next night the music might be detestable to him and he may not know or care if it really sounds as badly played as the evidence of his senses would suggest. And if a solitary mortal critic is encased in relativity, with his " standards " sometimes as though vain and illusory, at the mercy of his blood pressure and adrenal, what of the orchestra which is not a machine conductors and composers keep on the premises to make music? It is composed of eighty and more men and women, each much like the rest of us, with his and her own temperament, degree of intelligence. Consider them all at a rehearsal on a cold winter morning, an aggregation of fiddlers, 'cellists, trombonists, trumpeters, oboe and flute players, drummers, tympanists and sometimes but not always, a man supporting a tuba. Also a trianglist. Some of them are young and unmarried; some of them are old and very much married; some have got out of bed feeling happy and some have not. Some are in the mood to play and others are sick of the sound of music. And nearly all of them believe at bottom that in a just universe they would be the conductor. Even amongst those who are keen to play there are differences of inclination; some are tired to death of certain works and some are tired to death of others. Let us suppose, on this dismal winter morning, that they are rehearsing the E minor symphony of Tchaikovski; the first violin nurses a grievance because it is not " Heldenleben "; but the first horn is expectant, at least he is not bored, because of the good show he gets in the second movement.

Here is where the conductor comes in to make or do something with a collection of diverse forces, beings of views and feelings bound now and then to be mutually exclusive. It is a familiar saying of the cynical layman that an orchestra could give a good performance if no conductor were present. I have certainly heard orchestral performances that have suggested they would have been better in the conductor's absence. The other month there was a public demonstration that a child could beat time throughout a symphony with no unusual disasters amongst the instrumentalists. This particular infant phenomenon recalled the story of the " prodigy " pianist who was brought by her mother to perform for Moriz Rosenthal. " She has already appeared in public with success," said her admiring parent. " And what did she play? " asked Rosenthal. " The B flat minor Concerto of Tchaikovski," said the parent proudly. Rosenthal took another look at the infant, then said, " Too old! "

It is the conductor who obtains unity of interpretation. Most experienced orchestras are capable, no doubt, of going through a standard work without palpable technical maladjustment, unassisted by a conductor. But they would not give an interpretation. How should they? No two musicians thoroughly agree about the plainest indications of tempi. Adagio might mean six different modes of feeling as well as six different modes of motion and energy, to six different minds. The conductor, according to his lights, has to establish unity of style, agreement as to nuance and tone-volume. In his mind is the score as a whole, and he must relate all the parts to it. Even when he has achieved as much synthesis as this—and most conductors fail to get much farther—he has only begun his work, if he is a great conductor. He has prepared his instrument, merely " tuned " it. Now he must play on it and transform correctly played notes into music. It is not

276

enough that a Gielgud should faithfully enunciate every word of " Hamlet "; he is expected to identify his personality and his art with the character.

I am now treading ground which is nowadays controversial. A play, I shall be told, is a matter of histrionics, of mimicry. Music is music; it is the conductor's duty to follow the score, the notes as written down on paper in the composer's lifetime. The composer, so the argument runs, has indicated by marks of expression all that is needed to render clear his smallest " meaning." It all depends on the composer. Beethoven, for one, had some trouble deciding between shades of " expression." The contemporary notion that notes of music are fixed symbols which fall as inevitably and symmetrically into place as the stars in their courses is not emphasised by a study of the notebooks of Beethoven, or the sketches of other composers. Most of us will remember how often Furtwängler was called over the coals for failing to observe tempi indications which the little Italian boy conductor would attend to respectfully and unhesitatingly. In the *Cavatina* quartet of Beethoven, if I remember, there are some fifty-eight nuances marked in some sixty-six bars. Even Furtwängler never indulged as many as that, in so short a space.

Criticising the Critics

A SYMPOSIUM in the useful periodical *Opera* discusses music criticism exhorting it to overhaul its catechism. The idea which inspired the symposium was excellent; unfortunately one or two of the contributors to it do not appear to have given much thought to the æsthetic position from which any critic worth while approaches his work. (I assume, of course, that the symposium is reviewing music criticism as it is to be found in serious journals outside of as well as within London.) Too much emphasis is laid by these contributors on the critic's fallibility as judge, on his helpfulness or lack of it to the creative artist, and on his influence on public opinion. That he tries to be something of an artist himself seems not to have occurred to Dr. Erwin Stein or to Mr. Benjamin Britten.

Dr. Stein goes so far as to state that " the critic's job holds power without responsibility, or rather with responsibility only at their own discretion. Moreover, they have the advantage over the artists of speaking in the public's own language." " Therefore," continues Dr. Stein, " their influence is enormous; they shape—potentially, at least, public opinion in matters of art. Yet their power is not derived from any merit of their own but from the mere chance that they have got the job."

For my own part, I have spent a good deal of a lifetime

at this " job," in preparation and in practice, and have, with increase of years and of humour, learned to bow tolerantly to the abuse which is the critic's portion and, let me add, his constant joy. But Dr. Stein is unusually hard on us, is he not? If we derive our " power " from no merit of our own, how do we obtain and retain our " jobs "? It is a familiar gibe that the critic is a " self-appointed judge." Apparently we need only go round to the offices of *The Times*, the *Manchester Guardian*, the *Scotsman*, introduce ourselves to the editor, and the rest is easy, including the salary. For, maintains Dr. Stein, those who employ the critics " are rarely competent judges of their qualifications." Possibly the editor of a newspaper might hold different views from Dr. Stein's on what are a music critic's qualifications. Much would depend on the standard of intelligence of his readers. But in every instance a certain requirement would be insisted on; and for lack of it nearly every contributor to the *Opera* symposium would, I fancy, be turned away jobless—at least he would be by any editor of the newspapers for which I myself have served as music critic.

The ability to write good English about music in such a way that the average well educated reader is kept interested is extremely rare. And by " average well educated reader " I mean one who concerns himself no more deeply about diminished sevenths when he is listening to music than about dactyls and spondees when he is giving himself to poetry. The *Opera* symposium could advantageously have called attention to the fact that at the present time musical criticism in this country is overloaded with technical language beyond the comprehension of people who are capable of enjoying V. S. Pritchett on Proust or Henry

James on Balzac. The most broadminded and sensible contributor to the symposium is Sir Kenneth Clark, who in his essay does at least pause to refer to " show-off " criticism, which rarely achieves its purpose of impressing other specialists and leaves the amateur completely bewildered.

Is it true that the influence of the critic on public opinion is " enormous " ? My experience is that so far as he has influence at all it is to the good: I mean that he can persuade the public to listen to a new work if he praises it, but is not likely by blame to keep them away from it if they are in the slightest interested. For it is a fact that it is when he is appreciating that the critic writes at his most persuasive; when he is not responsive and warm æsthetically his pen is likely to run dry, or take refuge in witticisms which seldom delight and hurt not. In any case, verdicts differ amongst critics as amongst doctors, leader-writers, politicians, and composers; and if one of us condemns a new opera by Mr. Britten (that is, if ever any of us ever does) another praises, so he is right and they are right and all's as right as right can be. A general supposition is that criticism is revealed as so much futile vanity if, say, half a dozen exponents of it should arrive at six different opinions on the same subject. It is a supposition arising from scant understanding of metaphysics and of the critic's æsthetic viewpoint.

The critic cannot, admittedly, always deploy or spread himself from this viewpoint as wholeheartedly as he would wish. Time and space fetter him. But at half a chance he tries to write an account of his reactions as artist to artist —and not as servant, or " inferior," to master. The counsel of perfection with him is to draw impressions of a work or performer into his own imagination, led there or attracted by knowledge and by sympathy with the creative artist's intentions. He is not content to deliver a " judgment " and leave it at that, though he is ready to swear to do his best here. He wishes most to " have a go " at some act of art of his own, a poor thing, maybe, less than a column of type, but still his own, conveying a heightened sense of what he has experienced at a concert or from hearing music in any way; he is urged to expression for the pleasure of writing or of clearing his mind or of casting illumination of words to darks of his consciousness where, perhaps, some idea has gone astray.

" Charles Lamb is just as much an artist in describing his personal sensation in the presence of Munden and Elliston at the height of their powers as he is in doing similar justice to his impressions of the old Christ's Hospital." So wrote C. E. Montague. Mr. Britten may be surprised to learn that some of us can get as much pleasure as literature from criticism by Hazlitt, Newman, and Langford as we can get from his compositions listened to as music. And I intend this as a high compliment to him.

Mr. Britten complains that in twenty years " my critics do not seem to have changed much. Of course some have been more welcoming (about 50 per cent at a guess), but practically all have been unobservant, if not actually inane. I can say with honesty that in every piece I have written, in spite of hard work, there are still passages where I have not quite solved problems. Not once have these passages been noticed, nor of course, suggestions made as to how I could have improved them."

Would Mr. Britten really like to be taught by a music critic, in a public print, how to compose? Most of us would consider it an impertinence to enter his workshop as collaborator. I would as soon expect him to tell me how to write music criticism.

Shaw as a Music Critic

In the year of Bernard Shaw's centenary, or any other year, those of us who are interested in music will dip yet again into his collected music criticism. To get the full relish of his fun, as well as of his acumen, we must always bear in mind that he was usually trying to make fools of the pedant and the pretensions of those who display technical knowledge for display's own sake. We must not imagine that in a passage such as the following he is not giving us a wink: " In the Scherzo, which lends itself to impetuous treatment, the tempo was perfect, varying between a normal 117 bars per minute and an exceptional 120." Shaw is here discussing a performance of the Ninth Symphony of Beethoven, conducted by Georg Henschel. " Later on," Shaw adds, with another wink, " Mr. Henschel rather astonished some of us by the apparently very slow tempo he adopted for the *allegro assai* . . . we are accustomed to hear this played exactly twice too fast, as if minims and crotchets were quavers and semiquavers. . . ."

Musicians in the 1880s and 1890s attended suspiciously to Shaw on music because obviously he wasn't a specialist. How should a man know music—that is, form and counterpoint and all the rest—if also he was running around the municipal chambers and vestries talking Fabianism, not to say Marx, expressing views on painting, drama, and even writing plays—and such plays, not fit for the eyes and ears of the Principal, let alone any student of the Royal College of Music? To this day musicians of academic office tend to eye dubiously the critic who is not cribbed and confined in technique and rooted to one place with scholarship. The critic who relaxes now and again into, say, cricket, is at once put on the spot; for all the world as though the credentials of a Strauss as a composer were questioned because he liked to spend lots of time but no money at a card-table. " A man can't play Skat all day," he said, when somebody asked him why he composed so much. And a critic can't listen to pianists and vocalists and fiddlers all day, especially when as so often happens, he finds he is descending to a less masterful and less honest level of skill, as he turns from a Hutton, a Compton, to the next tremolo of a soprano, or the next gesticulation of the latest interpretative conductor.

" I require to be certified by authorities like Bachelors of Music," wrote Shaw, " to prove that I know the difference between a tonal fugue and a real one. . . ." We have, of course, advanced beyond a narrowness and prejudice of this sort; but not very far beyond. To this day a critic without much understanding of music as a language in which a genius seeks to give an account of himself as mortal experiencing man, can make an impression of learning, and even of relevant learning, simply by referring to the fact that at the sixty-fourth bar of the first movement of the Ninth Symphony of Beethoven a theme repeated in canon leads in three extra bars to the dominant of B flat. I have exploited this gambit myself in my more sterile moments; the public swallow it whole. Shaw years ago made his famous satire on the " analytical " kind of criticism, demonstrating how the method might be applied to a soliloquy of Hamlet: " To be or not to be "—" Shakespeare, dispensing with the customary exordium, announces the subject at once in the infinite, in which mood it is presently repeated, after a short connecting passage, in which, brief as it is, we recognise the alternative and negative forms on which so much of the significance of the repetition depends. . . ." In 1957 this kind of hocus-pocus survives, and is read with a gullibility almost affecting: " Mr. Poppett's new concerto for harpsichord, flute, and three blow-pipes, reveals an intensifying of his polyphony with a greater freedom of modal harmony. . . ." Abracadabra and Mesopotamia.

Shaw was, of course, much more interested in ideas than in any notes of music. He is supposed to have found in " The Ring " of Wagner all manner of economic and sociological significances " which are not there." In *The Perfect Wagnerite*, he describes Nibelheim this way: " This gloomy place need not be a mine; it might as well be a match factory with yellow phosphorus, phossy jaw, a large dividend, and plenty of clergymen shareholders. Or it might be a whitelead factory, or a chemical works. . . ." Of the Tarnhelm, the magic helmet, he says, " Alberic wrests it from Mime, and shows him . . . that he who wears it can appear in what shape he will, or disappear from view altogether. This helmet is a very common article in our streets, where it generally takes the form of a tall hat. It makes a man invisible as a shareholder, and changes him into various shapes, such as a pious Christian, a subscriber to hospitals, a benefactor of the poor . . . when he is really a pitiful parasite on the commonwealth. . . ." Shaw dismisses those for whom *Das Rheingold* is only " a struggle between half a dozen fairy-tale personages for a ring, involving hours of scolding and cheating, and one long scene in a dark, gruesome mine . . . and not a glimpse of a handsome young man or pretty woman. Only those of wider consciousness can follow it breathlessly, seeing in it the whole tragedy of human history, and the whole horror of the dilemmas from which the world is shrinking to-day."

Nobody with the sketchiest knowledge of Wagner as a man, and in his muddled way, a serious thinker, will argue that he spent a lifetime working at a conception the main concern of which is with giants, dragons, and other wild-fowl, magic helmets and swords, merely for their own pantomimic sakes and effects. What, in a gallery of mere fantasy, is Wotan doing, a god caught in the snare of his own legality? Whoever reads *The Perfect Wagnerite*, a paraphrase of genius, will never again suffer boredom from Wotan. In a Wagner music-drama it inevitably happens that the words at times are of more importance than the music set to them. Yet it is seldom that I meet a musician who, as he describes Wotan as " that interminable bore," can give me the briefest précis of what Wotan is talking about.

Here is Shaw on the Wotan idea: " Godhead, face to face with Stupidity, must compromise. Unable to force on the world the pure law of thought, it must resort to a mechanical law of commandments to be enforced by brute punishments and the destruction of the disobedient. And however carefully these laws are framed to represent the highest thoughts of the framers at the moment of their promulgation, before a day has elapsed that thought has grown and widened by the ceaseless evolution of life. . . .

Yet if the high givers of that law themselves set the example of breaking it . . . they destroy all its authority with their subjects, and so to break the weapon they have forged to rule them for their own good."

With these words and ideas in mind we can never again contemplate the " Treaty " scenes and music and not have a heightened and enlarged imaginative perception. I doubt if Wagner himself would substantially disagree with any imputation Shaw brings to *The Ring*, or with any of his great range of human and dramatic ideas which were stimulated in his mind by close study of, first Wagner's life, and then, Wagner's words and music.

There were, no doubt, serious limitations to Shaw as a writer on music. We may read him for hours, enlivening our minds and wits; but not always, if ever, are we allowed to remember that music is an art occasionally related to beauty and sensitiveness. He was obliged, admittedly, to write of the musical scene as he found it in this country in the eighties and nineties. Few composers challenged him as a thinker and critic of life in those dark ages of " musical England." Shaw in fact was perhaps fortunate to be able to enjoy his " danse macabre " in the graveyards of oratorio and counterpoint, rattling the bones in the sepulchres. This was the perfect material for a diabolist. I can't quite see Shaw coping a decade or so later, after he had given up writing on music, with the subtle chemistry of a mind such as Debussy's, or the later Schönberg's. He was inspired to his most valuable music writings by Wagner, for here was a basis of more or less concrete ideas for his mind to work on; and it was not a truly musical mind at bottom —which music-critic's mind is?—but a literary one, with a genius for dialectic. In music, as in all things, as this cleansing, vivifying, scarifying mind of Shaw's played and probed, he distributed as much healing ointment as acid; for if not the most profound and scholarly of music critics, though he knew more of music than most, he was certainly the most genial and wittily endearing.

The Critic and Beethoven

SHOULD THE music critic devote most of his time and space to the discussion of music or to performances? It is an old controversy, and surely it all depends on the circumstances in which the critic writes. Is he dealing with a concert "on the night," or composing a weekly column at leisure, or—can he write at all? A concert on the night is "news," but even in this instance the critic should relate performance to a consideration of music as an art. To talk technique in the abstract and not as a way of illuminating an æsthetic idea is an impertinence. No matter how scanty his space, the critic will enjoy himself most and arrest his readers' attention if he is able, though only writing of Blank's umptieth performance of the Tchaikovski piano concerto, to indicate that the occasion was worth while, memorably good, or memorably and comically bad.

A weekly or periodical article is another matter altogether. Here the critic may escape from his routine and find a means of free and private contemplation. Here he need not keep his nose to the topical grindstone. A column article, not about a given event, can be regarded as the critic's confessional. Now let him momentarily forget the fashions and the market place. And the more he retires to his own session of silent thoughts, the more he forgets "current tendencies" and controversies, the more he withdraws to himself and expresses himself professionally on holiday, so to say, the more his readers will find him engrossing. That is, as we keep on saying, if he can write at all.

With these thoughts in mind, I turn for material for another " Survey " to two piano sonatas of Beethoven— both in two movements, opp. 90 and 111; and the first technically, or in the physiology of its forms, prepares the way to the last and greatest, in C minor, though it presents an entirely different world. Op. 90 contains some of the most lyrical and stylish of Beethoven's writing for the instrument. It is an error to think that he was a man perpetually morose or boorish. This E minor Sonata was dedicated to Count Moritz von Lichnowsky, who was only one of many of Beethoven's aristocratic friends. The point I wish to stress about op. 90 in the context of a discussion of op. 111 is that it is continuous in its development, with organic extension or transformation of small groups of notes and wide-flung key changes, simplicity and multiplicity to perfection. In the B flat Sonata, op. 106, composed some four years after op. 90. Beethoven allowed himself a final virtuoso fling, bringing the " grand " piano, which was now his joy and new toy, to play on the dramatic conception of the concert-sonata, in which the clash of themes and tone values is a matter for external manipulation: the appeal is essentially rhetorical.

In op. 111 we are taken to realms where the drama or " argument " is spiritual or metaphysical, if old-fashioned language may nowadays be used without apology. The development here is necessarily from within: in other words, contrasted themes or tone substances are not so much brought into conjunction and conflict with the dramatist's eye or ear on crisis and resolution: rather the music grows from mental and psychological concentration on one or two melodic, harmonic, or rhythmical entities which are positive and negative aspects of a single tonal symbol. If we could explain in words what is conveyed by this symbolism we might, as Beethoven himself said, be able to explain the meaning of the world.

Every great genius, as he gets older and comes to control over the technique and substance of his art, arrives at a certain simplicity of expression. Beethoven, in op. 111 creates from the barest parts of musical speech. So with Shakespeare; when Lear is broken on the wheel Shakespeare flaunts no purple period at us: over the dead body of Cordelia Lear merely says:

> Pray you, undo this button: thank you, sir.
> Do you see this?

In op. 111 Beethoven uses elements of fugue and variation, and is content with two movements. He begins the first movement with such old tricks of the trade as chords of the diminished seventh and sforzato bass. " The startling effects which many ascribe solely to the natural genius of the composer," Beethoven is supposed to have said to a friend, " are quite frequently easily achieved by the right use of the chord of the diminished seventh. " The strenuous notes of the opening of the first movement of op. 111, the thunderous bass in the distance; then the charging main theme—these factors in the scheme are followed by a softer and supplicating period; but we cannot rightly refer here to formal " subjects " or contrasts. This is a musical dualism; Beethoven shapes his motifs into the stuff and texture of the whole movement. It is action and reaction of mind and spirit. And if such language as this is reads suspiciously as an example of writing romantically "round" music, I can only answer that Beethoven spoke of his music in exactly the same way.

The struggle for long is indecisive. The stamping notes shatter attempts towards peace and appeasement. Beethoven subdues himself for a while by the discipline of a fugal passage, but he cannot contain himself in scholarship. There is a remarkable passage of four unison octaves; if I can trust memory, we have to go back some fourteen years to find unison writing of this extended recklessness in Beethoven's piano works. It is by study of a composer's many ways of using music, his traits of style over different periods, that we learn to understand what he is talking about. The contemporary musical crossword-puzzle solvers are satisfied that Beethoven and the rest wrote music qua music—which needs none but abstract contemplation, and can be reduced to so many wonderful self-subsistent " patterns." A man hears as much in Beethoven as his musical experience and imagination will attend to.

In the coda of the first movement of op. 111 Beethoven puts forth his power to come to some resolution and understanding; there are dissonant chords, a diminuendo, ending in bodeful stressful notes. Only a musical barbarian would make these sounds and use tone so drastically, if he were set on " pattern," or on music of no extra-musical association-values. Beethoven exploited tone exactly as Shakespeare exploited language; to give spiritual account of himself.

The transition is prepared for the adagio in which the world of time is left behind. In a sequence of variations the music seems to go on a higher plane of consciousness; the way it is all done is simple, even mechanical; the trills of high notes suggest vibrations of light. But the movement has been explained and written about, once and for all, by Samuel Langford:

> The final variations approach so nearly to a mechanical perfection that the contemplation of its nearness almost brings a shudder. Yet where shall we find music more divinely separated from the mechanical than in those first variations? . . . those various transitions and ranges of emotion for the height and parallel of which we could go nowhere in poetry but to the *Paradiso* of Dante. We have likened that apotheosis of the shake, with which this sonata ends, and in which the whole mechanical construction and subtlety of this sonata finds its solution, to those studies of light with which Turner in his last years baffled his beholders. The comparison is not far-fetched nor yet the comparison with the moving glass, the smoothest of all poetic rhythms, in which Dante turned his verse.

That, at any rate, is one way of writing about music and defining the music critic's " function.

Arthur Johnstone

MORE THAN fifty years ago, on 16th December, 1904, readers of the *Manchester Guardian* were shocked to learn of the death of the paper's music critic, Arthur Johnstone. On Thursday, 8th December, he had written his usual notice of the Hallé concert and was in his forty-fourth year by only thirteen days. To serve the *Manchester Guardian* as music critic during this period—and later, if it comes to that—was not a profession but a vocation, hieratic, sacer-dotal. On Friday mornings a column of small type would brood upon Bach and Beethoven, the performance men-tioned at or towards the end, as a sort of afterthought. Richter was conductor and All-Father of the Hallé then, yet it is a fact that notices of the concerts were known to appear next morning containing scarcely a mention of his name. None but subscribers to the society was really welcome to the Free Trade Hall on Thursday evenings—carriages at 9.30—and a handful of shilling benches near the back doors was supposed to accommodate the " general " public. Everybody in the front seats wore dress clothes: the men in " tails " and white ties. If a man dresses nowadays for a Hallé concert, likely enough he'll be mistaken for a trombone player.

Arthur Johnstone succeeded George Fremantle in 1896, and, with Bernard Shaw and John Runciman of the *Saturday*

Review, was the first writer in this country to discuss music humanely and relate it to a broad way of living. He discussed music in fact as a connoisseur " discusses " wine; the contemporary critic doesn't seem so much to flavour music as to sell or auction it, arguing the " Body " of a 1931 Walton against a 1942 Britten. By the good deed of a friend I have come upon the collection of Johnstone's music criticisms published in 1905 by the University Press of Manchester. I had lost my own copy in Australia—I took it with me there. I have more than ever been impressed by the main tone of these writings, for it is entirely different from the tone of music criticism of the present, taking it by and large. Johnstone is obviously cultured in the art, but he never exhibits his knowledge, never drags technique in irrelevantly or superfluously. He takes it for granted that the reader is not illiterate, so need not be schoolmastered. Of Strauss's *Zarathustra* he wrote:

" The plan of the tone-poem that gradually unfolds is one of the clearest. It is on the same plan as the discourse of St. Francis on " La Joie Parfaite " quoted by Sabatier from the " Fioretti," where the holy man, the better to impress upon Brother Leo wherein perfect joy consists first enumerates a series of things in which it does not consist, and then, having disposed of the erroneous opinions corresponding to various stages of the upward path towards true wisdom, tells us what perfect joy is."

Of Beethoven's *Fidelio*:

" It focuses a certain range of poetic ideas that nothing else of its kind touches, and stands—with its Wordsworthian simplicity and moral goodness—among other operas like a Sister Clare amid a group of fine ladies."

Of Moszkowski's piano playing:

" Though not the highest thing in music, technique is a very important thing, and, when carried to such a pitch of excellence, has a kind of self-sufficient beauty that may be compared to the lustre of pearls or diamonds. Perhaps it does not mean anything; but it is beautiful, cheering, enlivening. It raises the spirits somewhat like champagne, but better than champagne, and it has all the arrogance and costly unreason that are so fascinating in fine jewellery. . . ."

How urbane! it all sounds civilised; we can almost hear George Sainsbury and Dr. Middleton and the clink of the wine-glasses. And when it is necessary to attend to a didactic and technical matter the mood of Johnstone remains easy and well-bred. Of Paderewski, he asked:

" Why will he insist on using a pianoforte with so hard a tone? . . . Why does he never play Bach? . . . Such are the searchings of heart to which Mr. Paderewski's public performances give rise, and to none of them —probably—is there a complete and satisfactory answer. The shallow-toned instrument admits of greater clearness in the bass, and has a more scintillating kind of brilliancy in the upper octaves, and Mr. Paderewski who likes all passage-work a little staccato, naturally favours it. The rage of his " con gran bravura " lends greater charm to his grazioso style, by the principle of contrast—a point on which he often lays emphasis by rapid alternations of the two styles. Iteration of show pieces, such as the second Rhapsodie (of Liszt) is excusable in a pianist who is incessantly touring the two worlds and playing to all sorts and conditions of men by land and by sea. As to the Bach question, we know nothing. He may even have played Bach in other parts of the world. . . ."

It is charming; to-day it is refreshing. The knowledge and the experience we can feel instinctively; but he is incapable of the modern critic's show of bad manners—a deliberate technical reconditeness, as though a host at dinner-table were to address himself to a chosen few in a language not known to all of his guests. Johnstone is always writing with something in hand, and at his severest avoids nagging; yet each passage from him I have quoted was written between the age of thirty-nine and forty-three. He lived when the tempo of the passing years was not as ruinously quick as now.

Johnstone was one of our first critics to get the sense of Elgar's importance in the music of the early 1900s. He was sympathetic to Strauss as far back as 1899, but obviously he felt obliged, while praising the composer, from the Düsseldorf Festival in 1899, to add: " Strauss is not likely to become popular in England, but two or three of his larger orchestral works, and especially the *Heldenleben*, would probably find favour with a section of the English public. To the mandarins and to the majority he is and must remain anathema."

In 1898, when Johnstone was a young man in criticism, in a period that saw English musical standards lower than ever before or after, he had the insight and faith to write as follows of Elgar's *King Olaf*, one of the most unpromising of any composer's early works:

> The cantata did not seem to make any great impression on the audience; but we should expect to find, if ever Mr. Elgar were so fortunate as to obtain a really good subject and a good book, and especially a subject adapted to his remarkable dramatic powers, that he would produce something of lasting value.

Johnstone wrote admiringly of *Gerontius* from the start, though shrewd enough to hear where it is partly derivative:

> We shall doubtless hear of plagiarism from *Parsifal*, and there is indeed much in the work that could not have been there but for *Parsifal*. But it is not allowable for a modern composer of religious music to be ignorant of *Parsifal*.

It is curious that Johnstone, having savoured the *Parsifal* flavours in *Gerontius*, should have written that in the prelude Elgar " reverts to an earlier Wagnerian type." The prelude to *Gerontius* is the prelude to *Parsifal* translated, in Bottom's sense of the word.

I have found Johnstone well worth re-reading. Ernest Newman was not far wrong in his generous tribute to Johnstone at his death: " The best and strongest Englishman of our time in his line."

Erich Hartleibig

It is thirty-two years since Erich Hartleibig died in Vienna at the age of forty-four, poisoned by eating an overripe salzgurke. His music is still a cause of controversy. A translation by Gutrune Schnupfen is now available in English of Dr. Hans Gehirnsturm's monumental and authoritative study (*Erich Hartleibig: Werke und Methode*) under the title of *Erich Hartleibig: His Music and Method* (Atonal Press, 76s.)

As Dr. Gehirnsturm points out, Hartleibig cannot correctly be described as the beginning and end of the Third Viennese School, despite that he withdrew from the so-called Second Viennese School, which consisted of Schönberg, Anton von Webern, and Alban Berg, the three masters in this school being its only reputable students. Hartleibig in his last period reacted against any strict adherence to the dodecaphonic serial formula. He in fact was occupied until the day of his tragically premature death with his system of the one-tone row, which he used empirically rather than theoretically in the great scene of his opera *Verstummung*, where Adele is murdered by her mother.

Hartleibig, in his first five chamber works, openly acknowledges the influence of Berg, so much so that the dedication of the op. 13 Trio to Berg was a case of polite supererogation. The opening theme in itself admits the lineage:

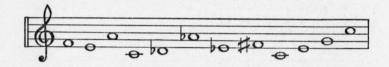

The Trio is for violin, harp and tenor tuba, and is prophetic of the later Hartleibig, even if it does contain certain dodecaphonic derivations. It is a far cry no doubt from the Trio, and from the chamber music in general, to *Verstummung*, but at the opera's mature and overpowering climax, the one-note motif, heard in the double bass, is really a transformation or variant of the D flat in the above quotation. Hartleibig's output was not large; like Hugo Wolf, he experienced periods of sudden creation followed by equally sudden relapses into complete sterility. Until he composed *Verstummung* he was silent for a year, and so far he had written only for small instrumental groups. *Verstummung* was composed in six weeks in one terrific spate of energy, and calls for a large orchestra. Hartleibig wrote his own libretto. The metamorphosis of Hartleibig's style, remarkable though it was, came from no arbitrary or doctrinaire theory or practice. On paper there might seem a rigidity here and there in Hartleibig's one-tone serial technique, but in effect and heard in the opera's dramatic context the rigidity is more apparent than real. In *Verstummung*, as I have suggested, the one-note technique is not pedantically employed. Hartleibig himself insisted that his music had to be heard, not seen, to be believed. One of his sayings has become a watchword among his followers: "Music begins where words leave off." But this epigram loses its pith and snap if translated from the German—"Die Musik beginnt in dem Moment wo die Bedeutung des Wortes aufhört."

Not until *Verstummung* did Hartleibig trust to his one-note technique as a central factor in the texture. He was curiously ambivalent. His chamber music aspires to the condition of drama: the music of *Verstummung* aspires frequently to an instrumental self-sufficiency, taking now and again definitely classical forms. One of the arresting moments on the stage in *Verstummung* is expressed in the orchestra by a Cancrizans; I refer to the scene in which Adele sets forth on her journey to kill her mother, and half-way there realises that she has forgotten the axe, so turns back to get it. On her way to the house of her mother, which is uphill, we hear

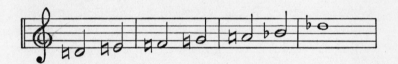

And on her frenzied descent and return for the axe we hear

It is clear from these musical examples that Hartleibig was free, when his genius instinctively directed him, to revert to an earlier and, for him, a generally outworn tonality. His

achievement was to make a synthesis of the old and, as far as he could discover it, the new.

With Hartleibig words and music certainly became, as his art integrated, one and indivisible. Music for him crystallised the world, as he would say, as " Will and Representation " (" Wille und Vorstellung "). When his Chamber Symphony in one movement was received in Vienna with hoots and cat-calls Hartleibig addressed the audience from the platform: " Ich hab' Sie alle schon komponiert." (" I have already got you all into music.")

The opera *Verstummung* is perhaps the least formidable way of approach to a study of Hartleibig's original use of the materials of music. As drama it is immediately gripping. Words, scene and music are fused into a whole, each a factor delineating on equal terms a musico-histrionic conception. The libretto tells of a Viennese girl, a student of psychology named Adele. She comes under an obsession to murder her mother, who is a widow living in the suburbs, while Adele has a town flat. Adele dreams she is actually killing her mother with an axe; but the edge of it is blunt and she cannot make an end of the grisly job, though she strikes time after time and the blood gushes and nearly blinds her. She awakes from the nightmare (Allegro ostinato) and rushes into the streets, where she encounters Hermann Schildkrötenschale, a taxi-cab driver, who succours her and at once ravishes her. Adele naturally is freed for the time being from the mother obsession: but next day she is reminded of her dread intent by the sight of the axe in her flat. She sharpens the edge (and here Hartleibig ironically inverts the " Nothung " motif in *Siegfried*). She sets out on her grim journey to her mother's house through the dark midnight streets. It is now that, half-way there, she realises she has forgotten the axe. She hastens back to her flat and finds Hermann waiting for her. He ravishes her, thus again putting the idea of murdering her mother clean out of her mind. She falls asleep in the arms of her lover, who, as the curtain falls on Act II sings the lullaby: " Schlaf und schnurre Lieb'chen mein."

The third act is violent and cumulative (Variations and Mirror Fugue and Waltz). Adele sets forth again next night armed with the axe, determined this time to settle the job and rid herself both of her mother and her obsession. On the way, crossing a waste piece of land, a figure emerges from the shadows and aims a blow with an axe at Adele, killing her. A moonbeam reveals that the murderer is Adele's mother, who also has become a victim of an obsession, to kill her daughter.

The mother drags the body of Adele into a stagnant pool nearby, then drowns herself in it. The day dawns. A child runs across the deserted scene, stops, sees an axe, picks it up, and happily imitating a soldier, carries it over the shoulder like a sword, and struts from the stage. As the curtain slowly falls we hear the bitter-sweet waltz refrain:

In a short article it is not possible to explain or even sketch the outline of Hartleibig's one-tone technique. He does not develop his spare thematic material by merely external devices such as instrumental interplay or rhythmical variation. The note itself is governed in its inflections, in its gravitations from the centre to the periphery of harmony, by Hartleibig's dynamic control, also by his formal allusiveness. I have referred to his inspired use of the Cancrizans. The fact cannot be pointed out too often that Hartleibig never allowed system to enslave him: no composer has shared his instinct for the adaptation of established musical forms to fresh imaginative needs.

Hartleibig does not employ in *Verstummung* the Alban Berg method of " Sprechgesang," which asks that notes, though written in the score at different pitches, are to be delivered as speech, but speech approximating to the musical pitches indicated. At the climaxes of action and emotion in *Verstummung*, Hartleibig uses his own " Sprechstillgesang." The singer suggests by subtle movements of the lips and mouth the words as well as the music. But the singer in these moments is vocally silent.

In a talk with Hartleibig about his system of " Sprechstillgesang," a friend from London playfully quoted Keats's lines about heard melodies and those unheard, but as Hartleibig knew no English the passage had to be rendered in German: " Melodien, die wir hören können, sind süss. Aber Melodien, die wir nicht hören können, sind noch süsser." (Keats inevitably loses something in translation.)

Verstummung is certainly a work which the B.B.C. should introduce to English listeners over the Third Programme. Whether the opera may be called decadent or not is scarcely a matter for æsthetic consideration. As Hartleibig himself said: " Die Musik ist ein Ding an sich—jenseits von Gut und Böse." From this simple wise remark we can all the more understand and appreciate the swift allusiveness of Hartleibig's mind, as quick to flash from Kant to Nietzsche in conversation as, in music, from the Cancrizans to the Waltz, from dodecaphony to the most familiar common chord.

TAILPIECE

A Rare Memory of Gigli (1935)

FEW ARTISTS with musical connections can hope to fill the Albert Hall nowadays: perhaps only Kreisler and Gigli. Last night the traffic to the place was enormous, the roads were congested; all London, certainly all Soho, seemed to be eager to hear Gigli. I could not get to my seat in time to enjoy his opening aria; I turned down the wrong corridor, and had to retrace my steps about three-quarters of a mile. When at last I found my destination Gigli was singing *Plaisir d'amour*, and by his soft phrases, light as the lightest and mellowest viola, he was transforming the Albert Hall into an intimate music-room; we felt the flavour of antique airs and graces from a world lighted by the sunshine of old Florence.

It was a remarkable experience to sit there and to see this vocalist, helped only by a piano, standing on the platform breathing forth his floating melody to the packed multitude reaching higher and higher to the remote galleries. Could they hear him there, could they do anything more than overhear, this gentle singing, almost as unselfconscious and lovable as that of a boy? Later in the evening Gigli showed that he is indeed an Italian opera tenor, capable of giving the full luscious line to Puccini's *Lucevan le stelle*; but I hope that I may always retain my first impressions of him, as I heard him at this concert, singing Gluck's air *O del mio dolce ardor*, and Cesti's *Intorno all idol mio*;

here was the beauty of a vocal art that is almost gone, even from Italy. Gigli is the most perfect lyrical tenor conceivable; it might almost be said that he really belongs to French and not Italian opera. He lacks the natural bombast needed in early Verdi and the tragic power needed in the Verdi of *Otello*. I can imagine that in Massenet he would charm even Mr. Newman into a brief acceptance of the composer's pussy-cat purrings. His tone is quite bewitching, a tenor without a touch of throatiness. His phrasing would cause the phrasing of a 'cello to sound stressful; he never bleats; throughout his splendid range there are no obvious registers. He never forces; he can make even *Vesti la giubba* sound musical. It is his lack of the familiar Italian bravura that causes him to fail in a comparison with Caruso when he sings *La donna e mobile*. But such a comparison is uncritical; Gigli, as I say, is a lyric, not a dramatic tenor. Now and again he concedes to the crowd—by hanging on to a top note, by an excess of portamento, but these tricks are external with him, not a part of his pure style. In an age that did not turn most things into commerce, his singing would probably never have become associated with the sentimental rhetoric of the opera-house. Gigli's voice is for quiet moonlit nights; he should have sung in Illyria to the Duke.

He sings and only sings. There is nothing in his art that extends consciousness of life, or, as the phrase goes, adds to the criticism of life. This voice is a natural happening, like a bird's song, a boy's laugh. Gigli has apparently no taste, as the word is generally understood. He will sing a vocal arrangement of Liszt's *Liebestraum*—and Leoncavallo's *Mattinata*. A little of him goes a long way; his perfection contains no enigma for us to attend to expectantly. And Gigli is nearly a flawless vocalist; I could hear only one " fault "—a certain " whiteness " in some of his high notes.

At first there seemed something depressing in the sight of a vast crowd attracted by Gigli, and hanging on to every note. Not a twentieth part of the multitude would ever dream of going to hear a Hugo Wolf recital. Yet, on second thoughts, I feel that there was something about this crowd for Gigli which placed them all on the side of the angels. Everybody sat in spellbound silence, broken only when a woman of his own country cried out, at the end of *Plaisir d'amour*, " Bella, bella, bella! " and when, as the evening came towards an end, thousands of requests were heard for favourite airs out of Verdi, Puccini, and the rest. On the whole, though, the immense audience were willing slaves to a beauty which was not unsweetened by modesty; a beauty not of our own period. It was like the unaffected blossoming once again of a culture almost forgotten to-day. The singing did not protest too much; it conquered by allurements that meant nothing but sweet singing. The crowd is not heading for the bottomless pit if it stops, amid all the noisy distractions of modern life, to listen to a lovely singer.

After the concert the Soho cafés were ecstatic. Waiters went about their work throwing their voices up and down with a magnificent recklessness. Not every waiter had been able to get away from his labours to hear Gigli. But it was enough for them all that Gigli had delighted us. They shared in his triumph; they were proud to be sons of Italy with him, and happy to cast huge smiles at us and to be of the same human family, all linked together by praise of Gigli.

INDEX

Abide with me, 55, 225
Adler, Larry, 83
Agate, James, 270
Agostinelli, 105
Aida, Verdi, 145, 148, 159, 180
Albanese, Lucia, 139
Alexander, Professor Samuel, 47, 202
Allin, Norman, 172
America, musical development in, 13, 14
American " Musicals," 247
Amfortas, Wagner, 255
Anakreons Grab, Wolf, 135
An die Geliebte, Wolf, 135, 136
Apollon Musagete, Stravinsky, 61
Appalachia, Delius, 250
Appassionata Sonata, Beethoven, 212
Arabella, Strauss, 93, 96
Arne, Thomas, 247
Arnold, Matthew, 204
Art of the Fugue, Bach, 76
Atonalism, 74, 76, 77, 191, 196-98, 238
Austen, Jane, 192
Austin, Frederic, 172

Bach, J. S. 21, 26, 45, 71, 175, 190, 195, 202, 204, 214, 226, 228
Bach, Philipp Emanuel, 190, 195
Ballet music, 62, 63
Ballet, Russian, 22
Balzac, 280
Bantock, Granville, 232, 245, 246, 249, 257
Barbirolli, Sir John, 36, 38, 111, 112, 227, 251
Bardi, Giovanni, 169, 265
Bartok, Béla, 191, 227
Barzun, Jacques, 207-210

Bax, Sir Arnold, 219, 251, 257
Beard, Paul, 83
Beaumarchais, 192
Beck, C. H., 103
Beckmesser, 94, 269
Beckmesser's Prize Song, 224
Beecham, Sir Thomas, 15, 18-25, 36, 37, 103, 111, 112, 114, 172, 251
Beethoven, 13-16, 22, 26, 27, 30, 32, 37, 46, 64, 66, 69, 79, 80, 82, 105, 106, 115, 121, 173, 179, 191-93, 202, 204, 212, 213, 217, 226, 229, 236, 254, 277, 283, 284, 289-93; 295; notebooks, 30; fifth symphony, 205
Beim Schlafengehen, Strauss, 89-91, 106
Bellini, Vincenzo, 125
Belshazzar's Feast, Walton, 25, 175, 176, 251
Bénédiction de Dieu dans la Solitude, Liszt, 118
Benjamin, Arthur, 260, 261
Bennett, Arnold, 184
Berg, Alban, 74-77, 193, 194, 265, 299
Berkeley, Lennox, 256, 261
Berlin Philharmonic Orchestra, 165
Berlioz, 37, 42, 54, 108-112, 120, 123, 258
Billy Budd, Britten, 94, 181-83
Bitter Sweet, Coward, 247
Bizet, 39-43, 140, 141-43
Bliss, Sir Arthur, 62, 184, 191, 256
Blom, Eric, 224
Blue Danube, The, Johann Strauss, 150
Boar's Head, At The, Holst, 178
Böhm, Dr. Karl, 149, 152, 164-66
Boïto, Arrigo, 146, 147

Borodin, 119
Boughton, Rutland, 176, 249
Boult, Sir Adrian, 251
Boyce, Bruce, 133
Bradbury, Ernest, 196, 198
Brahms, 13, 27, 37, 42, 43, 46, 78, 89, 108, 115, 116, 128-33, 179, 204, 228, 230, 243, 244, 255; tempo indications, 47
Brian, Havergal, 257, 261, 262
Bridge, Frank, 250, 257
Brigg Fair, Delius, 250
British National Opera Company, 26
British Opera, 172-80
Britten, Benjamin, 54, 94, 171, 172, 174, 175, 177, 179-84, 191, 218, 244, 245, 249, 256, 260, 261, 278, 280-82
Brown, Ivor, 199
Browning, Robert, 204
Bruckner, Anton, 53, 60, 64, 78-82, 88, 158
Bruckner and Mahler, 52
Bruno, Walter, 158
Butler, Samuel, 254
Butt, Clara, 41
Butterworth, George, 245, 246

Calvé, Emma, 140
Capell, Richard, 81
Capriccio, Strauss, 93-96, 110
Carmen, Bizet, 39-43
Carner, Dr. Mosco, 58
Carroll, Lewis, 213
Caruso, 310
Casa, Lisa Della, 39, 91, 157
Cervantes, 213
Chabrier, 76
Charley, Herr Fr., 272
Charpentier, 22, 64
Chesterton, G. K., 188
Chevalier, Albert, 247
Chopin, 121-27, 256, 258
Clark, Sir Kenneth, 280

Columba, Mackenzie, 180
Come Away Death, Quilter, 244; Sibelius, 68, 244
Conducting: use of score and baton, 44-47
Cophtisches songs, Wolf, 246
Copland, Aaron, 54
Cortot, Alfred, 126
Cosi fan Tutti, Mozart, 192
Covent Garden Opera, 22
Cowan, Sir F. H., 42
Coward, Noel, 247
Critic, The, Stanford, 22
Crook, John, 247
Crozier, Eric, 184
Crozier, W. P., 227
Crown Imperial march, Walton.

Dante, 202, 204, 213, 293
Dante Symphony, 119
Das Lied von der Erde, Mahler, 51, 52, 75, 166
Das Rheingold, Wagner, 285
Debussy, 183, 191, 219, 220, 229, 244, 258, 265, 287
Delius, 18, 22, 128, 175, 176, 178, 219, 250, 257, 259
Der Rosenkavalier, Strauss, 90, 96, 97
Dibdin, 247
Dickens, Charles, 202
Die Frau ohne Schatten, Strauss, 100, 102, 155, 159
Die Liebe der Danae, Strauss, 90, 93, 94
Die Meistersinger, Wagner, 15, 36, 98, 150, 161, 162, 180, 182, 225, 245
Die Schöne Mullerin, Schubert, 245
Die Walküre, Wagner, 173
Dies Natalis, Finzi, 244
Dieren, Bernard van, 246, 251
Domestic Symphony, Strauss, 104
Don Giovanni, Mozart, 70, 156-59, 192
Don Juan, Strauss, 46, 92

Don Quixote, Strauss, 109, 213
Donne, John, 260
Dream of Gerontius, The, Elgar, 25, 26, 104, 175, 177, 255, 298
Düsseldorf Festival, 1899, 297

Einstein, Alfred, 230
Elektra, Strauss, 91, 97
Elgar, Edward, 42, 83, 84, 98, 175, 177, 218, 232, 249, 250, 255-57, 259, 297, 298
Elkin, Robert, 272
Eliot, T. S., 254
Elliot, J. H., 112
Elliston, Robert William, 281
Elson Memorial, Louis Charles, 207
English Opera Singers, 172
Enigma Variations, Elgar, 256
En Saga, Sibelius, 67
Ernani, Verdi, 146
Eroica Symphony, Beethoven, 226
Etudes d'exécution transcendante d'après Paganini, 118

Façade, Walton, 176
Fairy's Kiss, The, Stravinsky, 62
Fall, Leo, 161
Falstaff, 172
Falstaff, Elgar, 177, 249
Falstaff, Verdi, 144, 145, 148
Fauré, 243
Faust, Goethe, 16, 96, 169
Faust, Gounod, 223
Faust Symphony of Liszt, 120
Feldeinsamkeit, Brahms, 244
Feneon, Felix, 108
Ferishtah's Fancies, Bantock, 245
Ferrier, Kathleen, 251
Feuersnot, Strauss, 174
Fidelio, Beethoven, 150, 152, 157, 173, 295
Figaro, Beaumarchais, 192, 245
Fingal's Cave, Mendelssohn, 219
Finlandia, Sibelius, 222, 224
Finzi, Gerald, 244

Fisher-Dieskau, 133
Five Tudor Portraits, Vaughan Williams, 84, 86
Fleet Street Choir, 260
Floradora, Stuart, 247
Foll, Professor, 101
Forster, E. M., 184
Four Last Songs, Brahms, 89
Four Serious Songs, Brahms, 27, 208
Franck, César, 234
Fremantle, George, 294
Fricker, Racine, 191, 239
Friedman, Ignacy, 126
Frühling, Strauss, 89, 90
Fühlt meine Seele, Wolf, 136
Furtwängler, Wilhelm, 15, 29-33, 46, 152, 274, 277
Furtwängler, Wilhelm, Curt Reiss, 29

Geh' Geliebter, Wolf, 136, 246
Gehirnsturm, Dr. Hans, 299
German music, contemporary, 192
Gesualdo, 238
Gielgud, Sir John, 32, 46
Gigli, 309-311
Glinka, 60
Gluck, 71, 94, 265, 309
Godowsky, Leopold, 124
Goethe, 16, 96, 134, 136, 159, 171, 203, 204, 213
Goossens, Eugene, 184, 250, 257, 261, 262
Gothic, The, Brian, 262
Götterdämmerung, Wagner, 99
Gounod, 223
Gramophones and music, 228
Gray, Cecil, 255
Greatness in Music, Einstein, 229
Gregor, Joseph, 94
Guiraud, Ernest, 139
Guntram, Strauss, 174
Gurney, Ivor, 245, 246

Hallé, Charles, 109, 112, **123**
Hallé concerts, 109, 294

Hallé Orchestra, 34-38, 42, 51, 111, 112; Sir John Barbirolli, 36, 38; Sir Thomas Beecham, 36, 37; Hamilton Harty, 34, 37, 38; Hans Richter, 34, 37
Handel, 21, 253, 263
Hardy, Thomas, 84, 87, 130
Harmonies poetiques et religieuses, Liszt, 118
Harold en Italie, Berlioz, 110
Hartmann, Rudolf, 106
Harty, Sir Hamilton, 34, 42, 51, 111, 112, 251
Haydn, 60, 145, 193, 226
Hazlitt, 281
Heb' auf dein blondes Haupt, Wolf, 136
Heine, 246
Hellmer, 167
Henschel, Georg, 283
Heroines of Opera, 177, 178
Herzogenberg, Elizabeth von, 132
Hess, Dame Myra, 45
Higgins, Colonel, 39
Hindemith, 176, 193, 239
Hoffmann, The Tales of, 22, 37
Hofmannsthal, Hugo von, 94, 100, 170
Holbrooke, Josef, 176, 249, 257
Holst, Gustav, 178, 179, 244, 250, 257
Horowitz, 123
Howes, Frank, 197
Hugh the Drover, Vaughan Williams, 26, 86, 245
Hymne to God the Father, Rubbra, 260

Ibsen, 193; *Doll's House*, 233
Ihr seid die Allerschönste, Wolf, 136
Il Trovatore, Verdi, 144, 147
Im Abendrot, Strauss, 89, 90, 106
Inge, Dean, 212
Ireland, John, 251, 257
Ivanhoe, Sullivan, 180

James, Henry, 204, 280

Jeritza, Maria, 99-102
Joachim, Joseph, 129
Job, Vaughan Williams, 86
Johnstone, Arthur, 270, 294-98
Jones, Sydney, 247
Jurinac, 39, 157

Karajan, Theodor, 111
Karsavina, 59
Kasser, Dr., 99
Kassner, Rudolf, 98
Keats, 244
Kennst du das Land, Wolf, 135, 136, 246
Kern, Jerome, 229
King Olaf, Elgar, 298
Klemperer, Otto, 33, 46
Krauss, Clemens, 95, 164
Kreisler, 309

La Bohème, Puccini, 180,
La Campanella, Listz, 118
La Clemenza di Tito, Mozart, 73
La Damnation de Faust, Berlioz, 109, 111
La Mer, Debussy, 219, 220
La Roche, 96
La Scala, 13, 14
La Traviata, Verdi, 144, 174, 245
Lamb, Charles, 254, 281
Lambert, Constant, 76
Langford, Samuel, 26, 41, 52, 53, 85, 177, 205, 234, 270, 281
Lark Ascending, The, Vaughan Williams, 83
Last Visit to Strauss, Hartmann, 106, 107
Lauder, Sir Harry, 247
Laye, Evelyn, 161
Leach, George, 205
Leeds Musical Festival, 25
Lehár, 161
Lehmann, Lotte, 99, 102, 105, 168
Leonora, Beethoven, 152, 153
Leopardi, 212

Le Sacre du Printemps, Stravinsky, 60, 61, 62, 109, 258
Les Illuminations, Britten, 182, 244
Les Troyens, Berlioz, 111, 112
Libretti, 170
Librettists, 181-84
Licette, Miriam, 172
Lichnowsky, Count Moriz von, 290
Liebestraum, Liszt, 118, 310
Lied von der Erde, Mahler, 89
Linden Lea, Vaughan Williams, 83
Liszt, 118-21, 126, 310; B Minor Sonata, 118; La Campanella, 118; Piano music, 118
Liszt Society in London, 118
Literature and music, 207-211
Lohengrin, Wagner, 239
L'Oiseau de Feu, Stravinsky, 59
London, George, 157
London Philharmonic Orchestra, 25
London Symphony, Vaughan Williams, 251
Louise, Charpentier, 22
Ludikar, Pavel, 105
Luisa Miller, Verdi, 148
Lully, Giovanni, 60
Lunn, Kirby, 172
Lush, Ernest, 133

Mackenzie, Alexander, 180
Madame Butterfly, Puccini, 245
Madame Pompadour, Fall, 161
Mahler, Alma, 43
Mahler, Gustav, 33, 34, 43, 51-58, 75, 78, 89, 97, 108, 128, 134, 157, 163, 166, 184, 211, 239, 253, 262; his influence on orchestral technique, 54; Symphonies, 51-54; 1st, 51; 2nd, 225; 4th, 113-17; 5th, 225; 9th, 42, 43, 55-58, 224
Man and Superman, Shaw, 227
Manchester and the Hallé Orchestra, 35
Manchester Guardian, the, 35, 41, 146, 205, 279, 294

Manns, Sir August, 42
March to the Scaffold, The, Berlioz, 111
Mass of Life, The, Delius, 175, 178, 250
Matthews, Thomas, 44, 83
"Max," 270
Mefistofele, Boïto, 146
Meine Ruh', Gretchen, 111
Mendelssohn, 219
Mérimée, Prosper, 140
Merrill, Robert, 139
Messiah, Handel, 253
Mignon, Thomas, 272
Milne, A. A., 229
Milton, John, 202, 204
Missa Solemnis, The, 256
Mitropoulos, 44
Modl, Martha, 152
Moncton, Lionel, 247
Montague, C. E., 281
Moore, George, 255
Moore, Gerald, 133
Morgen, Strauss, 91
Moszkowski's piano playing, 296
Moussorgsky, 119, 244
Mozart, 15, 22, 37, 64, 69-73, 76, 88, 127, 157, 192, 198, 222, 223, 226, 228, 229; tempo indications, 47; last compositions, 73
Mullings, Frank, 172, 245, 246
Munden, Joseph Shepherd, 281
Music: contemporary, 62, 187-95, 229, 236-39, 256, 259-62; British, 188-91, 243; German, 192; relative values, 201; and literature, 207-211; meaning of, 212-16; and nature, 217-21; vocal, 243-47; period, 248-82
Musical Critic's Holiday, A, Newman, 189
Musical life in England, 104
Musicians, Incorporated Society of, 196
Musicians of To-day, Rolland, 104

Naïl, 22
Nash, Heddle, 172
Nazi ideology, Fürtwangler and, 31
Newman, Ernest, 75, 103, 110, 189, 270, 281, 298
Nichols, Agnes, 172
Nielson, Florence, 133
Nietzsche, 36, 142, 143
Nikisch, 33
Now sleeps the crimson petal, Quilter, 244
Noyes, Alfred, 144

Offenbach, 76
Olzewska, 168
Omar Khayyám, Bantock, 232, 246
O Mistress Mine, Quilter, 244
On Hearing the First Cuckoo in Spring, Delius, 83
Opera, 13, 22, 139-84; Sir Thomas Beecham and, 22; Russian, 22; opera æsthetic, 168, 169; words and music in, 168-71; passing of the prima donna, 168; English opera singers, 172; British opera, 172-80; heroines of opera, 177, 178; libretti, 181-84
Opera, symposium of music criticism, 278-80
Opera Glass, Charley, 272
Oratorios, 175
Orchestras: technique, 13, 14, 41; rehearsals, 34, 42; development in numbers and scope, 41; conductors, 39-43; conducting from memory, 44
Orpheus, Stravinsky, 62
Otello, Verdi, 144-48, 310

Pachmann, 125
Paderewski, 125, 296
Paganini, 129
Paradiso, Dante, 293
Parker, Robert, 172

Parry, Sir Hubert, 78, 175, 245, 246, 248, 249
Parsifal, Wagner, 76, 89, 111, 255, 298
Pathétique Symphony, Tchaikovski, 44, 46, 202
Pater, Walter, 170
Pastoral Symphony, Beethoven, 193, 217
Pastoral Symphony, Vaughan Williams, 251
Peerce, Jan, 139
Pélleas and Mélisande, Debussy, 177, 183, 265
Pergolesi, Giovanni, 60
Peter Grimes, Britten, 177, 180, 183, 218, 221, 249, 260; influence of Mahler, 52
Petroushka, Stravinsky, 59-62
Pfitzner, 238
Pianists and playing from memory, 45
Piano music, 118, 119; Chopin, 122-27; Brahms, 128-32
Pierrot Lunaire, Schönberg, 75
Pierrot of the Minute, Bantock, 232
Pilgrim's Progress, The, Vaughan Williams, 179
Plaisir d'Amour, 309, 311
Planets, The, Holst, 250
Portsmouth Point, Walton, 219
Preislied, the, Wagner, 224
Priestley, J. B., 184
Pritchett, V. S., 279
Promenade Concerts, performance of Mahler's Symphonies, 51
Proust, 203, 228, 279
Puccini, 16, 176, 178, 180, 226, 261, 263, 309, 310
Purcell, 247

Quilter, Roger, 244, 245

Raaff, 72
Radford, Robert, 172

Raff, Joseph, 121
Rake's Progress, The, Stravinsky, 61
Ravel, 227, 243
Rawsthorne, Alan, 191, 256, 261
R. C. A. Victor Orchestra, 139
Reger, Max, 211
Reiner, 139, 162
Requiem Mass, Verdi, 145, 147, 225
Requiem, Mozart, 73, 88
Richard Strauss: Dokumente Seines Lebens und Schaffens, Beck, 103
Richter, Hans, 34, 36, 41, 44, 69, 98, 99, 163, 294
Riders to the Sea, Vaughan Williams, 86
Rienzi, Wagner, 147, 190
Riess, Curt, 29-31
Rigoletto, Verdi, 147
Rig Veda hymns, Holst, 250
Rimbaud, 108
Rimsky-Korsakov, 32, 59, 85, 232
Ring, The, Wagner, 15, 22, 220, 285, 287
Rodgers, Richard, 229
Roi de Thule, Berlioz, 111
Rolland, Romain, 104
Roméo et Juliette, Berlioz, 110, 111
Ronald, Landon, 42
Rosenkavalier, Der, Strauss, 93, 95, 105, 106, 170, 172, 173, 177, 182, 251
Rosenthal, Moriz, 124, 125, 238, 276
Rossini, 22, 146
Rowse, A. L., 248
Royal Philharmonic Orchestra, 62
Rubbra, Edmund, 191, 256, 259-61
Rubens, Paul, 229, 247
Rubenstein, 123
Runciman, John, 270, 294
Ruskin, John, 94, 170
Russell, Bertrand, 204
Russian ballet, 22; opera, 22

Sachs, Hans, 266

Safonov, 44
St. Matthew Passion, Bach, 210
Saint-Saëns, 32, 83
Salome, Strauss, 97, 106
Santley, Sir Charles, 223
Sapphische Ode, Brahms, 133
Sappho songs, Bantock, 246
Sargent, Sir Malcolm, 24-28, 251
Saturday Review, 270, 294
Savitri, Holst, 250
Scarlatti, 118
Schnabel, 33
Schnupfen, Gutrune, 299
Schöffler, 162
Schönberg, Arnold, 23, 74-77, 188, 191, 193, 194, 196, 198, 205, 228, 229, 239, 258, 287, 299; twelve-note technique, 74
Schorr, Freidriche, 168
Schubert, 21, 64, 79, 80, 88, 133, 188, 239, 243-45
Schumann, 133, 243
Schwarzkopf, Elizabeth, 133
Scriabine, 85
Sea Drift, Delius, 219, 250
Sea Symphony, Vaughan Williams, 219
Searle, Humphrey, 263, 266
Seefried, Irmgard, 39, 153, 157, 162
September, Strauss, 89, 90, 92
Serenade to Music, Vaughan Williams, 86
Shadow of Cain, The, Sitwell, 263
Shakespeare, 203, 209, 212, 213; songs, 244
Shaw, Bernard, 70, 72, 140, 177, 203, 227, 283-88, 294
Shostakovich, Dimtiry, 54, 227
Sibelius, 22, 23, 34, 37, 42, 64-68 83, 222, 244
Siegfried, Wagner, 22
Silent Noon, Vaughan Williams, 244
Simon Boccanegra, Verdi, 145
Sitwell, Dr. Edith, 263, 266

Smyth, Dame Ethel, 176, 179, 248, 249
Somervell, Arthur, 246
Songs, contemporary English, 173
Songs of Hugo Wolf, 133-36
Stanford, Sir Charles, 22, 176, 189, 246, 248, 249
Stein, Dr. Erwin, 278, 279
Stendhal, 194
Sterb' ich, so hüllt, in Blumen, Wolf, 136
Stevens, Rise, 139
Stevenson, Robert Louis, 177
Straus, Oscar, 161
Strauss, Johann, 150
Strauss, Pauline, 102
Strauss, Richard, 22, 29, 37, 46, 59, 64, 83, 85, 88-111, 116, 120, 155, 164, 170, 174, 176, 182, 191, 211, 213, 217, 222, 228, 229, 232, 265, 284, 295, 297; Strauss-Hofmann-sthal letters, 173
Strauss, Last visit to, Hartmann, 106, 107
Strauss, Richard: Dokumente Seines Lebens und Schaffens, Beck, 103
Stravinsky, Igor, 34, 59-63, 109, 175, 177, 239, 258; ballet music, 62 63; Royal Philharmonic Society Gold Medal, 62
Stride la Vampa, 147
Stuart, Leslie, 228, 247
Sullivan, Arthur, 42, 102, 180
Swift, Jonathan, 203
Symphonie Fantastique, Berlioz, 109
Symphonies pour Instruments à Vent, Stravinsky, 60
Symphony of Psalms, Stravinsky, 175

Tale of Two Cities, A, Benjamin, 260, 261
Tallis, Thomas, 83
Tasso, Goethe, 159
Taylor, Bayard, 169
Tchaikovski, 41, 44, 46, 202

Tempest, The, Sibelius, 68
Tempo indications in Mozart **and** Brahms, 47
Tennis at Trianon, Sibelius, 68
Thomas, Ambroise, 272
Thomas, Edward, 87
Tiefland, 22
Tintagel, Bax, 219
Tippett, Michael, 172
Tolstoy, 203
Tom Jones, 227
Toscanini, 13-17, 21, 25, 31, 32, 40, 44
Toye, Francis, 145
Traherne, Thomas, 244
Trenner, Dr. Franz, 103, 105, 106
Tristan und Isolde, Wagner, 15, 76, 111, 125, 145, 147, 172, 177, 189, 190, 215, 220
Troilus and Cressida, Walton, 26, 176, 180, 199, 200
Turandot, Puccini 200
Turner, Laurance, 83

Und willst du deinen Liebsten sterben sehen, Wolf, 136

Valse Triste, Sibelius, 64
Vaughan Williams, Ralph, 26, 40, 83-87, 104, 116, 179, 219, 236, 244, 245, 251, 256; Symphonies, 85-87
Verdi, 83, 88, 93, 111, 144-48, 174, '79, 215, 225, 310, 311
Verklärte Nacht, Schönberg, 75
Verlaine, 246
Vienna: 149-67; opera, 39, new Opera House, 149-65; Philharmonic Orchestra, 91, 153, 156, 157, 164, 171, 265
Viennese School, Third, 299
Vier Letzte Lieder, Strauss, 89-91, 106, 110
Village Romeo and Juliet, A, Delius, 22, 178

Virtuoso vocalist and the opera, 168

Voltaire, 203

Wagner, 15, 22, 70, 75, 79-81, 89, 94, 98, 106, 108, 110, 111, 119-21, 125, 142, 147, 148, 163, 168, 169, 171, 173, 174, 176, 182, 189, 190, 193, 194, 199, 219, 220, 224, 225, 228, 239, 266, 285-87

Wagnerian opera æsthetic, 168

Wagnerite, The Perfect, Shaw, 285, 286

Waldesrauschen, Liszt, 118

Walkley, 270

Wallace, William, 248

Walter, Bruno, 43, 46, 157, 164

Walton, William, 25, 26, 172, 175, 176, 179, 191, 199, 219, 236, 251, 256

Warlock, Peter, 246

Weber, 29, 194

Webern, Anton von, 299

Weingartner, 163

Well-Tempered Clavier, The, Bach, 210

Wenlock Edge cycle, Vaughan Williams, 244

Where Corals Lie, Elgar, 219

Widdop, Walter, 172

Wiener Staatsoper, 1955, 98

Wilhelm, Kaiser, 106

Winterreise cycle, Schubert, 133, 245

Wireless and music, 228

Wodehouse, P. G., 203

Wolf, Hugo, 52, 133-36, 163, 167, 243-46

Woman Without a Shadow, Strauss, 158

Wood, Sir Henry, 26, 51

Words and Music, 263-66; in opera, 168-71

Words into Music, Barzun, 207

Wordsworth, William, 87

Wozzeck, Berg, 74, 171, 177, 194, 265; solo voices in, 168

Wreckers, The, Smyth, 179, 249

Zarathustra, Strauss, 295

Zauberflöte, Mozart, 71, 165, 172

Zelzer, Harry, 216